COMMUNICATIONS AND MEDIA STUDIES SERIES
Robin Andersen, series editor

Charms That Soothe

CLASSICAL MUSIC AND THE NARRATIVE FILM

DEAN DUNCAN

FORDHAM UNIVERSITY PRESS
New York
2003

Communications and Media Studies, No. 9
ISSN 1522-385X

Library of Congress Cataloging-in-Publication Data

Duncan, Dean W.
    Charms that soothe : classical music and the narrative film / Dean Duncan.—1st ed.
        p.   cm.—(Communications and media studies series ; no. 9)
    Includes bibliographical references (p.   ) and index.
    ISBN 0-8232-2279-9 (hard cover : alk. paper)—ISBN 0-8232-2280-2 (pbk. : alk. paper)
    1. Motion pictures and music.   2. Motion picture music— History and criticism.   I. Title.   II. Communications and media studies ; no. 9.
ML2075.D83   2003
781.5'42—dc21   2003011363

Printed in the United States of America
07   06   05   04   03   5   4   3   2   1
First edition

CONTENTS

ACKNOWLEDGMENTS

I WOULD LIKE TO express my sincere gratitude to the many people who have contributed to this book. Drew Casper, Richard Jewell, and David Shepard provided valued direction and support at its inception. Kathryn Kalinak was instrumental in turning a general interest in the field of film music into something more urgent, and hopefully more substantial. Betty and Erik Barnouw offered much valued advice, as well as giving me great examples of honorable scholarship and gracious intellectual pursuit.

I am grateful to my many friends at Glasgow University for their patience and encouragement during the early stages of this process. The efforts and insights of Sean Cubitt, Simon Frith, Karen Lurie, and particularly John Caughie are deeply appreciated. I am no less appreciative of support by family and friends who made our Scottish experience so much more than educational. We are grateful to the members of the Glasgow Ward for their fellowship and affection. We treasure the friendships of our neighbors at the Gartnavel Hospital. We remember with tenderness our associations with Scots family members who welcomed and cared for us so wonderfully.

I would also like to acknowledge the contributions of my colleagues at Brigham Young University. Department Chairs Eric Fielding and Robert Nelson were unfailingly supportive. James D'Arc, Darl Larsen, Tom Lefler, and Sharon Swenson provided much needed instruction and guidance, and much valued friendship. Many students also contributed through their vigorous discussion, enthusiasm, and friendship. They remind me that research without a teaching component is conspicuously incomplete.

Special thanks go also to those at Fordham University Press for their expertise and efficiency. I owe a special debt to Robin Andersen, who has worked very hard and selflessly on my behalf. Felicity Edge, Anahid Kassabian, Robert Oppedisano,

Mary-Lou Peña, and Harrison Shaffer have all contributed their skill and effort to make my work more presentable, and to make this book better.

Finally, my deepest thanks go to the members of my family. My parents, Don and Mona Duncan, brought me up in a loving and enriching atmosphere that I will always remember fondly, and for which I will always be grateful. They, together with my parents-in-law, Wallace and Anne Anderson, have been unfailing in their emotional, moral, and material support. I express my affection for my brother, Scott, my sisters Susan, Lisa, and Sharon, and for their families. The same goes for my dear brothers and sisters in-law and their families. Most of all my love and gratitude go to my wife, Sharon, and to our children Caitlin, Drew, Sarah, Spencer, Mathieson, and Claire. As nice as it is to participate in scholarly discussions, all these beloved people remind me how much more there is to life than research, and how glad I am for that fact.

Charms That Soothe

Introduction

THE TITLE of this book is adapted from the familiar opening lines of William Congreve's 1697 tragedy, *The Mourning Bride*: "Music hath charms to soothe the savage breast, to soften rocks, or bend the knotted oak."[1] This quotation-book staple is the definitive idealized expression of music's benevolent powers, and of course it relates to more than just music. Straightforward declarations like this, and the straightforward use we often make of them, speak to our deep desire for simplicity and comprehensibility. They evince an ancient and persistent faith that there can be a parallel relation between a statement and its object, between a set of conditions and the sentiments, ideas, and applications that arise therefrom.

From another perspective it might be observed that these reassuring, apparently universal parallels have been much questioned for a very long time now, and not altogether without reason. We may have had such a direct experience with music, and with other things besides. Ideas and the experiences that give rise to them, or that emerge out of them, can surely be congruent. But congruency does not exhaust every possibility, and ambiguity lies always in wait. When we investigate Congreve's statement further we find ourselves confronted with a pair of common quotation-book complications. The first of these is that for almost every position we urge there is sure to be an equally urgeable counterposition. The other is that this counterposition is often to be found at the source of the original statement, and that the roots of received wisdom are generally more tangled than we'd like them to be.

Almeria, Congreve's mourning bride, illustrates this idea as she opens the play with her well-known statement, which she then immediately contradicts.

> What then am I? Am I more senseless grown
> Than Trees, or Flint? O Force of constant Woe!
> 'Tis not in Harmony to calm my Griefs. (6–8)

Here is a problem with famous quotes, and with platitudes in general. We often use them to prove our position or even to by-pass any proving process. We seek to establish fixed points, or even a single fixed point, when the context out of which the observation emerges is in a state of constant and multiplicitous flux.

Sometimes it is possible to sort these threads, to reach a synthesis of opposing yet complementary ideas. In this instance we might say that Almeria's opening monologue demonstrates that music can both calm and disturb, that the very same tones might strike one person as being harmonious and another as being dissonant. It suggests that these properties of harmony and dissonance, or at least our apprehension of them, are subject to our own dispositions or circumstances, both individual and cultural. Leaving the terms of the debate to consider the process by which we reconcile them, we might draw an important conclusion that also extends beyond this particular discussion. When we interrogate, when we go beyond the well-known expression or the truncated idea, we find that there are more positions, and more to each position, than we had ever suspected.

These are uncontroversial points, but they bear repeating because of the way they reflect the subject at hand, as well as the insistently partisan discussions that still surround it. This is a book about parallels and perpendiculars, and about what can happen when apparently opposing concepts clash. It illustrates these outcomes by considering quotations, the uses we put them to, and the contexts out of which they emerge. The quotations in question are musical, so that the book also addresses the places of music in narrative and in the transmission of meaning generally.

These last are familiar questions, widely debated through recent centuries, and still of central concern to the come-lately communities of film composition. Until recently the question of film musical quotation—of music originally created for one particular purpose being used in a separate, cinematic setting—has not had much of a place in these discussions, whether they be broadly musical or specifically cinematic. One important reason for this is that whereas many musicians of various stripes have an investment in totalities and musical idealisms, quotation is almost unavoidably fragmented and even disruptive. Far from clarifying or covering its contexts, this repurposed music has had a consistent and decidedly disconcerting effect on a number of music cultural factions.

As we will see, the idealists have some justification, and we will not pretend that all of the effects of quotation are straightforwardly salutary. In passing through some of its complications, however, we will find that this is more than just a troubling trend with which we must come to terms. Rather it will be argued that the institution of musical quotation in film narrative is quite central in its resonance and relevance, and that it holds the possibility of real instruction and enjoyment.

It is possible to find these things when we take the trouble to investigate a quotation, when we trace it back to a source or consider its transformations in a narrative, or in the way that a spectator receives it. In doing this we will very often find that what has begun in fragmentation can lead us to a certain resolution and to an illumination of broad contexts and common experiences. Congreve's platitude and counterplatitude is emblematic of most any intertextual interchange, and even of our own attempts to relate our own particular experiences and partial knowledge to the broader settings around us. We are surrounded by fragments, removed from roots, troubled and tempted by echoes of plenitude, disconcerted by the possibility that these echoes are only an illusion, or a deception. Seeking reassurance, we may incline toward clichéd expressions and conceptual reductions, even filtering our experiences and perceptions through such selective lenses. Conversely, and in reaction, we may tend toward negation, seeking alternatives to and even denying the viability of conventional affirmative impulses.

These are precisely the contradictory impulses that motivate and characterize the main traditions not only of narrative film generally, but most particularly of film music. Harmony and dissonance, parallelism, and what has most commonly been called film musical counterpoint, together constitute both the prescribed practice and the most standard critique of classical film music.

These are binary oppositions, and they were important in establishing and giving definition to some of the first film music discussions. Initially these oppositions invited staunch advocacies, as well as corresponding antipathies, all of which bore fruit in both the theory and practice of film music composition.

The positions, or at least the received representations of these positions, are familiar. Closer scrutiny will follow, but the standard versions bear repeating in this introduction. The practitioners and theorist-historians who together codified the conventions of classical film music accepted certain institutional imperatives. As a rule golden age Hollywood produced fairly simple narratives that provided, through numerous straightforward cinematic means, a clear and unobjectionable experience for the audience. Continuity editing and what has been called Aristotelian structure—clear protagonism and antagonism, unambiguous objectives—were some of the devices that became standard in studio output, which was designed both for entertainment and profit and not to overly tax the viewer. In exchange for these considerations it was hoped the viewer would feel comforted and cared for, and that his patronage would continue.

To safeguard this relationship, the film music community did its part, adopting and expanding the notion of parallelism, which is to say that it provided movie music that charmed and soothed. To work as efficiently as the rest of the cinematic apparatus, film scores were to be congruent with and subordinate to the narrative; what you heard was dovetailed to what you saw, though the correlation was to be quietly communicated and subconsciously processed. Further, lest this correlation of music to image, and more importantly of narrative to reality were to seem strained and inadequate, it was determined that audiences were not to know of the taming processes to which they were being subjected. And for the most part they seemed not to recognize them: the subjugation was successful, audiences were subdued, and Hollywood, industrially, economically, and ideologically, prevailed.

This is a defensible characterization—a usable quote—taken out of a more complicated context. There is more to this story than Hollywood hegemony. Opposing production alternatives arose to the film industry's guiding and smothering devices, and in the stalls there were many who were able to read against the intended industrial grain. At the core of the contrary reading was the idea that commercial, conventional film's parallel processes and straightforward representations may have been simple and comprehensible, but they were not adequate to the complexity, richness, or direness of art and experience.

So it was that the musical community, when it condescended to take notice of film music, consistently decried its subservient state. Musicians and musical scholars believed and had a stake in the independence and integrity of music, but they felt that these things were, and were likely to remain, nonexistent within the confines of the film industry. Other voices, more sympathetic to cinematic projects, nevertheless sided with the musicians in their perpendicular relation to and their general rejection of film musical parallelism. For film modernists of formalist persuasion the effects of conventional film music were aesthetically impoverished. For the ideologically and politically minded, these effects were even more serious: the conventional devices of film music, and of commercial film generally, had a dangerous influence on both spectators and citizens. These films left audiences domesticated and enervated, with the result that audience members were circumscribed in the expression, apprehension, and exercise of freedom, and of freedom's responsibilities.

A good deal of time has passed since these first formulations were made, and a good deal of more measured theoretical and practical activity has taken place. The need for this more reasonable discussion has at least something to do with the totalizing tendencies that inform the seminal film music statements. We find in these a seemingly unwavering faith in commerce (Hollywood and its apologists), or in communism (the early statements of the Soviet modernists), or in the ineffability of abstract music (Romantic elements of the music community). The certainty in these statements is undeniably appealing, and dangerous as well, and it is still present in the trenches of media production and public perception. As it was in the early debates, so it is sometimes today; salesmen and artists and their respective defenders can all be restricted by platitudinous self-images, which not incidentally distort their notions of the other side. And scholars, myself included, are not immune, as these last, slightly monolithic

thumbnail sketches indicate. Our antagonism, even our mild dis-
inclination toward opposing positions can blind us to some of the
complexities of these positions, and to the possibility that we are
not in such opposition after all.

It need hardly be pointed out that notwithstanding their many
constraints and vulgarities, Hollywood and other commercial
centers have produced a great many excellent films, full of nuance, subtlety, and beauty. Likewise the classical film score has
played a frequently beneficent part, providing much of convic-
tion and emotion even in its most conventional story support. If
on the other hand it is true that there is much that is inadequate
in commercial film production, then it might be argued that the
contrapuntal alternatives of the film modernists could be, in their
conceptual homogeneity and inflexibility, as limited as that
which they opposed. The standard accounts of the positions of
various film music communities are something like the quotes
already discussed; these are famous expressions and truncated
ideas, essential and incomplete, in need of interrogation and susceptible to real synthesis and even reconciliation.

If a single quote can signify more abundantly when we trace it
to its source, then these broad accounts can likewise benefit from
contextualization and comparison. A book about musical quotations in film is in some senses a very particular, very specialized
investigation. But in tracing the consistently disapproving attitudes that firmly constituted and widely diversified film music
factions have had toward quotation, and by outlining the nature
of and the motivations behind these attitudes, this book also becomes an alternative history of film music itself. What is perhaps
new is that this alternative is both revisionist and conciliatory; it
reaches for and finally posits a kind of synthesis of several very
valid and ultimately incomplete positions. After the history
comes a contemplation of possibility, taken from the fragments
of things already partly said, and partly done.

This book is divided roughly into three sections, corresponding to three important ways in which serious music interacts with
film and film culture. The first, as portrayed in chapters one and
two, is critical and cultural. In these chapters we will find film
music advocates squaring off against the musical establishment
over the subject of classical music in film. In this debate each

community will reveal much of its values, and much of the social and historical context in which these values operate, and out of which they emerge. We will also consider some of the more measured, less factional scholarly accounts of the subject, some of which will inform the direction of my own eventual argument.

The second point of film-to-classical music contact is figurative. In chapters three and four we will discuss film music analogies, metaphors that have suggested, as well as a new one that will suggest, ways in which film and music might actually have similar aims and effects. The first analogy, the influential and confounding idea of film-musical counterpoint, emerged out of the Soviet cinematic avant-garde. With its bold prescriptions and refusals, this is a faction as surely as the other two just mentioned. As such, and as might be expected, its analogy, or at least the way in which it has most frequently been wielded, is far from conciliatory. But the counterpoint analogy will lead us to another, largely unmarked figure that encloses and gives place to both film and classical music cultures, and which presents an alternative to the largely divisive, pugnacious exchanges that have tended to prevail on the subject.

This latter film-musical analogy is built upon the institution of program music, which reminds us that some kind of narrative, some set of assumptions or expectations generally predates and informs almost every expression, musical or otherwise. This informing can clarify, or it can be incoherent, but in either case the results can be both interesting and instructive, and they are at the least emblematic. Programs lead us finally to the book's last section and the final way that film and classical music have acted together—in actual practice, in the production and the receiving, which practice has been and continues to be most broad and varied. Films, and music, and the places where both combine, may return us to the standard positions and analogies, but they will allow us a refreshed look at and helpful alternatives to the familiar paradigms.

Finally, a word about the parameters of this study. It is not intended to be an exhaustive list of films in which classical music appears. Such a list would be useful as a resource for further study, but it would necessarily leave aside the critical work needed to provide theoretical context. Instead, as I have suggested, I will consider a number of texts and contexts, attempting to draw therefrom some general patterns and their implications for the ways films are made, both at the level of production and reception.

For "classical music" I will use the term in its generally, popularly accepted sense. It is art music which has, either in its time of composition or by some evolutionary process, come to be accepted as "serious," and that has been composed by the formally trained to be played by the formally trained, with a few exceptions. It includes that which usually falls within the standard concert hall repertory, comprising mostly the Baroque, Classical, and Romantic periods. In relation, it is generally that which has been composed and canonized long before the production of the film in which it appears. There will be some consideration of twentieth-century forms as well, especially those that derive from the traditions and culture of classical music. I will not generally deal with opera, though its utilization in film has been very frequent and raises many of the same issues that will be discussed here. As for compositions and composers which have become serious after the fact (such as George Gershwin or Kurt Weill), there will be only passing mention.

Even more loosely utilized will be "narrative film," that which tells a story of some kind, which is of course true to most fiction and much of nonfiction production. Narratives can range from the most familiar conventions to the most stringent boundary stretching. Narratives both transparent and opaque fall within the purview of this study, and though avant-gardes are officially outside the present scope, there will be some reference to these traditions as well.

NOTES

1. Congreve, 1967, 326, lines 1–2.

1

Interdiscipline and the Place of Classical Music in Film Studies

As VIEWED FROM WITHOUT, the disciplines of music can appear to be very resistant to external and interdisciplinary influence, and occasionally even hostile to it. These outsider's perceptions can be ascribed to a couple of conditions that exist within the musical community, though they by no means account for the whole.

One of these perceptions is that, semiotics, *carnaval,* and postmodernism notwithstanding, "serious" music is still in many ways an elite, elitist field, held above and held to be above the fray by a good number of its adherents. While faithful to outmoded though not entirely illegitimate notions of mastery and at least partial imperviousness to social and historical influence, and while properly preoccupied with formal properties and expressive purities, musical practitioners can forget that they are inevitably, in some way, affected by their material existence. As they are affected, so is their work, if only indirectly.

Even when attitudes are not quite elitist, it is still true that music, and musicology in particular, is a specialized field. The microscopic examination of any object can obscure that object's setting and the circumstances external to it. Musical insularity proceeds from here, and indeed like conditions can be found within any specialization. There is a tension between the specific and the fairly generalized knowledge typical of popular discourses. Broad surveys can miss the details and contradictions that make academic scholarship so important and, sometimes, so enjoyable. But scholarship can also resist the contextualization that the general can provide, thereby blocking possible connections with lay constituencies.

The relevance of such tension to this study is that resistance can also inhibit relationships between specialists in different fields. Initiates can be impatient with a newcomer's scholarly baby steps, and the outwardly banal insights that they lead to. But baby steps are essential to the beginner; as one enters into a new discipline, undue attention to that discipline's specialized cutting edges may obscure its more fundamental, if unexceptionable, roots. Clearly, without roots, connections that spring up are in danger of withering quickly away.

It is not only the newcomer that needs to step back from elite or specialized sensibilities. Specialization's inward look also can mask the salutary effects of others' elementary investigations. Even received wisdom can be groundbreaking, when innovation occurs in new combinations of the received. A film scholar's study of classical music holds this possibility, especially in the ways that music interacts with the motion picture medium. More than in music, specialized research in media and literary studies has focused on popular perception and reception. Transposed to a musical setting, such research would remind us that listeners not only hear the music in the midst of their own social and historical circumstance, but a vast majority of us do so at a musicological level very much below the thin-aired engagement of the experts. Yet that hearing is also essential to an understanding of music's meaning, as well as its emotional and cultural affects. This study will attend primarily to film-music interactions, both theoretical and actual. However, interpretive strategies and specific interpretations discussed in later chapters imply, through my own response, how important setting and reception are not only to the understanding of classical music in film, but to the understanding of music itself.

In academic practice, musicology has attended fairly exclusively to musical content. Context—the extramusical conditions under which music is composed and heard—is mostly left to other commentators.

> Musicology is perceived as dealing essentially with the factual, the documentary, the verifiable, the analyzable, the positivistic. Musicologists are respected for the facts they know about music. They are not admired for their insight into music as aesthetic experience.[1]

Conventional musicological activity is important and needs no justification, but music scholar Joseph Kerman asks whether musicologists do enough.

> Why should analysts concentrate solely on the internal structure of the individual work of art as an autonomous entity, and take no account of such considerable matters as history, communication, affect, texts and programmes, the existence of other works of art, and so much else?[2]

For Kerman, musicology's collection of facts and details masks a reluctance to interpret and thus to engage with the world which gives music significance.[3]

There have been alternatives to this kind of musical positivism, but musicology has generally been very unsympathetic to them. Donald Tovey, Deryck Cooke, and Leonard Meyer are notable contextualizers whose work has had some extramusical attention and influence. Recently musicologists have tended to concentrate on their perceived inadequacies—respectively, an overdependence on elaborate extramusical metaphors, scrambled semiotics, pandering.[4] As a result these figures have sometimes been slighted or even ignored, but as Kerman points out, for all they may have lacked, they did something vital. These writers sought to connect to popular audiences, regardless of what elites might think.[5]

Whatever these writers' shortcomings, I will hope to take from them something quite essential. As Kerman points out in reference to Meyer, they deal "with music as perceived by listeners. The theory is oriented towards the receptor rather than the stimulus, to the listener who experiences 'emotion and meaning' rather than the composer who puts them in."[6]

This is the sensibility informing the musical components of my own study. I will consider composers and listeners both, but I will do so primarily as an informed but lay listener, one who is not in a position to add to the valuable literature of musicological detail. I will seek rather to elaborate on the other, underdeveloped side of the equation: context. I will set forth some theoretical and critical strategies for dealing with music in a setting which is not strictly musical. I will demonstrate said strategies through some film/music content analysis, and then venture some

interpretations, of various sorts and predicated on various traditions, that will situate that content more clearly. These interpretations are intended for other lay listeners with similar
backgrounds, and to musicians who don't yet share them.

The background to which I refer is characterized by Edward
Said in his book *Musical Elaborations* (1991). In this work Said
applies literary/cultural tools to music, observing that music has
not applied valuable advances from these fields (such as the work
of theorists like Raymond Williams, Roland Barthes, Michel
Foucault, Stuart Hall, Jacques Derrida, and Frederick Jameson),
and that it has harmed itself in not so doing. Said observes that
when even hermetics like James Joyce and Stéphane Mallarmé
are being read ideologically or psychoanalytically, music can and
should receive similar scrutiny.[7]

But there are difficulties attached to this kind of border crossing. Before continuing with the main body of this study, I wish
briefly to address some of the challenges and benefits of interdisciplinary study, especially in the areas of film and music.

The London *Sunday Times* had the following to say about film
music. "At its best, the big idea [about film music] is not simply
to get the music to sell the movie, and vice versa, but to use the
power of one to enhance, and make explicit, the mood of the
other."[8] Again, in reference to the British Broadcasting Corpora-
tion (BBC) 1994 television production of Charles Dickens's
Martin Chuzzlewit: "If there was music, it was perfect, because
I can't remember hearing any."[9] These comments, respectively
introductory and slightly facetious as they are, suggest a number
of intriguing things about the status and function of film music
in general popular discourse.

The Culture section of the *Times* proclaims reasonably expert
correspondents and assumes a broadly informed readership. In
view of this it is interesting to note how a fairly obvious, banal
insight—that music enhances mood in film—should be seen by
the author as something fresh, or that he should present it as such
to his readers. Whether the lack lies with the writer, his grasp of
reader background, in the experience of the readers themselves,
or in some combination of the three, something is suggested
here. Despite its long participation in the making and inflecting
of meaning in movies, music remains in many ways and in many

instances an unconsidered, un-understood, unsung component of the cinematic equation. That this is so is at least partly due to the persistence of an ancient film-musical platitude, which abides despite a good deal of theorizing and practicing suggestive of other possibilities.

The second quote from the *Times* reflects the platitude, briefly touched upon in my introduction, that in film music must be subordinate to the image and to the narrative impulse, that music's role is to meekly reinforce these more important players, and to not call attention to itself as it does so.[10] That this has been, and continues generally to be the case is not disputed.[11] What is interesting is that the *Times* writers should take it so much for granted. That they do so leads us to a dilemma that motivates the present project, which seeks to overcome the dilemma even as it inevitably suffers from some of its effects.

It is not my desire to denigrate these writers, but rather to suggest through them a very pressing problem, a central challenge to writers in any cultural field. Critics of popular music and of television state painfully obvious, or patently incomplete, notions about film music. Their gaffes are not unique, nor are they signs of any special inadequacy. Given today's exponentially expanding repertories of information and the staggering proliferation of writing in every discipline, the difficulties of merely keeping up have become very great, even in a single area of study. The challenge of currency in additional media is a very daunting one indeed.

I am aware of the possibilities and problems of poaching from enclosed disciplines. Said acknowledges these as well, but nevertheless expresses faith in the value and validity, even the necessity of this course. He does so through recourse to the concept of transgression, or of daring to venture where one does not belong.

> In its most literal sense transgression means to cross over, but rather than simply leave it at that I want to insist that the notion does not necessarily imply some irrevocable action against law or divinity. Secular transgression chiefly involves moving from one domain to another, the testing and challenging of limits, the mixing and intermingling of heterogeneities, cutting across expectations, providing unforeseen pleasures, discoveries, experiences.[12]

For all the errors incident to traveling in unfamiliar critical territory, it is just this venturing forth, this kind of transgression that provides the solution to the exclusivities and irrelevancies feared by Joseph Kerman. Said continues:

> The transgressive element in music is its nomadic ability to attach itself to, and become a part of, social formations, to vary its articulations and rhetoric depending on the occasion as well as the audience, plus the power and the gender situations in which it takes place.[13]

In other words, music is multivalent, emerging from numbers of contexts and susceptible to numerous recontextualizations, though social/musical custom may blind us to the fact.

If this is the case, a challenge still presents itself. Where do we find these instructive transgressions? How do we connect music to social formations, or rather, how do we draw out the connections that are already in place but which tend to remain effaced? Said refers to a practice transgressive enough to trouble most every constituency along the musical continuum. "*References and allusions*, negative and positive, create the context of musical presentation and representation."[14] This of course relates to the institution of quotation, musical and otherwise, the status of which has already been discussed at length.

Musicology may not yet be fully attuned, but for their part films are already built on references and allusions, both textual and intertextual, as much study in recent years has demonstrated. This being so, it seems especially useful to investigate serious music through film, and as it is appropriated in film. Here is where transgression, or border crossing and fruitful cross-pollinization, can take place. Here is where references and allusions are more customary, can be made more explicitly, and where associations and affects can perhaps be seen in greater relief.

By applying methodologies from a popular discourse to a culture (or to the products therefrom) that has tended not to be popular, we will uncover some of the contextual and ideological roots of classical music. We will also discover some of its unsuspected expressive possibilities, as revealed through the wide and sometimes surprising range of its uses in the narrative film. I hope that these explorations will reveal how this music, combined with the narrative manufacture of meaning in the movies, actually multiplies that meaning, leading to a richer, more complex play. It multiplies feeling, or affect, as well. I wish to state what unfortunately does not seem to be obvious enough: appropriated movie music can function as it does in its customary setting, rigorously, meaningfully, and susceptible to a very great many insights and enjoyments.

It can be argued that there is a predominating lack of context and social engagement in musicology. Since this is the case, Said says that "it must fall to rank outsiders with no professional musicological reputation at stake to venture the risky, often impressionistic theorizing and descriptions" that are required.[15] Commenting on music from outside the discipline can be risky, but attached to the risk are perspectives that promise great value and insight.

MAPPING THE FIELD

To begin, I would like to survey the literature, generated from film and film music communities, dealing with classical music in film. Is there precedent for this kind of study? Positive attention has been infrequent; since the advent of sound the use of classical music in film has been almost universally condemned, by commentators and practitioners alike. Early commentaries and compilations show that film music in the silent period drew broadly, even predominantly upon the classical repertory.[16] These publications list columns of composers, along with scores of their compositions, and very specific suggestions about how to use the music in films. Tony Thomas quotes Max Winkler, "the man who invented the film music cue sheet," on the nature of that use.

> We turned to crime. We began to dismember the great masters. We murdered the works of Beethoven, Mozart, Grieg, J. S. Bach, Verdi, Bizet, Tchaikowsky, and Wagner—everything that wasn't protected by copyright from our pilfering. Today I look in shame and awe at the printed copies of these mutilated masterpieces. I hope this belated confession will grant me forgiveness for what I have done.[17]

Partly because of the tone of Winkler's frequently quoted confession, compilations have not been very favorably, or even carefully, considered. Kurt London, whose *Film Music* (1936) is seen as the first self-consciously critical account of movie scores, introduces the typical response, seeing the end of borrowing as the beginning of film music maturity. "The system of compiled film illustrations remained, even in its greatest perfection, only a makeshift."[18]

London was attempting to prove that film music could be an art in itself, and so puts the best face on things, but illustrations fell *very* far short of perfection.[19] By the time Hanns Eisler's seminal *Composing for the Films* (cowritten with the uncredited Theodor Adorno) was published in 1947, allowances are no longer being made.

Eisler and Adorno briefly and dismissively discuss the use of classical music as part of their book's opening offensive, "Prejudices and Bad Habits."[20] "One of the worst practices [in film music composition] is the incessant use of a limited number of worn-out musical pieces that are associated with the given screen situations by reason of their actual or traditional titles." They see this practice as more than just an annoyance, though, and they elaborate on the consequences throughout the book. Borrowing is emblematic of all that is rootless and inferior about film music.

> It is preposterous to use words such as 'history' with reference to an apocryphal branch of art like motion-picture music. The person who around 1910 first conceived the repulsive idea of using the Bridal March from *Lohengrin* as an accompaniment is no more of a historical figure than any other second-hand dealer.[21]

The writers note that the practice of appropriating classical music is these days retained only in "cheap pictures," but still find it "a nuisance." "It is only a special instance of the general practice of rummaging through all our cultural inheritance for commercial purposes, which characterizes the cultural industry."[22]

Among other things, a kind of modernist elitism (to be discussed further in the next chapter) operates here. Writing in the same year, British film music writer John Huntley offers a different kind of caution.

The associations which individual members of the audience may have in relation to a certain piece of well-known music are quite beyond the control of the director of a film in which it is used; indeed it may produce an effect on the individual entirely different to the one he wants, or it will almost certainly produce a distraction (which may occur at a vital moment in the plot and spoil the whole effect of the film), because of these private reminiscences which are evoked by the music.[23]

Huntley is motivated by more than just snobbery. For him it is not only that quotation is tired, it is also dangerous. Precomposed music can upset film hierarchies (narrative explicit, ideology effaced), and unduly open up the traditional narrative film.

These two sets of dismissals and warnings set the tone for a whole generation of film music commentators to come. To one degree or another, they all repeated the same refrains.[24] Writing on early film music practice, Charles Berg observes that

the employment of mechanical pianos and random phonographic accompaniments . . . indicates the rather narrow and arbitrary attitude toward music that prevailed. These mechanical accompaniments which were not capable of responding to the shifting moods and situations on the screen eliminated the possibility of music giving any substantial dramatic support to the film.[25]

Berg's observation, written in the 1970s, is based on historical documentation, but his judgments about dramatic support are similar to the sentiments of his own contemporaries. Many commentators from this period are not so much historians or rigorous scholars as informed and passionate aficionados. As a result, instead of observing patterns and identifying causes, much of what they write aggressively advocates, prescribes, and forbids. Their views on classical music are much affected.

Roy Prendergast is skeptical about the usefulness of previously composed music. "The music for [concert music films], however great on its own merits, was really the antithesis of good film music, for it was certainly not conceived with the dramatic requirements of the picture in mind."[26] Is this true? Frequently what we intend is not the same as what we accomplish, and yet something is accomplished. Prendergast's objection does not hold, until we look more closely at what underpins it.

We would not underline a dramatic film with a Beethoven symphony because, no matter how good the film, the audience might
end up listening to Beethoven. In short, good film music is a purely
functional aspect of . . . drama.[27]

Here is a strangely conflicting statement, with a defensive fear
of Beethoven coinciding with the too-modest view that film
music should be purely functional, and not call attention to itself.
Much film music writing still betrays this conflict, with inferiority complexes exacerbated by lack of ambition. The result is that
very practical, how-to concerns can flare up into disproportion-
ately strong feeling.

Irwin Bazelon objects to the use of the standard repertoire for
mere "emotional saccharine." He expects the musician to object
too.

To a music-loving purist the use of concert music in films of this
type is *offensive* because the original mood and tone, organic to the
composition's formal structure, are altered when combined with
oversweetened narrative.[28]

Ernest Lindgren echoes John Huntley, summarizing this still
standard view about the possible duplicities of film music, and
then using some remarkably emphatic language.

The use of well-known music is . . . distracting, and has the
additional disadvantage that it often has certain associations for
the spectator which may conflict entirely with the associations
the producer wishes to establish in his film. . . . The use of classical music for sound films is entirely to be deplored.[29]

Lindgren's strong sentiments are almost universal among the
film composing community, which adds a new issue to the mix.
Composers repeatedly emphasize how precomposition is an emblem of various dire philistinisms.

Producers will rest content [to tolerate mediocre film music] so
long as movie critics, like the movie-going public itself, continue
to exhibit their altogether remarkable insensitivity to all film music
except popular songs, folk tunes, ballads or familiar concert and
opera classics; and so long as music critics continue to ignore film
music completely.[30]

It can be said that this statement equates philistinism with the
mistreatment of artists, in this case film music artists. Precom-

posed tunes are an emblem and element of this mistreatment. So it is that many complaints against this music emerge as statements of solidarity for put-upon members of the composers' fraternity.

Tony Thomas defends Alfred Newman, whose contribution to George Stevens's *The Greatest Story Ever Told* (1965) was much derided.

> The more snide among the critics sneered at Newman's 'attempting to glorify his own music by incorporating Verdi and Handel' but once again it was a case of the blame being laid at the wrong door. Stevens had defeated his own purpose by insisting on the *Hallelujah Chorus*; all it did was accentuate an already overly-theatrical film. Sprinkled as it was with dozens of cameo performances by famous faces the film emerged as a rather monstrous vaudeville act.[31]

Jerry Goldsmith comments on a different example of the same problem.

> I remember seeing Stanley Kubrick's *2001: A Space Odyssey* and cringing at what I consider to be an abominable misuse of music. I had heard the music Alex North had written for the film. . . . It is a mistake to force music into a film, and for me *2001* was ruined by Kubrick's choice of music. His selections had no relationship, and the pieces could not comment on the film because they were not a part of it.[32]

Goldsmith is addressing the familiar problems of appropriateness, the need for music to support images, the ambiguity of familiar music, which ambiguity is taken to be negative. But inseparable from his *contra*-Kubrick sentiment is the *pro*-North one. The travails of Alfred Newman and Alex North are just a part of a larger fraternal problem.

> I have no tolerance for the critics who put down film music. The film composer today functions in much the same way as did Mozart, Haydn, and Bach with their weekly commitments to the church or their patrons, except that we haven't yet produced a Mozart, a Haydn, or a Bach. But it can happen.[33]

Goldsmith's meaning is clear: to the critical listener, "Stop putting us down;" to the composer (and the film producer), "Don't use the greats, become great yourself."

The connection between classical quotation and composer trib-ulation is very important. For composers, especially during Hol-lywood's heyday, using classical music increased their sense of alienation and frustration, as it took them further away from their own goals and development as composers. Later, after the break-down of studio orchestras, use of prerecorded music meant, for both composer and musician, unemployment. There was no need for live bodies when a recording would do.[34]

A related challenge is that classical music actually adds to the prejudice, the "snobbism," and ignorance that keeps film com-posers from receiving their full due.

> The snobbism comes from outside the industry, from so-called serious music lovers who have always tended to regard that which is written for films as being of less value than what is written for the concert hall, the opera, the ballet, or the theatre.[35]

Given prejudices like these, the film music community policy, and the policy of its staunch defenders (such as Thomas, Ba-zelon, Prendergast), makes complete sense.[36] "I . . . believe that original composition, not the adaptation of music from other sources, is the answer to effective film music."[37] That's the sense of the standard view; Bernard Herrmann articulates the feeling behind it. "I think it's stupid [the use of preexisting music]. What's it got to do with the film? Nothing. Cover it with choco-late ice cream, that's about it!"[38]

This then is the dominant thinking with regard to classical music in film, and in many ways it remains current. However other possibilities have appeared. Irene Kahn Atkins's book, *Source Music for Motion Pictures* (1983) is built on the con-straints we have just been observing. Echoing the language of the golden age composers, and probably echoing their motivation as well, Atkins says

> there is really nothing very creative about playing a record to ac-company a film, even if there is a phonograph or radio on the screen. This criticism is also applicable to the use of records in nonsource background scoring, as in *2001*, *The Exorcist*, and *Barry Lyndon*. One argument against the use of records, particu-larly orchestral ones such as 'Blue Danube' and '*Also Sprach Za-rathustra*,' is that they have a frozen, congealed-in-aspic quality;

another, that they are a throwback to the clichés of silent theater music, with 'tried-and-true' classics from 'the old masters.'[39]

Using records is not creative, presumably, because no one created any new music, and therefore they were not paid, and they were not enhanced in reputation, and neither was the film medium itself.[40] I will hope to show through this study that, beyond a not insignificant concern for the livelihood and reputation of film composers, these sentiments are simply not true.

Atkins's book is designed "to show the way in which source music can enhance the dramatic elements in a film."[41] For her, "source music" is that which "is audible to the characters of the film" regardless of its point of emanation.[42] It is almost always precomposed, prerecorded music. For Atkins, "enhance" implies an evaluative model evident throughout the book, and throughout the work of other writers quoted in this section. There is recurring consideration of music that works and music that doesn't, "working" meaning to reinforce meaning and unify disparate cinematic elements.

It is out of notions like these that many of the central questions of my own study emerge, as well as many of its main points of departure. Though one can argue about more or less successful music, my contention is that all music enhances, if we take enhance to mean that it inflects and affects, whether for unity or multiplicity. If unity of meaning has been invoked for the sake of better and more profitable films, then an opening up of meaning and of the sources from which meaning derives can expand our ideas about, and our experiences with, both quality and profit.

This opening up also relates to Atkins's use of the term "source music." Actual instances of musical elaboration far exceed the constraints of audible emanations, or even the standard splits between diegetic (audible to the characters of the film) and nondiegetic (audible to the audience but not to the characters) sound.[43] Claudia Gorbman points out the frequent presence of "metadiegetic" film music, which straddles the inner and outer narrative spaces that are so often characterized as being strictly separated. For her film music maintains a complex and shifting relationship of "mutual implication" with the image track, the permutations of which result in a rich and constantly negotiated "*combinatoire* of expression."[44]

In this light the traditional formulations described by film music advocates in this section become limiting. Not only is music expressive all the way across the sound track, so too can image express regardless of its accompanying music's temporal or compositional origins. With the possibilities, and realities too, of Gorbman's mutual implication, it is clearly not necessary to so smother notions of music's affect, nor is it necessary to proscribe the music being used.

I do feel that Atkins's book is valuable for the way it hinted at other possibilities beyond the accepted film-musical norm. She is one of the first writers to call attention, in a serious and sometimes sympathetic way, to the possibilities of using source, or precomposed, music in films. This is a shift which, followed by a rush of other film-musical elaborations (to be discussed in the next section) opens up a place for the present work. Following Gorbman's terminological lead, I have expanded Atkins's definition of source music to include any piece—in this instance classical—composed previous to the film's production, and occurring somewhere across the cinematic soundscape (non-diegetic, diegetic, or metadiagetic). On that broad spectrum distinctions must—and will—be made between different articulations and variations. But now I wish simply to take Atkins's original focus on preexisting music, and through it demonstrate some of the many ways attention to this element of the *combinatoire* enhances and enriches the cinematic equation.

FINDING A PLACE FOR SOURCE MUSIC IN FILM

As we have seen, much writing on film music, and on source music in film, simply states what the writer prefers and then condemns that which departs from it. Beneath this tendency lie whole histories of evaluative criticism, of advocacy and taste-making and interpretive virtuosity, of eccentricity and mediocrity, of the buying and selling that always underpins popular critical discourse. In response there have also been waves of opposition and reaction, new methodologies and new criticisms, more measured and scholarly approaches to texts and to their interpretation, or explication. These also may have had their own tendentious roots and unacknowledged, even unconscious agendas. I will not take time here to set forth any kind of critical history, but I do wish to present a distillation of methods that emerge out of these numerous contending, incomplete impulses. I wish to briefly set forth, and then go on to make use of, some strategies that seem to be useful for the question at hand, and more useful than the kind of highly opinionated prescribing and proscribing that have dominated the discussion. Some of these strategies pertain directly to film music, while others come from different settings and require some transposition.

In setting forth these ideas I should emphasize their relation to my earlier comments about interdisciplinary scholarship. We will presently go on to explore new theoretical ground, but these first introductory notions will all be familiar to scholars of various literary or cinematic stripes. This relates to the present orientation, as well as to other discussions in this book.[45] Some of these scholars may even find the ideas to be overly familiar and of diminished usefulness in contemporary critical discussions. While open to the potential of this point, I will still stand by my warhorses, and for two simple reasons. The first of these is that the initiate's platitude is of great value to the disoriented neophyte, including perhaps the experienced musician. The other is that notwithstanding their familiarity, I remain satisfied that these pearls of received wisdom still contains much that is wise, and that even specialists need cardinal points for their ongoing navigations.

How can we begin a more useful, open-minded discussion about classical music in film? The boosters of the film music community might benefit from the following four ideas. First I suggest that the familiar demands and advocacies should give way to a kind of subordination, where the viewer/listener stops wrestling and simply tries to understand. C. S. Lewis's invaluable *Experiment in Criticism* (1961) calls for an alternative to the evaluative criticism we have already seen. Instead of critical prescription and the imposing of personal, sometimes ill-fitting sensibilities upon a work, Lewis recommends the enlargement of self through sincerely seeking to understand a text on its own terms. What is the nature of the book, or, if we might venture to adapt, the film? On what principles is it operating, and how might the reader conform to these principles? Having asked these questions, the reader/viewer simply, and humbly, tries to learn.[46]

This strategy is of course familiar from the writings of André Bazin. Bazin felt that, though medium specificity (Rudolf Arnheim, the Soviets) had been important at one point, the cinema was mature enough to stop having to separate itself from the other arts. He allowed for the occasional subordination of cinematic impulse to a preexisting text, sensibility, or philosophy. With such subordination, the other element of the equation could not only be recontextualized in an enlightening fashion, but film itself could be enriched as well.[47] The implications for considering classical music in film in this way are obvious.

Lewis and Bazin bring us to other complementary strategies. The title of Susan Sontag's influential essay "Against Interpretation" (1964) offers a rebuttal to overly fussy film musician prescription. Sontag suggests that to interpret is to wrest or justify a work that requires neither. Interpretation is not absolute, and

> in most modern instances, interpretation amounts to the philistine refusal to leave the work of art alone. Real art has the capacity to make us nervous. By reducing the work of art to its content and then interpreting *that*, one tames the work of art. Interpretation makes art manageable, comfortable.[48]

With regard to our present topic we might admit that classical music can clearly make some film types uncomfortable. We might then suggest that this discomfort, or the attempt to legislate for the sake of its elimination, finally, harmfully limits film itself. Opening eyes (or ears) can open up the medium. "The function of criticism should be to show *how it is what it is*, even *that it is what it is*, rather than to show *what it means*."[49]

David Bordwell and Kristin Thompson have developed these strategies in their wide-ranging neoformalist studies. Without advocating an absolute end to interpretation, Bordwell suggests "that art is an affair of perception, and as such it presents the perceiver with problems of unity and disunity." But these problems need not be solved; conflicts in art are frequently unresolved, and struggle and strangeness are not stages to pass through, but valid destinations. Instead of finding meaning that delimits, Bordwell seeks to articulate, to explicate, and to leave open aesthetic experience.[50]

Again, the relevance of this course to film music study is obvious. Commentators would do well to stop objecting so much and just start observing. Even Eisler and Adorno suggest as much when they point out that strict universal criteria cannot be applied to uses of film music. Drawing on Hegel, they see potential harm in bringing "one's own yardsticks and [applying] one's personal intuition and ideas to the inquiry; it is only by omitting these that we are enabled to examine the subject matter as it is in and for itself."

Having presented and established these clear, cautionary positions, we return to a selective survey of film-musical scholarship. In doing so we find that in the work of a number of more recent scholars the partisanship of the pioneering scholar/advocates is giving way to just this kind of an evenhanded approach. Claudia Gorbman's groundbreaking 1987 study, *Unheard Melodies: Narrative Film Music*, takes important film music contexts—narratology and film music, the reasons music is used, its relationship to the spectator, the classical Hollywood model, and the Eisler/Adorno critique—and describes them, all in dispassionate detail, all the while resisting the urge to evaluate or to rate. In thus comparing preexisting models Gorbman also brings about an important expansion. The primordial division of film music between poles of parallelism and perpendicularity becomes, in Gorbman's *combinatoire*, a much more open and interesting system. In terms of the object of study here this means that whatever the musical source of idea and affect, it deserves our attention.

In the same way Kathryn Kalinak's 1992 book, *Settling the Score: Music and the Classical Hollywood Film*, also takes a more objective view of Hollywood scoring conventions. While detailing the way things have been, Kalinak implicitly suggests that what *has been* is not what *must be*. Although neither of these books deals primarily with source music, or classical source music, their scholarly openness does provide a context where this music can be and even must be observed, calmly and sympathetically. Also antecedent to this study is *Film Music I*, a collection published in 1989 and edited by Clifford McCarty. This excellent collection of essays helpfully extends its inquiries into a number of diverse film-musical settings, without priority or hierarchy.

The work of film music scholar Royal Brown is helpful for similar reasons. Brown's chapter in Gary Edgerton's book on film and the arts is one of the only works to consider at any length the specific relations between film and classical music.[51] While he quickly turns his attention from classical music to the classical film score, it is finally his open attitude, his willingness to wander into seemingly unrelated but ultimately enlightening areas that is most of value to the present study. By avoiding hasty judgment and undue delimitation Brown is able to more clearly place the music he hears, regardless of its source or substance.[52] In his book *Overtones and Undertones: Reading Film Music* (1994), Brown expands upon this idea, advocating and modeling an active engagement with film music. We should not only listen to and think about the music on its own textual terms, but we should do as Joseph Kerman suggested, making clear the links between the music and its social and material bases, connecting artistic expression to industrial production, and to our own reception and use.

This clearly takes us beyond neoformalism, beyond the new-critical, closely textual strategies that Lewis, Bordwell, and Sontag have described for us. If their explications, their principled noninterpretations serve to counter the stubborn rejections that had prevailed on this film-musical subject, they still fall short of exhausting its possibilities. The question of connection, of returning audiovisual combinations to some kind of praxis likewise takes us beyond the open-minded and evenhanded work of these just cited film music scholars. Their studies are expansive in attitude, but they are also effectively delimited. As a result they do not take on some of the challenges unique to source music, nor do they consider some of the questions essential to its understanding. How, then, do we effectively map this largely uncharted territory? Ultimately no methodology is adequate to the present proliferation of film and film-musical activity or accounts for every individual instance. Given contemporary complications, I venture to say that it is in a systematic survey of approaches, in a balanced and measured utilization of all the best critical constructs that the scholar, the practitioner, and the spectator will be best served, and will best serve.

What are some of these constructs? For newcomers and seasoned readers alike, some of the basic methods remain useful. One of these is artist-centered. If scholars have in the past been inattentive, it is important to point out that production practice has frequently pushed theoretical boundaries and opened new ground for the study of classical music in film. Classical music is integral to the provocative soundscapes of Jean-Luc Godard or Werner Herzog. It contains some of the compelling oppositions and thematic cores in the work of Ingmar Bergman and Pier Paolo Pasolini. It is one of the sites of Luis Buñuel's dark ironies, as well as his incongruous expressions of tenderness. The music carries much of the majesty and mystery of Robert Bresson's work. In it we locate the tragedy and humanity in the films of Jean Renoir or Louis Malle. It reveals ideological structures beneath narrative surface in the work of Max Ophuls, Luchino Visconti, and Martin Scorsese.

These last examples of classical music use obviously evoke a kind of high modernist auteurism. Inevitably the prospect of masterful authorship tempts us toward the Romantic and the ineffable and to their undoubted insights and pleasures. Still, the auteurs themselves and their various expressions will also lead us to weighty aesthetical and historical questions that the industrial run-of-the-mill will seldom summon. Classical quotations frequently do the same, and can thus be seen as sharing the aims of the art film. They practically force these big issues—preenlightenment plenitude, individualistic ideologies, and the myth of the Romantic artist, formal fragmentations and the possibility of far-reaching reconciliations—into the customarily isolated, defensive precincts of romantic music and commercial film. If all of these things are not necessarily in critical fashion, then their insistent cyclical resurgence reminds us that critical fashion, like industrial practice, can benefit from occasional jolts and reorientations.

My chapter five will demonstrate that these interesting devices and the ideas they summon are being taken up and transformed in modern production practice. For all the decrying of its apparently harmful distractions, quotations continue to deepen films and our experiences with them. Of course, there is more to quoting than depth and unity. The big questions and the masters who ask them may maintain currency, but the academics are correct in being wary of idealistic auteurism. Present industrial realities remind us that there are many other less heady settings in which we can increasingly find and study classical music, and more pressing reasons for us to do so.

In the age of the compiled sound-track album we find a proliferation of such pieces in more commercial films, and we are thus reminded that the music industry is becoming increasingly important to our film scholarship. Its presence, and what it suggests of media conglomeration and new horizontal integrations, reminds us that things musical are emblematic of a general shift in film culture. The language, our understanding and use of it, the infrastructures in which conversations take place, all are changing across the board. These changes have required and invited different critical strategies, so that what appears as destabilization has also led to helpful multiplication, and a greater understanding of music in cultural contexts. New film-musical topographies have allowed us to make use of work (by Simon Frith, Dick Hebdige, Susan McLary, Angela McRobbie, Phillip Tagg, for example) that had previously appeared to be extra-disciplinary.[53] Recent books by Jeff Smith and Anahid Kassabian have been helpful in describing the shape of the new sound track and in proposing critical methodologies adequate thereto. Movements such as these have begun to affect musical insularity to some degree. The latest edition of the *New Grove Dictionary* (an institution to which we will return at length in the next chapter) has become positively—or at least partially—sympathetic toward film music, allowing its wide range of possibilities and acknowledging it as a worthy object of scholarly and musical attention. It even gives slight ground on the subject of source music.

Given such advances in scholarship and interdisciplinary sympathy, we can see that difficult or confusing industrial circumstances have not kept us from a critical best-of-times, and in some ways have contributed to it. We are understanding music in culture as perhaps never before, and this brings us to a final critical methodology and closes our survey of attitudes toward classical source music. We began with the defensive dismissals of film-musical spokesmen and practitioners and suggested that their totalizing responses to source music were both understandable and inadequate. We spoke of the disadvantages of hasty interpretation, and found value in stopping short of definitive judgments. Notwithstanding all this, it is interpretation that closes the circle and brings source music fully in touch with its most important contexts.

That context is personal, which is to say that it resides in the individual spectator, or in a community of individuals. Having considered the insights and advantages of textual criticism, having allowed for auteurist intent and the influences of industry and culture, we finally return to the reader, and to how he makes use of or finds benefit from what he is reading. The use and benefit comes from these multiple approaches, and from the more measured interpretation and application they allow. We will grant that interpretations can be dangerous. David Bordwell for one has demonstrated how frequently excessive and even silly the interpretive impulse can be. But what is possible is not necessarily inevitable;[54] I advocate the seeking and weighing of numerous possible answers, and I feel that multiple interpretations, presented as options for understanding, can be extremely useful. They show us how rich and multivalent a work can be, and give us, and others, multiple points of access and use.[55] These multiple points can also encourage a reader or viewer who may have been cowed by absolute interpretations or daunted by the indeterminacies of formalist analysis, to join in, finding a place and a voice. In addition to letting art be, it can also be desirable to join, as a reader or viewer, in the art-making process.[56]

In addressing these multiplicities, French sound theorist Michel Chion provides a final inspiration for this work. In his 1985 work *Le Son au Cinéma*, Chion suggests, as in the possibilities of the metadiegetic category, a way out of the parallel/perpendicular impasse that has bedeviled film music.[57] A third category, "anempathetic" music, allows us to do more than simply support and oppose, but rather to see, and hear, how music shifts and confounds in the ways it relates to meaning.[58]

In his 1994 book, *Audio-Vision*, Chion goes beyond the films themselves to make a similar distinction between *critical* approaches to film music. He posits three receptive categories. Causal listening seeks the source of sound, and its specific meaning. Semantic listening, which is based on codes and language, contains the possible extravagances (personal interpretations) of the causal alternative. And reduced listening, like formalism, seeks only to observe and account without recourse to interpretation or semiotic rationalization.[59]

Which approach is validated? All of them. Chion rejects methodological hierarchies, and compositional ones as well. He too effaces distinctions between diegetic and nondiegetic music, between original compositions and excerpted ones. Each option means, and each deserves attention; I agree. There are numerous points to consider when studying classical music in film. Few of them have received any substantial attention. Rather than following previous courses of prescription and proscription, I will present a broad survey of approaches. It will be left for the reader to choose and follow what he or she feels to be the most productive path.

NOTES

1. Kerman, 1985, 12.
2. Ibid, 18.
3. Ibid, 31–59, 79–90.
4. See Tovey, 1937, Meyer, 1956, Cooke, 1959. For criticism see Monelle, 1992, 1–30.
5. Kerman, 1985, 107.
6. Ibid., 108. The phrase "emotion and meaning" refers to the title of Meyer's 1956 book, *Emotion and Meaning in Music*.
7. Said, 1991, xiv–xvi. Elaboration is by no means a new concept. Donald Tovey's musical criticism contains many striking extrapolations from extramusical discourse. See for instance his comments on the relations between Mendelssohn's incidental music to *A Midsummernight's Dream* and Shakespeare's play. Tovey, 1937, IV, 102–9.
8. Sandall, 1994, 19.
9. Gill, 1994, 3.
10. This idea was first and most influentially stated in London, 1936, 37.
11. The title of Claudia Gorbman's *Unheard Melodies: Narrative*

Film Music is very suggestive of the subservient, even subjugated status of film music throughout the history of the medium. Her book is just one of many convincing works that trace the whys and ways of this kind of musical functioning. See "mapping the field" section in this chapter, and the discussion on parallelism in chapter three.

12. Said, 1991, 55.

13. Ibid., 70.

14. Ibid., 90. Emphasis added.

15. Ibid., xvii.

16. See George, 1912 and 1914, Becce, 1919 (cited in London, 1936, 55), Lang and West, 1920, Rapée, 1924 and 1925. It should be noted that, while I have and will make some reference to silent film music, my emphasis for the most part will be on the sound film.

17. Thomas, 1973, 37–38. See also Karlin, 1994, 156–57.

18. London, 1936, 62. Cf. film composer Leonard Rosenman, quoted in Thomas, 1979, 237.

19. London, 1936, 78–79.

20. Chapter one in Eisler, 1947, 3–19.

21. Ibid., 15, 49.

22. Ibid, 15–16, 49, 82. See also their introduction, ix–xi. Eisler and Adorno do note the potential "charming disproportion" of, say, "Pluto galloping over the ice to the ride of the Walkyries." (17) For more on such oppositional possibilities, see "counterpoint" section in chapter three.

23. Huntley, 1947, 53–54.

24. This is not to say that their repetitions were unconsidered, but as I hope to demonstrate, there are other ways to look at these issues.

25. Berg, 1976, 17.

26. Prendergast, 1992, 70.

27. Williams, Martin, "Jazz at the Movies," in Limbacher, 1974, 42. Cf. composer Ernest Gold: "I wouldn't use classical music as a score, I think it interferes. If you know the music, it draws more attention to itself than it should. . . . If you don't know the music, it doesn't support the picture because it wasn't written for the picture." Quoted in Larson, 1987, 351–52.

28. Bazelon, 1975, 133. Emphasis added.

29. Quoted in Flinn, 1993, 37.

30. Thomas, 1973, 21.

31. Ibid, 62.

32. Quoted in Thomas, 1979, 227–28. See Cooke, 2001, 806, for a similar sentiment on the same issue, and relating to the same source.

33. Ibid.

34. On alienation of Hollywood musicians see Eisler, 1947, 45–61 (especially note on 55–56), 112–13; Faulkner, 1971, 22, 44–57. On unemployment and other related issues see also Chanan, 1995, 82–86.

35. Thomas, 1979, 7.

36. For the advocates' view, see Thomas, 1973, 1979, Limbacher, 1974, Bazelon, 1975, Prendergast 1992.

37. Franz Waxman, in Thomas, 1979, 55. See also British film composer Clarence Raybould, quoted in Prendergast, 1992, 20.

38. Quoted in Brown, 1994, 291. In contrast to this overwhelming rejection Brown (1988, 177–80) briefly discusses a strain of acceptance for this music, continuing from silent practices well into the sound period. This acknowledgment, however, is fairly unique in the current literature.

39. Atkins, 1983, 58.

40. Cf. Bernstein, Elmer, 1972. Also in *Film Music Notebook* 1, Winter 1974, 10–16.

41. Atkins, 1983, 17.

42. Ibid., 13.

43. See my chapter five for a fuller discussion of diegetic, nondiegetic and metadiegetic issues.

44. Gorbman, 1987, 15–16, 20–26. In this connection Gorbman also discusses the dialogue and sound effects tracks. These are obviously important elements of these image/sound relationships. Notwithstanding, this work will concentrate mostly on musical uses. See Kassabian, 2001, 42–49 for a helpful discussion about the elements of Gorbman's *combinatoire*.

45. I.e., my discussion of montage and semiotics in chapter three.

46. Lewis, 1961, see especially 104–41.

47. Bazin, 1967. See particularly "In Defense of Mixed Cinema" (53–75), "Theatre and Cinema" (parts 1 and 2, 76–94, 95–124), and "*Le journal d'un curé de campagne* and the Stylistics of Robert Bresson" (125–43).

48. Sontag, 1983, 97, 99.

49. Ibid., 104.

50. Bordwell, 1981, 3–4, 60–61, 186. See also "Why not to read a film" in Bordwell, 1989, 249–74.

51. Brown, 1988, 168–69, 179–80, 184–92 (see section titled "Styles and Genres of Interaction").

52. This survey should also include Caryl Flinn's *Strains of Utopia: Gender, Nostalgia and Hollywood Film Music*, which among other things discusses classical film scoring in relation to musical romanticism and its various ideologies. Flinn also briefly discusses Hollywood antipathies to the use of classical music. Flinn, 1992, 13–50.

53. See Romney and Wooton (1995) for an excellent example of this felicitous interdisciplinary meeting.

54. Bordwell, 1989, 254–63. For an example see quotation in Flinn, 1992, 67.

55. In another setting, and as only one example out of the many possible, see two compelling and contradictory accounts of Orson Welles's *The Magnificent Ambersons* (1942): "Oedipus in Indianapolis," in Carringer, 1993, 5–32; and Jonathon Rosenbaum in Welles and Bogdanovich, 1992, 454–56.

56. The interpretation by P. Adams Sitney of some very difficult and slippery avant-garde film texts is exemplary in this regard. Sitney's interpretations can (and should) be debated, but it is by interpreting and then debating that he makes these challenging films accessible and personal for viewers who might otherwise be excluded. See Sitney, 1979.

57. Once again, classical Hollywood vs. the kind of oppositional, "contrapuntal" practice advocated by Hanns Eisler. See chapter three.

58. In Gorbman, 1987, 151–61. Gorbman clearly acknowledges her debt to Chion, and returns the favor in her translation of *Audio-Vision*. Incidentally, Chion is not the first to think of anempathetic possibilities in music. Eisler, quoting Busoni, notes the similar function of the *Barcarolle* in Offenbach's *Tales of Hoffman*. Eisler, 1947, 27. See also the concept of "essence and appearance" in ibid., 29, 79

59. In Chion, 1994, 25–34.

2

Film Music and the Musical Community

IN THE FIRST CHAPTER I discussed the challenge of interdisciplinary study, and this second chapter will illustrate a particularly thorny example of that challenge. We have seen the responses of film composers to classical music, as well as the observations of several writers and scholars. We have seen that the former group has predominantly condemned direct use of classical cues. However, that condemnation notwithstanding, film musicians have consistently sought to appropriate other elements of classical musical culture within their own work.

I will briefly discuss some of these strategies, and then go on to consider some of the ways that *musicians* and *music* critics have responded, both to specific instances of poaching, and to film music in general.

In addition, I will seek to situate music criticism within a larger critical context. We have already seen how traditional musicology has tended not to go beyond purely musical facts. The thoughts of other cultural figures will help us to place and understand some of these facts, and the way musicology inflects their interpretation in film settings. With that broader cultural ground illuminated, I will go on in later chapters to discuss ways that both film and music, as well as their respective communities, can benefit from mutual association.

We begin with a typically unsympathetic musical response to film music. In his foreword to a UNESCO catalog of films for music education, John Madison is sarcastic about music's traditional subservience in film. "Stronger mortals may abjure what they feel to be the irrelevancies of how musical sound is produced; certainly where visual stimuli come between the creative artist and his audience they are to be deplored." Madison here touches upon the common feeling that the material realities of this visual medium, together with the narrative preferences of filmmakers (and audiences), marginalize music.

His solution does not account for the possibility that these realities and preferences might be valid. Piqued by music's traditional subordination, Madison goes on to suggest that film's greatest service to music could and should be to reinscribe the materiality of music, the facts of its production and enjoyment, in the viewer's consciousness. Films should at least partly be about the making of music. "Film techniques can, at their best, recapture what may be called the social dimension, recalling and revivifying the personality of a great musician or quickening the sense of occasion, whether of a chamber recital, an opera, or a grandiose festival."[1]

This is essentially a musical version of André Bazin's discussion of photographic ontology, and valuable as far as it goes.[2] But from Madison's music-first position there is no awareness of or concern for whether film might not have its own ontology, its own ways of expressiveness, its own artful destiny. What Madison suggests, a half-century after film culture started to reject the notion, is a validation of film through validation of the nonfilmic.[3]

The UNESCO catalog concentrates on filmed musical performances, a few documentaries, and the odd low-budget narrative made for educational purposes. The only feature films listed as using music educationally are rare exceptions to the usual philistine run of things.[4] For the rest, according to this account, film dishonors music.

This is the situation, then, or at least the face of it. Such discounting has been fairly typical. "Film music can do a great many things but something it apparently cannot do is overcome its own rather dubious reputation. Most musical intellectuals regard film scoring as a medium of slick, conventional, cliché-ridden composition. . . ."[5]

Naturally the film music community took issue with this view, and it took action as well. We have seen that one legitimating strategy was for film composers, after a certain point in time, to avoid precomposed cues, especially if they were classical. But if borrowing was rejected for the subordination and the inferiority that it implied, then another key strategy in the bid for musical acceptance involved a more fundamental appropriation of the classical than any mere quote. This form of appropriation was seen by a key cadre of musicians and musical scholar/critics as being not only unmusical and obsequious, but as positively transgressive. "Transgression" is not used here in Edward Said's sense of a discomfiting but ultimately productive crossing over. For the critics in question, sin literally lay at the door. Film musicians ignored, or were even ignorant of, dire cultural conditions to which they were ultimately contributing, for which they were finally at least partly responsible. I will return to these criticisms, but for now I will set forth some of the actions that gave rise to them.

Film music rationalization appears in a number of guises. One of the most important of these is demonstrated by Max Steiner.

> Often complimented as the man who invented movie music, Steiner would reply, 'Nonsense. The idea originated with Richard Wagner. Listen to the incidental scoring behind the recitatives in his opera. If Wagner had lived in this century, he would have been the Number One film composer.'[6]

Film composers sought to appropriate the reputation and culture of their forebears, or at least the most respectable of them. Steiner's comment is not as modest as it might seem, for he was very much aware of film music's lowly reputation. Rather than being monarch of that paltry kingdom, Steiner deftly conflates high opera and melodramatic movie scoring, thus bringing himself into fellowship with Wagner, and bringing the entire film composer fraternity with him.

This connection is urged throughout early film music discourse. Steiner, again:

> In my early days in Vienna, Richard Strauss and Gustav Mahler had enormous influence on all budding composers, and theirs were the styles everyone tried to emulate. Later we became aware of the French school, of men like Debussy and Ravel, followed by the great impact of Stravinsky. And of course Beethoven, Mozart, and Brahms were all basic to us. We sort of inhaled them as we grew up.[7]

The refrain of legitimation by association is taken up frequently by the first generation of film music scholarship as well. Tony Thomas deftly indicates how this Viennese abundance made its way to Hollywood.

> While both were richly melodic and obviously Viennese, Steiner was the product of an operetta background and [Erich Wolfgang] Korngold came from somewhat further up the street—from the opera house and the concert hall. . . . Vienna, *like Hollywood*, was an artistic mecca.[8]

Just as early film sought legitimization by adapting respectable authors and their works, so film music used the validated to attain its own respectability. After the silent period the use of actual classical music was officially discouraged, but the boosters' comments strongly suggest that this is no great loss.[9] Being that the film composers are real heirs to their classical—or more properly romantic—forebears, past bounty gives way without a break to present musical reality.

Another important variation of this theme can be marked through sound film's first decades. A common rebuttal to musical snobbery is similar to the previously cited, and not necessarily very cinematic, UNESCO course. Kurt London's seminal study contains an emblematic chapter, titled "Prominent European Film Composers and Their Artistic Significance."[10]

A constant refrain in John Huntley's *British Film Music* is the continuous avowal of serious composers working in the cinema. Where in the silent period it was hoped that the film medium in general would be exalted through proximity to dead musical masters, we see in Huntley's work a certain progression.[11] Now it is film music itself, and British film music specifically, that benefits in the company of revered *living* composers.

In these themes there is some truth, but there is a tangible discomfort in stating it. The tone is apologetic, and the terms of favor are distinctly dictated by the music community. The question of terms leads us to an even more fundamental and egregious classical usage. Film composers borrowed more than just traditions and reputations. Throughout the classical period of Hollywood film composition, classical music *forms* were also wholeheartedly if not completely rigorously utilized.

Romanticism and Modernism as Relating to Hollywood Film Music

British film music pioneer Muir Mathieson, to whom Huntley's book was dedicated, observed in a 1971 interview that film fulfilled the notion of *Gesamptkunstwerk* to an extent never envisioned by Wagner.[12] This is at least part of the point of Max Steiner's previously quoted comment about Wagner. In the first decades of sound films the techniques and conventions informing the work of Wagner, along with Richard Strauss and Gustav Mahler and the rest of the composers Steiner cites, were consciously and vocally applied to film music problems.

One of the most important of these techniques, and a staple of classical Hollywood composition, was the leitmotif, a marked melodic phrase or short passage by which characters and situations were identified and elaborated. The leitmotif was also a means by which otherwise diffuse and gap-filled scores were given musical unity. Of course, use and defense of the leitmotif partook also of the legitimizing influence already discussed. Once again it was not only Wagner's technique, but Wagner himself that was being appropriated.

This at least was the idea. As years passed, however, observers became less convinced of claims by film music to Wagnerian vigor and validity. Hanns Eisler and Theodor Adorno asserted that because scores and films alike were generally substandard, leitmotif in film was doomed to mere and maddening repetition.[13] Wilfred Mellers, writing in *Grove's Dictionary of Music and Musicians* (1954), echoed the argument, finding film to be too fragmented and episodic to successfully utilize a technique designed after all for large musical structures.[14]

As with the leitmotif, so too the idea of the integrated artwork, at least as conceived by Wagner, came to be seen as foreign to film realities.

> It is worth reconsidering here Wagner's interest in *Gesamtkunstwerk* and Hollywood's own investment in unified, coherent texts, since both maintain that textual components should work toward the same dramatic ends. . . . The difference between Wagner and classical film commentators, however, comes from the fact that while for Wagner the unity of the music drama was achieved

through the synthesis of its elements, with the total effect equaling more than the sum of its parts, classical film critics and practitioners believed cinematic unity was retained through redundancy and overdetermination, not through a true synthesis of elements.[15]

The gap between theory and reality that Caryl Flinn observes here has a couple of important consequences, for the music as well as for those composing it.

The romantic style to which many Hollywood composers felt themselves heir provided a musical separation from vulgar realities. This is the classic formulation about Hollywood aims and results as well, and in this way the romantic idiom seemed to be ideal for Hollywood films.[16]

The musical conventions were as follows: "nondissonant if mildly chromatic harmonies, monophonic textures, broad, sweeping melodies, and lush instrumentations."[17] Romantic music tended toward large forms and appealed generally to the sensuous, the emotional, and the inexpressible. These were exalted nineteenth-century notions, and they applied across cultural fields. Byron and Shelley, Delacroix and David, the titanic Beethoven, Bayreuth, all bespeak a kind of heroic individualism, and the notion of art that transcends context and external consideration.[18]

By the birth of film in the late nineteenth century, however, many cultural observers and artists and even musicians were feeling that the time for these things had passed. Other impulses had come to the fore. The outsized forms of Wagner or Gustav Mahler coexisted with smaller, more humanizing alternatives: in the narrative and visual arts with Ibsen and Chekhov and the Impressionists, in music with the ethnomusicological efforts of Béla Bartok, Sabine Baring-Gould, and Ralph Vaughan Williams, for instance.

They also coexisted with more troubling, and even more agonized, expressions. Positivism, along with Darwin, Marx, and Freud, was giving way to naturalism, cubism, and especially the crises rising out of the First World War (Dada, not to mention overwhelming destruction): all came to collide with what now seemed oblivious Wagnerian largeness, which was felt to reflect

only upon the largeness of Wagner (the unique, increasingly irrelevant artistic sensibility) or upon other bourgeois obscenities.
Given this trajectory, and the weight of social realities surrounding it, the romantic notion of a complete, self-contained artwork
simply broke.

By one definition romanticism leans away from the topical and
toward the ineffable. It can be said, though, and in this period it
was certainly felt, that this ineffability was disingenuous and
even dangerous. According to Elie Siegmeister,

> if these [Romantic] doctrines are unhesitatingly accepted by those
> concerned with music, as for the most part they actually are, musi-
> cians will not question the social bases of the conditions under
> which they work, nor the social function of their work. . . . Com-
> posers will go on creating in the same way . . . contemplating the
> 'inner soul' and never questioning the society under which such
> activity is doomed to frustration in advance.[19]

This account suggests that late romanticism was out of touch
even with its own time, which is why modernism fled from it.
Functioning these decades later, romantic film music was twice
removed. Escapist mandates and their consoling consequences
not only distracted audiences from their frustrations. Siegmeister's statement pertains particularly to Hollywood music makers
themselves. There is a paradox in the fact that film composers
used and defended the idiom of individuality in an industrial context that completely effaced the individual. It is at least partly
true that the celebration of romantic ideologies masked for the
composers the indentured realities of their own creativity.[20]

Music criticism, then as now, did not often underscore these
ideological matters. Yet they were an important subtext in the
music community's criticism of film music and its various appropriations. A close reading suggests that for many critics, the inadequacies of classical film music were emblematic of broader
musical/cultural ills. In other words, condemnations reflected
deeper biases. If criticism addressed, and continues to address,
inherent film music failings, it also has a foundation of extramusical discontent with the conditions of art and its reproduction in
the twentieth century. We will now look closely at an important
and influential music institutional critique of film music and at
some of the currents crossing beneath its surface.

THE GROVE DICTIONARIES

In the late 1870s, the great Victorian engineer, editor, and educator Sir George Grove undertook to prepare a comprehensive musical reference for the musical amateur. Grove's innovation and importance lay in part in the fact that he was himself an enthusiastic and informed amateur. "I wrote about the symphonies and concertos because I wished to try to make them clear to myself and to discover the secret of the things that charmed me so; and from that sprang a wish to make other amateurs see it the same way."[21]

Grove's first *Dictionary* was published in four volumes in 1879–80. After this ambitious and kindly beginning the *Grove's* continued to evolve, passing through four more editions (1904–10, 1927–28, 1940 and 1954) before the twenty-volume *New Grove Dictionary of Music and Musicians* was published in 1980. By that time it had become "the standard and the largest comprehensive music encyclopedia in English and the work to which all others are currently compared."[22]

As has been mentioned, in 2001 a second edition of the *New Grove* was released in twenty-nine volumes, with a film music section completely rewritten by Mervyn Cooke. While this entry still shows traces of strictly musical allegiance, and of conventional film-musical notions taken as absolutes, Cooke generally demonstrates an unprecedented sympathy for film music conditions, an interest in film music practice, and an optimism about film music possibilities.[23] I will continue to refer on occasion to the *New Grove* 2nd edition, but the bulk of my attention, particularly in this chapter, concerns the findings and attitudes of the 1954 and 1980 editions.

Naturally over these one hundred years the tone of *Grove's* changed considerably, and one of the most significant shifts pertains to the audience being addressed. Although *New Grove* editor Stanley Sadie declared his own intent to continue speaking to the dictionary's traditional, partly amateur, public, it can be argued that with the passage of time, and with the increasing volume and sophistication of musical scholarship, the dictionary became in many ways a reference written for specialists, and by specialists.[24] "This [1980] edition clearly favors the interests of music scholars rather than those of informed amateurs and performers."[25]

This partial change can be seen in many ways, and it has a number of important consequences. A colleague noted that Sir George "undertook his task in the spirit of a lover of beauty rather than in that of an antagonist." As D. W. Krummel observed, however, this open sentiment was eventually succeeded by a more adversarial one, and later editions gave themselves over increasingly to "invidious comparisons" and value judgments.[26] This antagonism was complex and not universal, but it can be at least partly ascribed to an increase in scholarly specialization, and to the elitism that sometimes goes with it, as I discussed in my first chapter.

Such elitism is not an absolute, however, but rather exists in relation to the things it purports to rise above. More important in this context than the severities of advanced scholarship are the dangers such severity opposes. The Eric Blom-edited 1954 *Grove's* is the location of the most invidious comparisons cited by Krummel, and its areas of opprobrium are predictable and significant.

Desmond Shawe-Taylor observes that the 1954 edition was particularly poor, and even parochial, in its coverage of ethnic and popular music. Richard Hill, in a contemporary review, described its tone as "insularity with a vengeance." Stanley Sadie goes so far as to call the 1954 *Grove's* xenophobic.[27] Nowhere is this attitude more evident than in the discussion on film music, which appears to be heard as ethnic (read *American*) and popular in the worst ways. Why the withering disapproval? There were, of course, valid musicological objections. But additionally, Sir George's amateur's love of beauty, and of communicating its pleasures, were no longer admissible when popular beauties had become so dangerous, and its aficionados had gone so far astray.

From the perspective of the film music writers, George Grove's music-for-the-people utopianism was no longer possible. In film music the beauties loved by amateurs—overwhelmingly the people composing and appreciating this music—could only be answered by antagonism.

Shawe-Taylor suggests that in using the *New Grove* specifically, "everyone is sure to come across details in his own particular field which are misleading or plain wrong."[28] This is perhaps even more true of Blom's edition, predating as it does the official establishment of film and media studies, at least in an official academic sense. Film music's previously cited pugilistic reactions to musical disdain confirm how troubling this kind of misunderstanding can be. My point is not merely to find fault with the attitudes expressed in the 1954 edition, however. Stanley Sadie describes the value and validity of those earlier expressions. "We recognize that every age needs its own reference works, not merely to absorb extensions in factual knowledge, but also to represent the attitudes, the interpretations, the perspectives, the philosophies of the time."[29] Some of the Grove attitudes remain with us and paradoxically, they also suggest ways out of contemporary dilemmas.

The 1927 edition of *Grove's Dictionary of Music and Musicians* does not have an entry on film music. In that year it was clearly too early to discuss the sound film with any degree of perspective. Still, it must have been well known that film and music, largely lifted from classical domains, had coexisted for thirty years. It may be imagined that the *Grove's* editors did not wish to dignify that relationship by their notice, especially since it could not have met with their approval. The 1954 edition bears out this suspicion.

Three writers, Ernest Irving, Hans Keller, and Wilfred Mellers, collaborated on the film music entry in the 1954 edition. Irving opens the entry by pointing out that in film exhibition, there was music from the first. "Some of the music was, *of its kind*, excellent in quality. . . ."[30] He says that in silent years music "had to be used" instead of dialogue, in order to make the action readable. Here we find Irving dismissing the music, and even more the film medium itself. There is a subtle intimation that the picture, even motion pictures, were insufficient to the telling of the story, and that conversely music could carry meaning on its own. The first suggestion is mostly not true, and the second contradicts the whole burden of serious music criticism in terms of music's dalliance with film, that burden being that music is not built for and should not have to carry narrative meaning. Such slightly bilious contradictions occur frequently in the *Grove's* film music articles. Mention is made of numerous pieces adapted by "talented hacks," and exalted names like Beethoven are quite consciously placed next to the ignominious uses to which their music was put ("aeroplane dives and Red-Indian chases").

Expressions are generally polite, but the fundamental attitude taken is clearly rendered in passages such as the following, which describes the selection of musical cues and their dissemination by the various musical forces. "The silent film thus made millions of people acquainted with classical music, even if in a diluted and degraded form, and certainly created a good deal of lucrative employment for the executive musician."[31] Dilution and degradation are defensible descriptions of much musical transformation in film presentation, but they are also ideologically loaded terms, containing much of contempt and condescension.

In the *Grove's* there are examples of a virtue being made out of what were perceived as film's inherent limitations. In *The Gold Rush* (1925) Charlie Chaplin is complimented for his musical "apotheosis of the trivial." As the tramp waits for the dance hall girls,

> the shabby music [of the motion picture music guides] reinforces the shabby poetry of the scene. The use of the 'Star of Eve' from 'Tannhauser' is a case in point; no subtler tune could so intimately relate the little man's dreams to the banality of the world in which he lives.[32]

The *Grove's* writers suggest that the musical implications of the coming of sound are a simple extension of the old *kinotek* techniques: heavy-handed correspondence, diegetic strum to justify the entrance of the orchestra, mickey-mousing, vulgar leitmotif, and excessive and inappropriate use of nineteenth-century symphonic styles. The functions are simply illustrative, geographical conventions that ensure an absence of depth or poetry.

The discussion of processes used for recording sound ends with an expression of disapproval at the "very regrettable mutilation" which the cuts and additions of cinema practice impose on the music. The music is given over to the mixer, "who proceeds to dilute it with dialogue, commentary, train noises, bird noises, car noises, footsteps, door bangs, and suchlike incidentals." In this rendering the music has rightful primacy, and it is in the

superimposition of "incidentals," of the aural agents of clear signification which is after all the narrative film's generally received
first responsibility, that music receives its greatest indignity.[33]

Again, this discussion is contradictory. Music is sullied by the
burden of signification in its silent period usage, and then when
it is relieved from that burden, its new subservience is even more
vigorously bemoaned. At heart are convictions about music's
rightful preeminence and lingering doubts about the possibility
of film being art. Perhaps this accounts for some of the dismissal
in the following quotation.

> For composers the first and most important result of the invention
> of the sound-film was the tendency to use special music for each
> film. This began to provide a steady and rapidly increasing income
> for all composers capable of equipping themselves with the neces-
> sary technique. Three months in each year spent in writing film
> music leaves them nine months to write such symphonies, concer-
> tos, and chamber music such as their artistic urge may dictate;
> music discarded from serious compositions can often be furbished
> up for use in films, its very flaws possibly rendering it more suit-
> able for the less austere medium. It is seldom that the same music
> can make a success on the concert platform and in the kinema
> [sic]. If it is good concert music it is essentially bad film music,
> and the converse is usually true. Nevertheless a good composer
> will write better music for even the crudest of dramatic scenes than
> a bad one, if only he possesses the necessary dramatic instinct.[34]

Here is the dubious reputation referred to by Tony Thomas.
This account provides for three months' film whoring which, as
soul destroying as it may be, at least leaves leisure for the kind of
composing that really counts, that which coincides with "artistic
urge." The rest can be fobbed off on the films. It is interesting to
note the depth of feeling in Irving's writing, a depth which in
some ways replaces a detailed defense of his position. What are
the "flaws" serious compositions are prone to, and why would
they be more suitable for film? Why is it, what makes it a "less
austere medium"? Why must good concert music be bad film
music? Why the apparent supposition that film drama is likely to
be "crude," and film composing as well?

There are reasonable answers to these questions, answers
which don't presuppose the inferiority, even the criminality of

music used in narrative. Donald Tovey speaks in more charitable terms, pointing out that theatrical music—to which category we might add film music—often seems to fall short when taken out of theatrical context because it was conceived as part of a musical/narrative/visual ensemble. Since its effect comes in combination, it is not quite fair to criticize only part of the combination for producing a diminished effect.[35]

If the populist Tovey is making this commonsense, not very exceptionable observation nearly twenty years before the film music entry, then whither the *Grove's*? As suggested by Stanley Sadie, encyclopedias provide as much insight into the perspectives of their time, or into perspectives that refuse the conditions of their time, as they do irrefutable truths. This idea helps us locate and understand the attitudes which inform the 1954 *Grove's* film music entry. Irving's comments suggest that one of these is an adherence to the romantic ideology which exalts the artist and renders the work immutable. This marked high-low division underpins the above-quoted assumptions and would also account for what seems an excessively critical tone. Irving also demonstrates a perhaps self-conscious or self-justifying musical sophistication and displeasure when composition is not rigorous, or formally correct (conventional). One of his great objections is that high art correctness is beyond the reach of film music's workaday realities.[36]

What is accomplished, then? Irving suggests that film music is used only to excite and subliminally influence audiences. "Its appeal must be eighty percent subjective because it has to operate upon a large body of people of whom at least eighty percent are non-musical."[37] This last sentence is more polemical than scientific but clearly, between broad lines, it is saying that film presentations are not conducive to the rapt reception that music properly requires, nor the reverence its best composers have a right to.

This last inflection very clearly coincides with the auteurist impulses that were soon to overtake film culture. The account of the "good" composers' experiences in the cinematic wilderness resemble quite dramatically discussions concerning the great Hollywood directors who spent careers languishing in fields of philistine incomprehension. This is the classical conception of the composer working in the studio era.[38]

Hans Keller goes on to cite the case of British film in the 1940s and early 1950s, whose fortunate circumstance was to draw upon the enthusiastic contributions of generations of great composers for a wide range of films in a number of genres. Some of those enthusiasms are cited, and yet it also seems that there is some sad head-shaking. Film music defenders such as John Huntley rejoice in the august participation of great composers. For his part, Keller expresses regrets, suggesting in great measure that the Baxes, Blisses, Brittons, Benjamins, Waltons, and Williamses are squandering their talents in a medium unable to bear those talents up. "One cannot have a highly organized unity without having enough to unite."[39]

Where merit is acknowledged—for example, Walton and his unusual success in using leitmotif in Olivier's *Hamlet*, and tonal coherence in Bax's "Oliver Twist" music—it is likewise treated in auteurist fashion. "Even the best Hollywood composer would just automatically . . ."[40] Walton and Bax, of course, do more than this poor Hollywood construct could ever have imagined. Keller's understanding of the issues of author and institution is quite nuanced, but his separation leads very directly to the language and attitudes of the 1970s film music enthusiasts already discussed. There the great composers are sentimentally characterized, genius laboring in its figurative garret, hatching miracles while the unheeding hordes run munching to the exit signs.

This is not to say that talent and genius, or institutional insensitivities to them, are irrelevant. These validated composers are validated for good reason, and much of their film work is doubtless superior to the hack-produced run-of-the-mill. But it is true that notions, or even facts of talent and genius can distract us from real conditions and real affects. This same difficulty is present in the *Grove's* account of American film music.

This account states that "perhaps the finest scores to complete film dramas yet composed are the work of," predictably, Aaron Copland. Referring to *Of Mice and Men* (1939), Mellers valorizes Copland's elaboration of Hanns Eisler's advanced, musicologically informed film scoring theories. Ironically, the thing most acclaimed is a simple stinger, a dischord accompanying the moment when Lennie crushes Curly's hand.[41] Of course this does not invalidate either Copland or Eisler, nor even the time-honored convention of stingers. It seems though that the qualities of Copland's film compositions are not at issue. The point is that the *Grove's* granting of exemplary status to Copland over, say, Korngold, relates as much to Copland's seriousness as a composer as to the qualities of his music.[42]

A tone of condescension, or at least paternalism, runs through the *Grove's* entry on film music, together with a kind of resentment typical of, and at least partly justified in, the patronized. There is a mild allowing for the artistic possibilities of film mixed with the assurance that those possibilities will not likely come close to musical actualities.

> The cinema is the one field where composers are regularly employed in considerable numbers, and where their music is regularly played if not listened to. However artistically frustrating the task of writing film music may sometimes seem, the honest composer cannot forget that the public which—however subconsciously or unconsciously—listens to his music may be immense, and that its musical and emotional health is to that extent in his hands.[43]

Toward the end of his discussion Keller quotes Ralph Vaughn Williams, who advocates more integration of the various artistic functions of film—dialogue, design, direction, and music. Keller likewise looks forward to this day, but not too optimistically. He continues, "once the film stops calling itself an art and starts to become one, its makers will realize that instead of teaching the musician his business they might learn some of their own from him."[44]

The 1954 *Grove's* entry on film music is perceptive and, ultimately, unsympathetic. The next official take suggests at least a certain softening. Desmond Shawe-Taylor notes substantial improvement in the *New Grove* over its predecessor, for the simple fact that this time the contributors seem to consistently have sympathy for their subjects.[45] To some degree the 1980 film music entry in the *New Grove* reflects this attitude. For instance, there is an admission that film is a *bona fide* art form, and that though nineteenth-century conventions continue to characterize its music, this music also has its own special characteristics and problems.

The article is as much adapted by Christopher Palmer and John Gillett as it is rewritten, though much of the previously dismissive language is softened. Still, auteurism and a superior attitude prevail. "A real advance was made when such composers as Milhaud, Honegger, and Shostakovich began to take an interest in the cinema."[46] In this there is certainly advance, or at least advantage, but much remains unstated. These composers became involved with film as young men, before they were who they were, so to speak, so the impression given of great masters coming to the infant medium's aid is not accurate. More importantly, emerging from the influence of modernists like Erik Satie and Jean Cocteau, and from a Soviet Revolution which exalted the despised-by-the-bourgeois forms such as film, these composers' film activities would have come out of a sensibility very distinct from the one informing the *New Grove* account.[47]

As in the 1954 edition, the writers go on to track improvements in film scoring through and because of the activities of the usual celebrated suspects: Prokofiev, Shostakovich, Kabalevsky, Milhaud, Auric, Honegger, Maurice Jaubert, Britten, Bliss, Alwyn, Benjamin, Walton, Eisler, Korngold, and Antheil.[48] Again, this is true enough, but it does not necessarily follow that because there are masters, the masterpiece tradition that most enshrines them is always and only the best explanation.

In fact, if we were to unpack this list of now noted composers and their various film-musical activities, we would find a wonderful and disconcerting diversification of background and practice and reception. These men did not, as a rule, look back to Mahler and Strauss for their inspirations, nor did they invoke Wagner to their justification. The echoes of late Romantic music give way in many of their compositions to more modern alternatives. They are redolent of bitonality and serialism, or they have rhythm or color taking precedence over melody, or joining it in a more neutralized ensemble of musical elements, or they are derived from popular or ethnomusicological sources.

As for the films, many of these scores are written for documentary or avant-garde settings, where the hypnotic and immersive conventions of Hollywood parallelism were often opposed and critiqued, both by the films and by their scores. Even when these composers do write for long-form commercial narratives, the results reveal anew how wide-ranging apparently conventional film music can be and always has been. It is a long way from *Zero de Conduite* or *Henry V* to *King Kong*, or from *King Kong* to *Kings Row*. All through the history of film music conversation we see the need to expand and sometimes to reject the standard accounts.

Nevertheless the music-institutional take on film music is still powerfully informed by these standard takes, and more particularly by two basic narratives. They are the Hollywood myth of its classic film composers being heir to and working abundantly within the Romantic tradition, and the Groveian rejection of that myth, along with its resulting and reacting caricature of rampant film philistinism. But neither of these stories fully reflect the realities, or are adequate to the roots that gave rise, and that continue to give rise, to film compositional activity.

Even the softened 1980 account continues to reflect the old prejudice, especially in the area that is most pertinent to the present discussion, and which in some way summarizes the attitude of much of the academic music community toward the movies. This concerns the functional use of concert music in film. According to the 1980 article there are three ways that this is done. First, there are illustrations of concert music in pictorial terms (e.g., Jean Mitry, *Fantasia*). Second are its uses by filmmakers "not primarily interested in the music," as in Delius's "Appalachia"—and Mendelssohn's "Midsummer" overture—clipped by Herbert Stothart for *The Yearling*, or Tiomkin's borrowing of "The Merry Widow Waltz" in *Shadow of a Doubt*. Finally there is a more dire kind of appropriation. "There was no . . . extramusical justification for David Lean's interpolation of Rachmaninov's "Second Piano Concerto" throughout his film of Noel Coward's *Brief Encounter*, and the use of existing music in such a context may be found distracting or even offensive."[49] This remarkably cranky expression quite willfully ignores a great deal of vigorous critical comment on this particular film, evidently to affirm, after all the attempts at understanding and fair consideration, exclusivity, and snobbery.

Who, then, are these elitists? Why are these generations of

music cultural spokesman such consistent film music haters? As we will see, the situation is not so easily reduced; elitism is only part of a complex cluster of attitudes and motivations behind musical suspicion of film. As such, it is obviously important to respond to the biases of the 1954 edition not as absolute expressions to adopt or reject, as for instance film composers and their defenders have been wont to do, but as statements inflected by setting and context.[50]

Sentiments expressed in the Grove dictionaries are not necessarily untrue: music has, historically, been subservient, and it has often been substandard. Romanticism in film music and clear-eyed observation as well may imply the effacement of individual expression within repressive capitalist economies. But it is also highly romantic and inaccurate to suggest that effacement eliminates meaning or its expression. Subconscious signification is signification nevertheless. The fact remains that what is mediocre in evaluative economies—the predominant reduction of films to either good or bad status—should still be subject to consideration that is more than just dismissive.

FILM MUSIC CRITICISM: UNDERLYING SENTIMENTS

Similarly, these same critical evaluations should be interrogated, as validations and condemnations both are illuminated by the conditions and ideologies that gave them rise. We will now look more closely at music community dismissals of film music, and particularly of the use in films of the classics. There are various voices and motivations, all opening up larger issues than we might at first see.

One of the writers of the 1954 *Grove's* film music entry, Hans Keller, criticized film music for *Music Review* from 1948 to 1959.[51] The apparent hostility found in Keller's *Grove's* entry can also be found in his *Music Review* writing. "That Hollywood music in and beyond Hollywood is the most powerful force unmusicality has ever commanded must be a truism to every musical mind."[52] He is skeptical about and often dismissive of original film composition, and these attitudes are a result of a great and demanding musicological sophistication.

Keller describes a belabored film attempt at modern music as "a pastiche with wrong notes duly injected."[53] He notes that Leith Stevens's "Piano Concerto in C min.," composed for the film *Night Song* (1947), "is no piano concerto and ends in F min." He finally and wrathfully declares it "nine minutes of stinking refuse." He finds that another subpar effort "makes one dream of America's first great thriller, *Scarface* (1932), wherein there was no background music at all."[54]

As with observers of early film who came from outside the discipline, Keller often seems reluctant to afford film full artistic status.[55] "[There] is no legitimate inartistic music, which is why naturalism, the art of remaining inartistic but expressive, will always be able to say more, rather than less, without music."[56] He damns with faint praise, talking in one case of "one of the least rotten American scores." Conversely, as commentators from the start of film had done, he valorizes the participations of real composers. Praising new composition in William Walton's *Hamlet* score he notes that "even the best Hollywood composer would just automatically have re-used the music."[57]

This dismissal of Hollywood film scoring may relate to one of its central tenets. Keller disagrees with Kurt London's oft-quoted maxim about film music being bad when one can hear it. "Any so-called artistic process or device that has to shun the light of consciousness is suspect in the extreme."[58] He disagrees with the handmaiden model, finding that when the score merely reinforces the images, musical tautology results.

Though he is critical of original composition and wants the music to be heard, Keller's greatest ire is reserved for the kind of music we are partly discussing in this study, the kind of music that, even in film, comes to the foreground. Keller decries especially "the notorious stratagem of hiding behind music from the concert hall, as if a picture had ever been uplifted by the music it degrades."[59] He observes how Lionel Newman "murdered" Mozart's "Clarinet Quintet" in the film *Apartment for Peggy* (1948) by, among other things, taking out the clarinet.[60] He laments Franz Waxman's "protracted and multiple murder" of Smetana's *Vltava* in *Man on a Tightrope* (1953).[61]

Keller finds that musical quotation often emerges as a "covert expression of simultaneous love and hate towards a parent figure—the quoted composer." This applies not only to individual instances but to the whole practice and what it says about film's relationship with the parent arts. For Keller quotation is a powerful evidence of film's perpetual adolescence.

> As in literature a quotation serves to authorise a wrong statement, so a musical quotation may answer the quoter's need for parental approbation; he feels that by thus honouring, and identifying himself with, daddy's holy words, he sanctifies his own. A rose thrown into a midden, however, does not improve the latter's smell, but rather starts to stink itself.[62]

For all the strong language, Keller was aware that film music need not be a force of unmusicality. He acknowledges how film has been uniformly successful in smuggling twelve-tonality into public consciousness.[63] On "The Function of Feature Music" Keller states that "as long as . . . 'good music' . . . is not used for any extraneous and unmusical purpose, or re-scored and 'arranged' or 'varied' by a composer in search of atmosphere, there is definite if limited scope for the filming of unfilmic [previously composed] music."[64]

But Keller is not just echoing the intransigent attitude manifest in the previously cited UNESCO catalog. He is interested in more than how film can further musical ends. Although at times his writing betrays a conflict in his own mind, Keller's best instincts seem to speak for a reconciliation of film and music communities, for the possibility of each edifying the other. Such would mean that "the narrow minded musician would have his eyes opened, the narrow minded film-goer his ears."[65]

Keller is not just a hostile critic, but a demanding would-be enjoyer of films and film music, if on his own specifically musical terms. Those terms include, as we have seen, a pretty complete intolerance for musical quotation. There is more to this sentiment, though, and to Keller's film music writing in general than education, expression, and enjoyment, and a jealous regard for classical music's rightful territory.

As with many of his critical contemporaries with similar backgrounds, Keller is motivated by more weighty matters. He quotes Antony Hopkins on the subject of underqualified film composers. "Who are these people, whose names never seem to appear on any concert programmes? What else have they written; what pages have they placed on the altar of Art, rather than on the lap of mammon?"[66]

Elitists, or even just art lovers, have always been concerned about philistine besmirchment of art's altars, but serving Mammon, sacrificing principle to material expediencies, can have more portentous ramifications. Hanns Eisler and Theodor Adorno describe these in their discussion of modern culture, as transformed into modern cultural industry.

> Taste and receptivity have become largely standardized; and, despite the multiplicity of products, the consumer has only apparent freedom of choice. Production has been divided into administrative fields, and whatever passes through the machinery bears its mark, is predigested, neutralized, leveled down. . . . All art, as a means of filling out leisure time, has become entertainment . . .[67]

Mass art diminishes the art object and dehumanizes those who contemplate it. During and after the Nazi period, that is, the time of the 1954 *Grove's* entry, these issues assume special weight. In the age of mechanical reproduction fascism had led to unprecedented holocaust. In this light what appears to us as elitism could be, or at least could seem to be, the last defense against disaster.[68]

The dire effects of the culture industry are a central preoccupation of Theodor Adorno's writing, and this preoccupation overwhelmingly informs Eisler and Adorno's *Composing for the Films*. We have discussed musicology's customary insularity, but Adorno is an important exception to this tendency; his musicology was inseparable from his sociology.[69] Adorno's most celebrated explication of the modern conditions of music in a social context is found in the 1938 article, "On the Fetish Character in Music and the Regression of Listening."[70]

In this article Adorno discusses the modern musical tendency of fragmented listening, whereby conspicuously recognizable—beautiful, famous—parts of larger works are keyed upon at the expense of the whole. In this way a fetishizing replaces real engagement and pleasure with the work's actual dimensions and implications. Of course, much more than music appreciation is at stake.

Musically the "isolated moments of enjoyment prove incompatible with the immanent constitution of the work of art, and whatever in the work goes beyond them to an essential perception is sacrificed to them." What this portends is that compositions become "culinary delights which seek to be consumed immediately for their own sake, as if in art the sensory were not the bearer of something intellectual which only shows itself in the whole rather than in isolated topical moments."[71]

So we have a loss of thought, action, and freedom. This mode of listening reflects a mode of living, or rather not living. "The romanticizing of particulars eats away the body of the whole." The result is that modern musical culture creates a general malaise of regression and misrecognition.[72] The triumph of the culture industry is that this social misrecognition is masked by mere brand-name recognition. The regressive state and its concomitant fragmentations become legal tender, and use gives way to exchange value.

> The feelings which go to the exchange value create the appearance of immediacy at the same time as the absence of a relation to the object belies it. . . . If the moments of sensual pleasure in the idea, the voice, the instrument are made into fetishes and torn away from any functions which could give them meaning, they meet a response equally isolated, equally far from the meaning of the whole, and equally determined by success in the blind and irrational emotions which form the relationship to music into which those with no relationship enter.[73]

The cultural inoculation, the "vulgarization and enchantment"[74] that Adorno outlines in this piece is seen as a general condition and a dire danger. It appears in numerous settings, like in film music. Given this context, strong words of criticism and disapproval suddenly appear as much more than cranky proprietary complaints about incorrect appropriation of the leitmotif.

Concerns like these are essential to understanding this period, its critics (and the tone of its criticism—Adorno, Benjamin, Horkheimer, Keller, and others). I do not wish to propose facile equivalencies. These critics do not constitute a homogeneous group, but they do hold some things to be self-evident. Defenses are needed against the dangers of the popular.

And what was the supreme popular art? The movies, of course.

Film for these critics is not considered just for itself, but as an emblem. Eisler and Adorno point out that

> music is supposed to bring out the spontaneous, essentially human element in its listeners and in virtually all human relations. As the abstract art *par excellence*, and as the art farthest removed from the world of practical things, it is predestined to perform this function.

Film's reduction of music to purely functional levels, as discussed in the *Grove's Dictionary* entry on film music and in Eisler and Adorno's book, not only blocks that destiny, but in so doing it blights human relations.[75]

In all these statements the underlying stakes are extraordinarily high. Thus, for instance, Keller's hyperbolically critical review of the score, by Daniele Amfitheatrof, for Max Ophuls's *Letter from an Unknown Woman* (1949), which he finds to be "utterly depraved, as well as stupid."[76] Once again Keller, naturalized British, but a Jewish Austrian refugee from Hitler, is not merely being elitist in his displeasure. As with Adorno, another refugee, he finds such encroachments to be emblematic of a general cultural disaster.

Keller criticizes Herbert von Karajan's eighty-minute version of the *Matthew Passion*, which juxtaposed paintings of Christ's life with Bach's music:

> A devitalized culture which has ceased to understand its own creations tends to explain one art in terms of another; hence the popularity of . . . Disney's *Fantasia* . . . and [the filmed] *St. Matthew's Passion*. To juxtapose self-contained works of art is to establish a meaningless relation between what is meaning-full-up, in a vain attempt to recover the lost meaning, 'new and unsuspecting beauties.' 'Thou shalt not make unto thee any graven image. . . .'[77]

This is Adorno's fetishism *in exelcis*. Film quotation of previously composed music infantilizes the listener and gives the power of selection and dissemination to the "publishers, sound film magnates, and rulers of radio," and to other such totalitarians.[78]

In response to all this we find the music community's seeming hostile elitism, which can now be see as being concerned with so much more than mere hierarchies. Cavalier cutting and careless quotation are mere symptoms of a more general malaise. These considerations explain in part why so much music theory of this time was concerned with the problems of composing modern music. Observers and practitioners both urged currency and cutting edges, and their urging can legitimately be read against the perceived reactionary backpedaling of film music practice. In a pre-John Cage world, this meant a kind of musical self-containment, a fortress defended by severity and inaccessible compositional complexity.[79]

This is where we find some of our protesting film music commentators. In his strictly musical writing Hans Keller was a systematic analyst, a musical new critic. He preferred close textual reading partly because of his concerns about the besmirchments of the extramusical. These feelings are contained within his film music writings. For Keller musical meaning was thematic, or rather, motivic, contained within the composition, and in purely musical relations. For him and for the tradition he represented, film music's signifying functions, not to mention the additive meaning of appropriated classical compositions, were suspect, and finally dangerous.[80]

These are also the reasons that Adorno so fiercely defended the absolute, and, among other things, criticized film music. He had seen music culture and its modern accoutrements—sound recordings, technology as taken over by culture—raising ephemera such as the three-minute single above the great longer forms that they could not properly render and distribute. Thus it was that the concert hall—since the courts and cottages, the musical cultures and political economies that created the music in the first place no longer existed—not only presented music as it was intended, but also insulated it from the vulgarizations of middle-class culture and the culture industry.[81] The alternative, the counter, maybe the end to this tenuous refuge was, of course, the movie theater.

On this issue Wilfred Mellers, who could be quite optimistic about the positive workings of music within culture, is in agreement. Before John Cage and Karlheinz Stockhausen, classical ideology was based on liveness. Recordings were documents of real performers, really performing, which is where Glenn Gould's flight from the stage could be seen as constituting a betrayal. It is partly for this that Mellers so admired the egalitarian and participatory nature of early English music. From that plainsong unity even the concert hall is a great fall, but for him the concert hall at least preserves some of the conditions and regard for things lost. Film, as the most literally canned of all the arts, was in this formulation irredeemable. Film music, bound up in technology and the workaday, was the apostasy embodied.

The music critics I have discussed are informed, articulate, convincing, and they favor what are for them purer universal narratives in music, or underscore its most pressing threats. This accounts for what sometimes seems a stubborn antifilm attitude. The medium, in its commercial manifestations, masks with its illusionary individualism the mere vulgar search for lucre that defines it.[82]

Music critics who disparage film music, then, use film as a plank in a larger platform. Especially taken in this context their arguments were and remain effective, valuable, even largely valid, but they are not the only possible perspectives. The following two chapters will focus on other areas where classical music traditions have special applications in modern film, and particularly film music practice.

NOTES

1. International Music Centre, 1962, 5.
2. Bazin, 1967, "The ontology of the photographic image."
3. Cf. the *films d'art* of cinema's early years.
4. The Archers' *The Tales of Hoffmann* (1951) (coproduced by "Emerio" Pressburger), Eisenstein/Prokofiev's *Alexander Nevsky* (1938) and Pabst/Brecht/Weill's *The Three-Penny Opera* (1931). International Music Centre, 1962, 104, 111.
5. Thomas, 1973, 18. See Eisler, 1947, 62–63 for a withering expression of this low regard.
6. In Thomas, 1973, 122. See Brown, 1988, 170, for a contemporary affirmation of the relevance of Wagner to picture music.
7. Thomas, 1979, 107. Steiner, ca. 1964, traces valid musical connections and sets forth the undoubtedly real accomplishments in Steiner's work. A simultaneous impression is that there is rather a lot of

name dropping, of protestations of legitimacy through proximity to august musical personages.

8. Thomas, 1973, 73, 107, emphasis added.

9. Though in fact usage remained frequent. I will go on to discuss these uses.

10. London, 1936, 211. Note the use of capitals. The *New Grove* summarizes Ernest Irving's career by noting that "he was responsible for engaging a number of distinguished [British] composers to write film scores" [for British films in the 1930s and 1940s]. For this Irving, as well as Muir Mathieson, are credited for finally making film music a serious proposition. See article on Irving in Sadie, 1980, 9: 329. For similar sentiments from another perspective see Previn, 1991, 91–99.

11. Cf. George, 1912, 1914, Lang and West, 1920, Rapée, 1924, 1925.

12. Interview with Ken Secorra, broadcast during the program "Carl Davis on Film Music," Radio 3, 21/3/95. *Gesamptkunstwerk* is Wagner's term for the integrated artwork, "in which all the arts [including music, poetry, and visual spectacle] were to be perfectly fused." Randel, 1986, 339.

13. Eisler, 1947, 5. Keller (*1946*, 136) says that, far from the potentially justifiable "theme with variations," Hollywood leitmotif is more often "a theme without variations, but with plenty of repetitions."

14. Mellers, 1954, 3: 105. Hollywood leitmotif may actually bear more resemblance to the notion of the *idée fixe*, "a melody representative of a character or feeling, which reappears in a variety of forms and develops with the changing circumstances." (MacDonald, Hugh, "Idée fixe," in Sadie, 1980, 9: 18.) Those unsympathetic to film music might point out how this musical figure slavishly reinforces the accompanied image, and overdetermines the musical material. In relation the superlative idée fixe (from Berlioz's *Symphonie Fantastique*) was an opium-addled artist's dream of his lost beloved, whom he'd murdered (at least in his dream). In French the term means, or has come to mean, "obsession." MacDonald notes that Balzac also referred to the idée fixe, and that it became a clinical term for unreasonable, even certifiable obsession. MacDonald, 1980, 9: 18. For a modern defense of the validity of leitmotif in film, see Brown, 1988, 165–66, 199–201.

15. Flinn, 1993, 34.

16. By "romantic" I mean the musical period dating roughly from middle Beethoven to the primes of R. Strauss and Mahler. Romanticism obviously pertains to more than just music. Many of the musical points made here could be cautiously applied to other discourses as well.

17. Brown, 1988, 184.

18. Not the only possible take on Romanticism; see, for instance, Rosen and Zerner, 1984. Siegmeister (1938) also discusses the progressive and democratic elements of early Romanticism. Here I am concentrating on its latter permutations.

19. Siegmeister, 1938, 12. See Faulkner, 1971, for a fine book-length study of the social conditions of Hollywood musicians.

20. For evidence see Levant, 1940, Raksin, 1989, Previn, 1991.

21. Quoted in Krummel, 1981, 762.

22. Duckles and Reed, 1988, 14.

23. "Ideally, the force of [film music] structures should be appreciated subliminally. . . ." Cooke, 2001, 806.

24. Sadie, 1975, 260. See also Shawe-Taylor, 1981, 218.

25. Duckles and Reed, passim.

26. Krummel, 1981, 764.

27. Shawe-Taylor, 1981, 218; Hill, 1954, 87; Sadie, 1975, 263. Blom's Britain-first strategy was one of the most remarked and controversial characteristics of the fifth edition. See Hill, 1954, 86. Also problematic was a related hostility to things American. Both of these attitudes are key elements to the film music entry in the 1954 dictionary. (Krummel [1981, 762] points out that the removal of anti-American biases was one of the main objectives of the supplement to Blom's 1954 edition.)

28. Shawe-Taylor, 1981, 220.

29. Sadie, 1975, 259.

30. Irving, 1954, 3: 93. Italics added.

31. Irving, 1954, 3: 94.

32. Mellers, 1954, 3: 104.

33. Irving, 1954, 3: 97. Alternatively such indignities can be seen as evidence of the film medium's maturing. George's guide (1912, 28–83) gives the approximate duration of complete musical selections, obviously assuming that the film musician would play them straight through. (See a similar view in Van Houten, 1992, 22, which suggests that audiences actually preferred this course.) Cinematically, or in relation to the standard prescriptions about film music, this practice was quickly condemned. However it would seem that musically, and in the music community, this respect is just what is longed for, even forty years later.

34. Ibid. "The truth is that no serious composer writes for the motion pictures for any other than money reasons. . . ." Eisler, 1947, 55.

35. Tovey, 1937, IV, 29, 31, 44.

36. With less strain, Wilfred Mellers also takes note of film composition's frequent formal naïveté. As with the leitmotif in film, Mellers points out that film composition is episodic, and cannot properly be

worked out (with developments and recapitulations) in the standard Sonata form. Mellers, 1954, 104.

37. Irving, 1954, 3: 97.

38. For more on this refer back to my chapter one. In the *Grove's
Dictionary* elaborate efforts are made to validate the work of the Hollywood auteurs and show solidarity within the ideologies of genius, without giving undue musical credit. "Chaplin produced another musically
insignificant but highly intelligent score to '*Monsieur Verdoux.*'" Mellers, 1954, 3: 108. Elsewhere (Keller, 1947, 31) Keller advocates the
prominent display of composers' names on marquees and in advertise-
ments, to "invite praise and criticism."

39. Keller, 1954, 3: 99.

40. Ibid., 3: 100.

41. Mellers, 1954, 3: 107.

42. It relates also to how quickly a reputation can change. Twenty
years earlier, just before Korngold's remove to the United States, his
reputation would have far exceeded the still relatively obscure American composer.

43. Mellers, 1954, 3: 109.

44. Keller, 1954, 3: 103.

45. Shawe-Taylor, 219. The trend continues through the 2001 edition, and is happily demonstrated in Cooke's film music article.

46. Palmer, 1980, 6: 549.

47. On French influences see Thomson, 1966, 52–61. For the Soviets, see my chapter three.

48. See also Sternfeld, 1960.

49. Palmer, 1980, 6: 552–53. Cooke (2001, 806) finally breaks ranks
and allows for a positive response to Coward/Lean's appropriation. On
the other hand, while giving slight ground to the possibility of classical
music being well or cleverly used in film, Cooke finally appears to come
down against it, if implicitly. After discussing the usefulness of source
music in setting a period tone and for providing structural underscoring,
Cooke emphasizes how such use is largely a temp track phenomenon,
the main product and most serious consequence of which is likely to be
composer casualties.

50. "It would be idle to pretend that *Grove* was being prepared for
use in a musicological vacuum." Sadie, 1975, 262.

51. The other writers' biographies are of interest as well, particularly
as they suggest some of the ways that specific criticism relates to larger
critical communities. Ernest Irving was the musical director at Ealing
Studios from 1935 to his death in 1953. Before that, between 1900 and
1940 he was an active London theater conductor, also giving seasons of

light opera on the Continent. Clearly he had an investment in, and evidently an affection for, popular musical expression, especially as it related to popular musical forms. It is also possible that as a popular musician/composer, he felt somewhat self-conscious in august Groveian company. Irving is the most dismissive of the three 1954 writers, and his attitude is similar to the sense of pugnacious inferiority often found in film musician discourse. On Irving see Sadie, 1980, 9: 329.

Wilfred Mellers' writing has none of this protesting-too-much, and he is not an academic absolutist. He has always been interested in music's social background, as evidenced by his first book, *Music and Society* (1946). His 1965 work, *Harmonious Meeting*, sympathetically investigated the relationship between music, poetry, and drama in the English baroque, and the music degree course he started at York University in 1964 pioneered the application of extramusical factors (social and historical determinants) to musical study. His book *The Twilight of the Gods* (1973) is a delightful musicological analysis and fan letter to the Beatles and their at once (unconsciously) sophisticated and fully accessible music. His editing of the series "Music and Society," (see Russell, 1987) bespeaks his continued interest in and commitment to the study of music in its context. I will return to Mellers later (see also Sadie, 1980, 12: 108–10).

52. Keller, 1951 (*Music Review*, XII), 324.

53. Keller, 1950 (*Music Review*, XI), 145.

54. Keller, 1949 (*Music Review*, X), 50–51.

55. I.e., Rudolf Arnheim and Erwin Panofsky. Both critics are in some ways sympathetic to film, but their tone can also be condescending. Arnheim, 1957; Panofsky, 1934, "Style and Medium in the Motion Pictures," in Mast, Cohen, and Braudy, 1985, 233–48.

56. Keller, 1956 (*Music Review*, XVII), 255.

57. Keller, 1948 (*Music Review*, IX), 197.

58. Keller, 1951 (*Music Review*, XII), 315.

59. Keller, 1949 (*Music Review*, X), 225.

60. Keller, 1951 (*Music Review*, XII), 223. See also Adorno on arrangement (1991, 36).

61. Keller, 1953 (*Music Review*, XIV), 311–12.

62. Keller, 1949, 25, 26. See Keller (1946, 136) on the related evils of pastiche.

63. Keller, 1951 (*Music Review*, XII), 147–49.

64. Keller, 1953, (*Music Review*, XIV), 311=12.

65. Keller, 1952 (*Music Review*, XIII), see 209–11. As with many other issues here considered, the desirability and difficulty of such compromise is not unique to film. Franz Liszt discussed the challenge posed

by program music to both professional musicians and men of letters. "Both parties set themselves against it with the same vigor, with the same obstinacy. The latter, looking askance, see their property being taken over into a sphere where, apart from the value *they* placed on it, it acquires new significance; the former are horrified at a violation of their territory by elements with which they do not know how to deal." Liszt, 1855, 130. For more on program music, see chapter four herein.

66. Keller, 1951 (*Music Review*, XII), 224.

67. Eisler, 1947, ix–x. Also 53, 82.

68. See Walter Benjamin's 1935 article, "The Work of Art in the Age of Mechanical Reproduction." Anthologized in Mast, Cohen, and Braudy, 1985, 675–94. For a noted study on fascism and the connections between art and politics, see Susan Sontag's "Fascinating Fascism," in Sontag, 1983, 305–25.

69. This is attributable to the fact that, with his really remarkable range of reference, Adorno was much more than a musicologist. See Adorno, 1991, author's preface in Adorno, 1973, xi–xv, and particularly his 1967 collection, *Prisms* (Adorno, 1967).

70. In Adorno, 1991, 26–52.

71. Ibid., 29.

72. Ibid, 36, 41–49.

73. Ibid., 34–35, 33.

74. Ibid., 36.

75. Eisler, 1947, 20. Film music is a classic example of what Adorno and Horkheimer criticize in their *Dialectic of Enlightenment* (1972). Use value had given way universally to exchange value, where "the intrinsic value of things (was displaced) for the sake of ends (capital accumulation) extrinsic to them." Introduction in Adorno, 1991, 3–10.

76. Keller, 1952 (*Music Review*, XIII), 55–56; this is an unusually long and pointed blast. Donald Tovey, who saw himself as an educator and looked for ways to make music accessible and more universally enjoyable (though he did not easily suffer besmirchment either) provides an important alternative to Keller's severity. See, for instance, Tovey's view of adaptation in his reading of Liszt's arrangement of Schubert's *Wanderer Fantasy* for piano and orchestra. Tovey, 1937, IV, 70–73.

77. Keller, 1954 (*Music Review*, XV), 141. In its initial release, and for many years afterward, *Fantasia* was not actually a financial success.

78. Adorno, 1991, 46, 31.

79. At this time Schoenberg's influence was still very substantial, and figures like Babbitt, Boulez, and Stockhausen were poised to continue that extremely specialized level of discourse. For a classic state-

ment on the subject of currency and the importance of moving past the aesthetic language of past periods, see Wassily Kandinsky's introduction to his *Concerning the Spiritual in Art* (Kandinsky, 1977, 1–6).

80. In fact, Keller went on to develop a nonverbal system of musical analysis, and then gave up writing about music altogether. Kerman, 1985, 73, 76–78.

81. Adorno was wary of the concert hall too; Schoenberg was his ideal modern composer, precisely because of his musical intractability, and the discomforts he caused the bourgeois concertgoer. Ultimately his pessimism was fairly terminal. "Between incomprehensibility and inescapability, there is no third way." Adorno, 1991, 31; also 38–39, on how the concert hall was not necessarily ideal.

82. See Mellers, 1946, chapter four, especially note 24.

3

Sound Montage and Counterpoint Analogies

IN THE LAST CHAPTER we saw how music critics have dismissed film music for a number of reasons that are not necessarily completely musical. The strict isolationism of Hans Keller and Theodor Adorno goes beyond mere musicological fussiness. Elitism in the face of dire modern reality is a response to and a defense against that reality. It is also in many ways a refusal of that reality.

This means that these critics, to a degree, are also refusing film itself. Fragmentation, as in musical quotation for instance, is not only the burden of modernism, it is the material fact of the cinema. Films are made from shots and scenes, out of pictures and dialogue, sound and music. They are made by those who produce them, by the infrastructures through which they are disseminated, and by the individuals and communities that receive and transform them. The commercial ideal, which is to see and to sell the film as a complete and untroubled whole, belies all this, and denies the extremely and inescapably piecemeal nature of the medium. Since films are fragmented, we can see that the unwillingness to consider the viability of these basic film properties is precisely where Adorno and Keller, and in part the musical community, fall short in their criticism of film music. In addition to their valuable views, for a more complete picture we need a perspective more accepting of and conversant with this fragmentation.

This chapter will deal with the film tradition—in broad terms, Soviet montage—that most articulately expressed and passionately pursued this idea. In doing so it will present an alternative to Adorno's terminal judgments concerning art and culture. In addition to representing that alternative, this chapter and the one that follows will also introduce the second of three ways that serious music interacts with film and film culture.

These were briefly mentioned in the introduction, and are reviewed here to help us mark our place. The first interaction was illustrated in the first two chapters of this study, where we saw direct theoretical and critical responses to film music and classical music's place in film music. The second way is more problematic, and it has in some ways been the most theoretically influential. Classical music discourse has also related to film practice and theory *by analogy*. This means that instead of discussing specific instances of film-music interaction, artists and theorists have elaborated ways that film is *like* music.

The most famous film-musical analogy is the Soviet notion of contrapuntal sound. The standard explanation of counterpoint in the sound film is that it built upon silent Soviet montage cinema, which elaborated formal strategies by which bourgeois social constructs were criticized and revolutionary alternatives presented. In this account film sound counterpoint functioned as an aural variant of Sergei Eisenstein's intellectual montage, so that disjunctions between picture and sound tracks led to uncovered apparatuses and empowering new conceptual syntheses.

This formulation posits polar opposites, criticizing bourgeois parallelisms as it favors revolutionary oppositions. It also favors intellectual meaning over emotional affect. I will argue that these perpendicular geometries are not adequate to the complexities of film-sound, and especially to the film-music relationship. This inadequacy is partly due to the appropriation of the musical term "counterpoint." There have been two primary uses of "counterpoint" in film. The first one relates to counterpoint's *musical* properties, but does not address issues of meaning. This use has received much less attention than the more dominant oppositional one, which is figurative, an analogy, and not very musical.

This chapter will present an important alternative that lies between these two: counterpoint as an analogy that partakes of *musical* sensibilities. By including Eisenstein's concepts of tonal and overtonal montage, as well as discussing the phenomenon of program music in the chapter that follows, I will suggest a way past the simplistic modernist dualisms and crude materialist dialectic that have prevailed, and which to some degree continue in film music theory. I hope to find a more complex and satisfying alternative to familiar and too frequent oversimplifications.

In this way, through revising and replacing the dominant similes of classical music, I will come to an effective way to deal with the third way that serious music has interacted with film and film culture: in the actual uses of the music in films. The last chapters will demonstrate ways that direct music and film criticism, as well as complicating but enriching film-music analogies, help us to understand and enjoy this underconsidered part of film music practice.

The Two Avant-Gardes

If Theodor Adorno represents one pole of modernist thought, advocating as well its corresponding artistic strategy, then the Soviet film artists are at the other end. The way Peter Wollen characterizes these two alternatives in his influential essay "The Two Avant-Gardes" is useful to this discussion. Wollen suggests that avant-garde art in the twentieth century split into two streams: the aesthetic and the political. Their ways and means were dramatically different: where one sought to remove itself from objectionable realities, the other moved to change that reality.[1]

Although Wollen states that the aesthetic avant-garde was derived from earlier experiments in painting, I wish to carefully place modern music, in the sense Adorno uses the term, in the same category.[2] "The suppression of the signified altogether, an art of pure signifiers detached from meaning as much as from reference" seems to me to describe the Schoenbergian severity that Adorno defends as much as it does the visual abstractions to which Wollen refers.[3]

Unlike its counterpart, the political wing of the avant-garde was most concerned with content and its application in a social sphere. All formal experimentation was to be in the service of progressive social ends. Instead of the strategic inaccessibility of the aesthetes, the political artist's aim was to communicate, and even proselytize. The artist's social role was very distinct as well. The heroic high modernist and the prophet crying in the wilderness were replaced, for instance, by the Soviet worker-artist, unalienated, valuable, and valued, in happy and productive service to the revolution.[4]

It is clear how serious music can coincide with Wollen's aesthetic avant-garde, but what of the political wing? In many ways Hanns Eisler's *Composing for the Films* is the key film-musical expression of this perspective. Eisler's collaborations with Bertolt Brecht confirm his interest and activity in the area of musico-political engagement, and indeed some of his oppositional suggestions for film music coincide very directly with Soviet theory.[5] But the book also deals very much with decried film music realities, as well as reflecting some of the isolation and pessimism of cowriter Adorno. In this book and in general it is a conflicted combination of the two avant-gardes that obscures some of the possibilities, as well as the problems, of the political side.[6]

For a more clearly defined example I wish now to concentrate on Soviet film. What does Soviet revolutionary cinema have to do with music culture? As I've suggested and will go on to demonstrate, one key connection is through the film-sound counterpoint analogy. But analogies can be uncomfortably abstract, so before discussing them I wish to briefly and concretely sketch a similar and significant artistic and social development pertaining to music. This expression of the political avant-garde helps put metaphorical contrapuntal elaborations on firmer historical and theoretical ground.

Adorno himself suggests a link to a political musical practice. In *Dialectic of Enlightenment* (1944) Adorno and Horkheimer discuss the "detail" in high art. A detail is some formal element—a postimpressionist brush stroke or fauvist use of color, or musical dissonance, for example—which leaps out from and disturbs the harmony of the unified artwork. The result of this disturbance is the unmasking of the illusory workings of the culture industry.[7]

We have seen how "transparency" and the illusion of unity were at the core of commercial film music's perceived mandate. These are some of the things most objected to by Keller and

Adorno, who have been seen to favor the aesthetic side of Wollen's avant-garde. Extremely important in this regard is a contemporaneous musical movement that advocates the *political* use of the disturbing detail. In doing so it contradicts substantially the perceived irrelevancies of romanticism and the effaced domesticity of film music, not to mention the severities of a Schoenbergian avant-garde.

In his introduction to *The Rise and Fall of the City of Mahagonney*, Bertolt Brecht discussed the now deadening effects of Wagnerian opera and, by extension, of conventional dramatic theater.

> So long as the expression '*Gesamtkunstwerk*' . . . means that the integration is a muddle, so long as the arts are supposed to be 'fused' together, the various elements will all be equally degraded, and each will act as a mere 'feed' to the rest. The process of fusion extends to the spectator, who gets thrown into the melting pot too and becomes a passive (suffering) part of the total work of art. Witchcraft of this sort must of course be fought against. Whatever is intended to produce hypnosis, is likely to induce sordid intoxication, or creates fog, has got to be given up.[8]

Clearly this criticism could also apply to the integration of *film* elements already discussed. Brecht's collaborator Kurt Weill had advocated a different place for music in the theatrical equation. Against illusion and the stupor described above, Weill spoke for the "gest," the idea that music must have a point, of which the audience must be conscious.[9] To accomplish this awareness Brecht posited a "radical separation of the elements."

> The set [works] as images rather than illusion, the story [becomes] less of an experience and [gives] room for meditation, the music [comes] not 'out of the air' but out of the wings and [remains] like a concert piece. Writing, music and architecture [play] their part as independent arts in an intelligible performance.[10]

Each constituent element, each "detail," was to be visible, audible, and noticeable. Musically this meant leaving "dramatic opera" for "epic opera," music that "dishes up" for music that communicates, "music which heightens the text" for music which "sets forth the text," music which merely illustrates for music "which takes up a position."[11]

All of this dramatically contradicts the received imperatives of film music: unheard melodies, subliminal heightening, smooth integration, cinematic leitmotif. For the artist/composer, Brecht's ideas demanded that confrontation replace hypnotic tale spinning. The confrontation was to be ideological as well, meaning that for both artist and viewer, passivity was to give way to activity and action.[12]

Brecht and Weill's ideas, as well as the works in which they applied them, caused a revolution in the theater and were felt generally in the arts. Their similarities to the general aims of Soviet cinema are especially striking. In either instance, formal details were to stand out, and all to progressive ends. Music, of course, was one of these details.

Hostile film music critics were responding to the Hollywood romanticism that rejected and then obscured these modernist possibilities. Likewise Brecht and the Soviet filmmaker/theorists were reacting to integrated illusionistic traditions in their own media, and in their own time.[13] Before elaborating on their reactions I will take a brief look at the classical cinematic integrations that the Soviet version of Brechtian modernism opposed. Its musical manifestations are especially telling, and will be returned to when I discuss the actual interpretation of classical music in film.

PARALLELISM

Brecht suggested that modern integration of the arts was a form of hypnotic, intoxicating witchcraft. The following are some of the recipes for spells cast by film music. Irene Atkins suggests that the key film-musical questions are as follows. "'Why is the . . . music necessary to the scene?' or, if the music is not really necessary, 'Does its inclusion still add something dramatically and emotionally?'"[14] Atkins's supposition is that music will or should "add somehow dramatically and emotionally." The implication is that adding means uniting, eliminating any rogue elements that might unduly distract from or open up the film.[15] These ideas are emblematic of musical parallelism, of polite and obedient musical accompaniment of visual stimuli. Modernism questioned the necessity of this correspondence, in part because it questioned the arbitrary and constraining suppositions that often lay beneath it. Silent music practice is full of these suppositions.

Edith Lang and George West's seminal 1920 primer, *Musical Accompaniment of Motion Pictures*, features the following illustration.

> There are certain keys such as A flat and E flat which suggest "warmth" or languor, such as B flat minor or G minor which fit a mood of sorrow and grief, such as A or D major which lend themselves to brilliancy, such as E major which suggests "clear skies" or "the ocean's wide expanse." . . . The key of C has nothing to commend it . . .[16]

With similar arbitrariness Lang and West link certain tone colors, or organ stops, to specific meanings: suspicion, clarinet solo with string accompaniment; entreaty, saxophone solo with string 8' and flute 8' accompaniment; temptation, clarinet or oboe with string accompaniment; defiance, reeds *mf*; treachery, reeds *mf*; torture, reeds *f*.[17]

It is unclear why all this should be so, beyond maybe convention and our susceptibility to the power of suggestion. Whatever the source, we see here a confidence in inevitable, inherent musical meaning. That confidence in musical matters extended to the films themselves, to their messages, and to the way audiences responded to them.

In the introduction to his influential film music collection *Motion Picture Moods for Pianists and Organists* (1924), Erno Rapée makes the following proposition.

> One third of all film footage is used to depict action; another third will show no physical action, but will have, as a preponderance, psychologic situations; the remaining third will neither show action nor suggest psychological situations, but will restrict itself to showing or creating atmosphere or scenery.[18]

Throughout this publication Rapée's "moods" and "situations" are consistent with this schematic rendering of film narrative, and are suggestive of music's functioning in the support thereof. These categories—action, psychology, atmosphere—are seen as discrete, inherently separate, nonintersecting. Meaning in film is assumed to be unambiguous and readily comprehensible. And whatever the sense of the screen action, whatever the emotional currents, there is music available that is adequate to its representation.

Rapée's model is representative of most contemporary views of film music. The early lexicons all served to shore up the narrative with musical reinforcements. The underpinning principle is that the image is primary, the music is secondary, and to accompany is to strive for correspondence and congruity. The nature of that congruity fascinates, and it demands further interrogation. In addition to the arbitrariness of abstract keys and colors, silent film music also depended on a rather more concrete musical inevitability.

We see this in a host of remarkably literal-minded musical selections, the motivation for which were generally referential and associative. Rapée, who was an influential compiler of music for silent film, suggests to accompanists that "for [films with] prominent people in Indiana use 'On the Banks of the Wabash,'" (a footnote points out that it also serves for natives of Illinois) "for the Mayor of New York—'The Sidewalks of New York' and for California personages—'California, Here I Come.'"[19]

Popular songs were not the only ones used in this way. Charles D. Isaacson, an early film musician, recommended a wide knowledge of the classical repertoire, and of program music in particular, as its inherent associative and illustrative qualities were ideally suited for interaction with image and narrative.[20]

The disadvantages of what was often excessive parallelism were emphasized by Siegfried Kracauer.

> Scores arranged from melodies with fixed meanings are apt to produce a blinding effect. There are popular tunes which we traditionally associate with . . . real-life events whenever these tunes, which long since have become clichés, are synchronized with corresponding images, they automatically call forth stereotyped reactions to them. A few bars of Mendelssohn's *Wedding March* suffice to inform the spectator that he is watching a wedding and to remove from his consciousness all visual data which do not directly bear on that ceremony or conflict with his preconceived notions of it.[21]

Despite Kracauer's objections, however, the effects he described were likely the intended ones. Containment and comprehensibility were the goals of early film, and its music participated in the attempt to fulfill them.[22] One of the negative results when this occurs is an equation—the music is equal to what you are seeing—that ignores, or is even unaware of the traces and remainders that equations almost always leave.

As Kracauer suggests, quotations could have a smothering effect, but musical associations could also have more serious ideological ramifications. Dismissive and even dangerous connections were made. Rapée includes in his *Encyclopedia of Music for Pictures* (1925) a section on "Rube Music," including "A Little Coon's Prayer," "By Heck," and "Hey, Paw!" ("also see '*Schottische*'"). For "Mad House" there are two selections, including Richard Strauss's "A Hero's Life."

This musical strategy is emblematic of a general lack of ambition and nuance evident in much early film. Contemporary rejections of the medium were often not much more than elitist tirades, but musical evidence suggests that there was indeed cause for much criticism.[23]

Rapée has detailed instructions about portraying villainy, but no thought about withholding that musical label for the sake of suspense or gradual disclosure. More significantly, the result of this strategy is that though many of the pictures themselves may not have allowed for much range or dimension in character, the music, at least in Rapée's influential prescription, goes even further, largely denying the possibility of nuance, ambiguity, humanity.[24]

This would seem to suggest a perception of audience desires and capabilities: film spectators want and understand black and white. It also suggests how Rapée himself, and presumably many of the musical directors who used his publications, saw film and films as functioning.[25] This underconsidered strategy can be seen throughout the silent music lexicons.

Rapée's encyclopedia contains the subject heading, "African, see 'Cannibal.'"[26] Chinese and Japanese music, both subsumed within a single category, is written by the well-known Asian composers Puerner, Clerice, Kempkinski, and Bartlett. Under "eccentric" we are referred to "clowns, dwarfs, and gnomes," and to the popular concept that difference is equal to deformity.[27]

Rapée's prescriptions are typical of silent film/musical parallelism. Parallelism says that music should exactly coincide with the images, the story, and the ideas behind them. But the reality is that images, stories, and ideas frequently contain gaps and ruptures, and great difficulties besides. Parallelism can mask elements that are insidious and even dangerous.

MONTAGE AND THE COUNTERPOINT ANALOGY

These at least were the ideas of the Soviet revolution, and of its film artists. Musical parallelism was merely emblematic of deeper, more widespread bourgeois offenses, to which their own work ran counter. Numerous correctives were proposed, including in the area of film sound. In 1928, as Brecht and Weill suggested new paths for musical narratives, Sergei Eisenstein, Vsevolod Pudovkin, and Grigori Alexandrov published the following "Statement on Sound":

> **Only a contrapuntal use** of sound in relation to the visual montage piece will afford a new potentiality of montage development and perfection.
>
> **The first experimental work with sound must be directed along the line of its distinct nonsynchronization with the visual images.** And only such an attack will give the necessary palpability which will later lead to the creation of an **orchestral counterpoint** of visual and aural images.[28]

The coming of sound to film was something of a technological crisis, and it caused a great deal of anxiety in international film communities. What made Soviet filmmakers most nervous, however, was the possibility that the challenges of sound would distract some from their proper course. They did not want the synchronizations of bourgeois narrative and reactionary ideology that for them ever characterized the bulk of commercial filmmaking, and from which they felt they had turned their own productions.

The Statement on Sound, together with other Soviet writings of the time, suggested that though technical adjustments would be required, a fundamental conceptual continuity would bind the silent period and new sound practices. Though it was a musical term, a kind of counterpoint had in fact already been central to the great Soviet silent productions. This was *montage*, which articulated rigorous formal devices by which revolutionary subject matter would be most effectively and meaningfully rendered.

Soviet film pioneer Lev Kuleshov proposed the key concept that came to underpin all montage theory: that all meaning in film comes from the juxtaposition of images, and not from the images themselves.[29] Kuleshov concluded that "we must look for the organizational basis of cinema, not within the confines of the filmed fragment, but in the way these fragments relate to one another."[30] Though a great number of variations would be played on this theme, Kuleshov's combinatory concept was the essential core, before and after sound; meaning is made in the juxtaposition of discrete film fragments.[31]

The contrapuntal possibilities of montage are suggested in the definition of the former term: "note against note."[32] This is as Kuleshov suggested; insight is gained through the juxtaposition of contrasting parts. It is significant that "counterpoint" was not the only dialectical simile, the only nonfilmic form that the Soviets found to be similar to montage. In his "The Cinematic Principle and the Ideogram," written in 1929 (1949).[33] Sergei Eisenstein discusses how Japanese picture writing conveys meaning by the combination of images that would seem at first to be unrelated. Thus "the picture for water and the picture of an eye signifies 'to weep'; the picture of an ear near the drawing of a door means 'to listen,'" and so on. He later points out that meaning can become the product and not just the sum of the two separate parts; concepts agglomerate around the combination, leading to a multiplication of association and meaning.[34]

In these examples we see how not only film fragments were combined, but also whole traditions and disciplines. Music and picture writing are two of the things that Eisenstein used both literally and figuratively to elaborate montage theory. They both utilize, in fact, telling juxtapositions, and the effects, metaphorically, are *like* those of cinematic montage.

Eisenstein's term for these multiplying juxtapositions was "intellectual montage." This was actually one of five types of mon-

tage that Eisenstein posited, but at the time he validated it as
the "high[est] category," and it certainly has received the most
attention.[35] Intellectual montage went far beyond a mere comprehensible syntax for film construction. For Eisenstein the dynamic
juxtaposition of images—montage—actually reflected the conflicts of the class struggle. Equations were inextricably interre-
lated: one image *plus* a second image *equals* a concept that
results from the collision of the two images, just as thesis *plus*
antithesis *equals* synthesis, as capital *plus* labor *equals* eventually, the utopian workers' state. Formal presentation and film
content were a mutual expression of the struggles that informed
social reality, a reality that was being transformed by the workers' revolution.

Although "counterpoint" suggests most immediately baroque
musical form—an established, classical model—the film version
is a modernist formulation, set contrary to the perceived illusions
and complacencies of bourgeois narrative. If musical counterpoint played note against note, then montage sets its own innovation against convention, its own constructedness against the
perception of things as natural, shock and alienation against comfort.[36] "Counter" is the key part of the appropriated musical
term.[37]

This, then, is a kind of musical manifestation of the political
avant-garde. Always the artful elaborations of intellectual montage are circumscribed by their social purpose and didactic function.[38] As for music, montage was a *figurative* "counterpoint,"
where line is played *against* line, and the collision results in a
new form, a new thought, a new society. In relation to the famous
Statement it was assumed, with some justification, that these
same additive, and more often multiplicative, strategies would
prevail when sound came on the scene.

FORMAL COUNTERPOINT

In the next sections I will discuss how this figurative, oppositional counterpoint has come to dominate discussions of sound
montage, and some of the difficulties connected with this dominance. In preparation for these sections, and as background to a

contrapuntal alternative that I will suggest, I would like now to discuss a less problematic film-sound counterpoint. There is precedent for this more formal, less figurative counterpoint in the original theory. Though this alternative has not been the most frequently heard, many applications and discussions testify to its viability.

The following criticism of Dziga Vertov's montage aesthetic gives us some idea of how film actually works musically.

> [Vertov] had failed already in the era of the silent films by showing hundreds of examples of most cunning artistry in turning: acrobatic masterpieces of poetic jigsaw, brilliant conjuring of filmic association, but never a rounded work, never a clear, proceeding line. His great efforts of strength in relation to detail did not leave him breath for the whole. His arabesques totally covered the ground plan, his fugues destroyed every melody.[39]

This critic's objection is that in Vertov's films clear oppositions and resolutions are lost to poetic detail. The consequences relating to montage and meaning are clear. Vertov's films are extremely individual, even eccentric in their forms and expressions. In addition, the unclear line insures that the viewer's response, as well as the action that may follow it, are also heterogeneous and unpredictable. Vertov's films do not merely affirm or oppose.[40]

This point will be pursued presently. What I wish to emphasize here is how this critic, decrying the obscuring of cinematic melody (narrative?) by elaborate fugue, rejects Vertov's superlative accomplishment, as suggested by the word "fugue," of a literal, formal cinematic counterpoint. To illustrate that accomplishment let us look once again more closely at the counterpoint analogy.

Roy Prendergast has said that "sound montage is, essentially, constructing films according to the rules of music."[41] Prendergast is talking about montage here, and in its traditional figurative sense. In this way, I disagree. Film and music are different media, and they play by substantially different rules. The effective application of one discipline's conventions and terminologies to another requires substantial modification and transposition.

In terms of a cinematic transposition of the musical, however, Prendergast has a point. Revolutionary cinema validated opposition in form and content, and we have seen how montage, and intellectual montage especially, embodied this very opposition. But in addition to this conceptual opposition, montage aesthetics provided for a more strictly formal, even unideological "counterpoint." Interestingly, though many writers since have seemed to assume otherwise, this is the counterpoint we find in the Soviet Statement on Sound cited above. To return to Peter Wollen's formulation, that description seems fairly exclusively formal, and original montage theory, as well as subsequent developments, had ample provision for such formal application.

> **Only a contrapuntal use** of sound in relation to the visual montage piece will afford a new potentiality of montage development and perfection.
>   **The first experimental work with sound must be directed along the line of its distinct nonsynchronization with the visual images.** And only such an attack will give the necessary palpability which will later lead to the creation of an **orchestral counterpoint** of visual and aural images

In his *Film Technique*, Pudovkin identifies "asynchronism" as the basic, presumably contrapuntal principle of sound film.

> It is not generally recognized that the principal elements in sound film are the asynchronous and not the synchronous; moreover, that the synchronous use is in actual fact, only exceptionally correspondent to natural perception.[42]

"Natural perception" is a phrase with ideological implications. The "natural" way of seeing and hearing is different from and superior to the more dominant "naturalized" way, to the bourgeois constructs of perception. In addition to this ideological construct, though, Pudovkin is also referring to naturalized *film* perception, or in other words an ossified sort of viewing. Asynchronism, aside from revolutionary precept, is simply an alternative to conventional cinema.

Béla Balasz said that the "formal problems of sound montage, the acoustic and musical rules which govern the effect of sounds are purely musical and acoustic questions . . ." This kind of sound montage is separate from intellectual formulations. When Balasz says "the asynchronous use of sound is the most effective device of the sound film," he is simply saying, in part, that a one-to-one correspondence between sound and image is not interesting.[43]

This is a recurring refrain in the early discussion of sound, and of music in film. Paul Rotha held that

> the old idea that music must fulfill the function of an undercurrent to the picture, just quiet enough to prevent distraction from the screen, being faded down when the commentator speaks, and faded up again when he has finished, this is as antiquated as the type of film for which it is still used. Modern music for sound film must be an integral part of the sound script, must on occasions be allowed to dominate the picture.[44]

Here is an important elaboration. If counterpoint is found in the asynchronous, then true cinematic counterpoint would require a radical reformulation of film elements, in which the image's traditional primacy would give way to a freer alternation of elements. This is very similar to Brecht's prescription, and it provides a way out of the effaced integration of formal elements he decried in the opera. Changing the setting from opera, cinematic counterpoint could be achieved when visual and aural lines, cinematic melodies, if you will, alternated in their predominance.

Is this an update of the previously cited Soviet oppositions, aural collisions to result in bourgeois debunkings and revolutionary conceptual syntheses? French film composer Maurice Jaubert wrote the following in 1936:

> We want music to give greater depth to our impressions of the visuals. We do not want it to explain the visuals, but to add to them *by differing from them*. In other words, it should not be *expressive*, in the sense of adding its quota to the sentiments expressed by the actors or the director, but *decorative* in the sense of adding its own design to that proper to the screen.[45]

Jaubert's mathematical metaphor is provocatively mixed. *Difference* is attained by *adding*, and deepening. Again we can see that this is film counterpoint, but without particular opposition. Music "differs" from the image without anything so drastic or concrete as the slaughter of cattle. The innovation is that, through nonsynchronization, a greater equality of cinematic elements is introduced as traditional picture/sound hierarchies are eliminated, or at least alternated. These things constitute, in a literal way, counterpoint.

CONFUSION: SOUND MONTAGE AND THE CONCEPT OF COUNTERPOINT

I have discussed how picture and sound tracks can interact contrapuntally. This interaction, though there are ramifications in the realm of meaning, is also substantially formal. I wish now to show how oppositional, figurative counterpoint has come to dominate the discussion, and how this dominance has had a complicating and even confusing effect.

Given montage precedents, it has been assumed that the "orchestral counterpoint of visual and aural images" would mean a further elaboration of intellectual montage. As with Kuleshov's original pattern, juxtaposition of sound and image was to create meaning, and then action. This assumption recurs throughout sound/music discourse. Hanns Eisler wrote the following in 1947:

> If the concept of montage, so emphatically advocated by Eisenstein, has any justification, it is to be found in the relation between the picture and the music. From the aesthetic point of view, this relation is not one of similarity, but, as a rule, one of question and answer, affirmation and negation, appearance and essence.[46]

This notion has prevailed. Kristin Thompson, writing in 1980, says, "[the Statement on Sound's] last two paragraphs do suggest that sound will be used to continue the tradition of silent montage, providing an additional material for the creation of ideas and feelings without an excess of words."[47]

Silent montage created ideas through the collision of images. Similarly Thompson identifies "abrupt sound cutting" as "the most varied, daring, and sustained use of contrapuntal sound" in a sample of eleven early Soviet sound films. Her examples of intellectual sound montage involve the ironic use of music, which stands plainly in opposition to the image.[48] These conclusions are consistent with common usage, and effective as such, but there is an important inconsistency that should be noted.

As Michel Chion and Claudia Gorbman have both suggested,

parallelism and "counterpoint"—and we might add concord and dissonance—are only defining points along a whole spectrum of meaning, tonality, interpretation, and application. If this is the case, since this is the case, then there is a confusing terminological incompatibility in the Statement on Sound, which most later discussions have also left unresolved. The problem is contained in the following question: *Does a cinematic montage predicated on dialectical oppositions have any correlation to the flowings of musical counterpoint?* Intellectual montage forms concepts through cutting, through the juxtaposition of images, and later of images and sounds, but counterpoint and its musical lines do not cut or collide—they flow.

"Counterpoint, with its emphasis on the linear or horizontal aspect of music, is sometimes contrasted with harmony, which concerns primarily the vertical aspect of music embodied in the nature of the simultaneously sounding combinations of pitches employed."[49] This simple distinction had been largely unremarked in film sound theory, until Chion pointed out that "many cases being offered up as models of [audiovisual] counterpoint [are] actually splendid examples of *dissonant harmony*, since they point to a momentary discord between the image's and sound's figural natures."[50]

This is a fundamental weakness in the counterpoint analogy: counterpoint implies horizontal movement, while harmony (or dissonance) is a vertical correspondence of simultaneous tones. A conceptual clash of sound and image creates a kind of multisensory chord and not a flow of intertwining melody. In other words, notwithstanding Chion's observation, in film and film sound discourse there has been and continues to be a confusing elision of montage and counterpoint, which, though taken to be otherwise, are not the same thing. The fact is that sound-image interactions are not just a matter of opposition through juxtaposition, but of simultaneous striking, with overtones that follow and increase.

This does not invalidate the counterpoint analogy, nor its many elaborations. In an analogy one object is only *like* another, and certain discrepancies are quite natural.[51] What I want to suggest is that an overliteral interpretation of the Soviet analogy has muddied montage discussions as they relate to sound and to

music. Film-sound counterpoint and especially the flow of concepts connected to it are more complex than we have generally
allowed. This is important to my work here, as this greater complexity, this more accurate notion of film counterpoint, will point
the way to understanding *classical* music in montage equations.

OVERTONAL MONTAGE

The complications and elaborations suggested above have their
origin in the original theory and the circumstances in which it
developed. The most noted Soviet filmmakers were not able to
practically apply the principles set forth in the Statement on
Sound.[52] Stalin, the rise of Soviet socialist realism, not to mention inferior sound technology and the popular inaccessibility of
the avant-garde filmmakers' works, cut short the shining period
before these grand sound film formulations could be executed.

It was not just history that hobbled the development and execution of sound film theory in the Soviet Union. Stalinist oppres-
sion gave the lie to the concept of neat historical dialectics;
contingency and cruelty showed that the product of any conceptual collision could not be safely, synthetically predicted, and
that montage oppositions were not any more reliable than parallelism had been. The historical and human results of these events
were of course overwhelmingly tragic, but conceptually, there
was some profitable result.

In montage theory, or at least in undergraduate caricatures of
the theory, there has been an undue emphasis on intellectual
montage, at the expense of other, more complicated possibilities.
By the time sound actually arrived, Eisenstein was going beyond
his first formulations of intellectual montage to a much more
complex and multivalent model. He sensed that things were not
as simple as his first statements had suggested.[53] Of course thesis
plus antithesis could still *equal* synthesis, but more musical terminology, not to mention the coming of sound, suggested to him
that there was much more in the air.

"Overtonal montage (grows) from the conflict between the
principal tone of the piece (its dominant) and the overtone."[54]
The overtone, in contrast to previous crude dialectical assump-

tions, allows for more than just for and against. It allows for the things in montage construction that we only subconsciously apprehend, but which are still there.

> The *central* stimulus . . . is attended always by a *whole complex* of secondary stimuli. . . . [In acoustics], along with the vibration of the basic dominant tone, comes a whole series of similar vibrations, which are called *overtones* and *undertones*. Their impacts against each other, their impacts with the basic tone . . . envelop [it] in a whole host of secondary vibrations. If in acoustics these collateral vibrations become merely 'disturbing' elements, these same vibrations in music . . . become one of the most significant means for affect. . . .[55]

Here Eisenstein allows for something insufficiently admitted in early montage theory, and some that comes later: unconscious process and affect, or feeling.[56] Unlike the first facile equations, the notion of a "dominant" montage synthesis, followed to its musical end, implies the presence of subdominants, even tonics—or that the dominant reading may not actually be in the home, or true key. And of course, as in modernist literature that subverts narrative, or modern music that eschews key signatures, chord progression, and tonality altogether, there is the possibility of some completely new landscape of signification, or unsignification.[57]

The significance of the overtone is that the parallels and perpendiculars of intellectual montage give way to far greater complexity and possibility. Though poles may be useful for definition, in actual communication and action we usually find ourselves in between extremes, even in a position to reconcile them.[58] Eisenstein says as much, quoting Lenin on the elements of Hegelian dialectics.

> . . . an endless process of *revealing* new aspects, relationships, etc. . . . of *deepening* human perception of things, appearances, processes and so on, from appearance to essence and from the less profound to the more profound essence . . . from co-existence to causality and from one form of connection and interdependence to another deeper, more general . . . *return, so to say, to the old.*[59]

Avant-gardes imply and are associated with opposition, and post-Soviet sound theory has validated opposition as the preferable of two alternatives—the other being parallelism—open to filmmakers. But as Eisenstein's overtonal ideas suggested, oppositions are not always completely authoritative, nor are the dominants that are opposed always easy (or necessary) to invalidate. Beyond that, and even more importantly, between and beyond the thin lines of opposition and genuflection lies a whole world not taken into account. It is in this in-between place that we find the difference between "counterpoint" as used, and as it would be used if applied to its logical, musical end.

MUSICAL MEANING AND CONTRAPUNTAL MONTAGE

To summarize, as montage theory overprivileged intellectual montage, so film/sound discourse overprivileged the oppositional implications of contrapuntal relations. In doing so it has sold short the complexity of music's relation to image, and to the play of meaning. Complicating formal flowings, *and their conceptual ramifications*, have generally been left out of the equation.

As demonstrated by the illustrations of formal counterpoint in film, when there is a *cinematic* transposition of *musical* counterpoint, it does not necessarily take place at the level of meaning. As demonstrated in our discussion of dissonant harmony in film, when sound (intellectual) montage is taking place, there is no strictly formal "rules of music" counterpoint, because formal, musical counterpoint does not collide. Finally, and paradoxically, when this figurative or conceptual counterpoint does take place, the resulting significations exceed standard, for-or-against notions of dialectical intellectual montage. In fact those significations flow and intertwine with practically contrapuntal complexity. No wonder that the "in-between place" I referred to above can be confusing.

Here are some reasons for the confusion, and some ways out. Pudovkin maintained that music should never just accompany the picture, but that it should retain its own line. He gives as an example the riot sequence in his 1933 film, *Deserter*, where Yuri Shaporin's music avoids slavish blow-by-blow illustration, instead maintaining a triumphant tone suggestive of the will to resist that eventually leads to the workers' victory.[60]

The picture, which presents the narrative, traces the fluctuations of the workers' struggles, while the music affirms the inevitability of the workers' victory. Here is formal counterpoint, as the image "melody" now departs from, now returns to, its musical counterpart, as Pudovkin's "lines" separate and unite and eventually resolve in a cadence of victory. The *figurative* counterpoint is found in the collision of what some of the images mean, and the music's seeming contradiction to that meaning. Significantly, it is that *collision* that Pudovkin most emphasizes, and in the collision that eventual resolution and intellectual synthesis are accomplished.[61]

Pudovkin implies two counterpoints, and presents both alternatives, but his work raises questions as to whether the formal and the figurative are compatible, at least with respect to the early theory. Discussing the music in this sequence from *Deserter*, Kracauer observes that original music does not enact a collision, nor create a concept very effectively. The flow of formal counterpoint undercuts the figurative function, and the audience simply does not understand. "Like sound proper, music is quite able to characterize . . . concepts and notions as are already given us; but it cannot define or symbolize them by itself alone."[62]

So, as we have seen, musical parallelism underestimates the complexity of meaning in film, and in the world that film reflects. The "contrapuntal" alternative falls short too. But Pudovkin and the Soviets generally theorized and practiced in order to find an alternative to the oversimplifications of parallelism and its social equivalents. As shown by Brecht's somewhat similar work, this impulse was not limited to film circles. As will be shown by the properties of music as they relate to meaning, success in this regard was still possible.

How? By a better, more realistic understanding of the properties of musical meaning. I will now elaborate on Edward Said's idea, introduced in my first chapter, that music can be contextualized through reference and allusion. Concurrent with early silent film practice, there was a movement in linguistics to counter its kind of overwhelming underdetermination. It is now generally related that before the pioneering work of Ferdinand de Saussure, linguistics concentrated on etymology, and that the actual articulations of language were taken for granted as natural. The account continues by representing, here on the brink of the abyss of modernity, an untroubled human subject, seeing and seen in classical perspective, in a world where things were as they appeared, God in His place and man in his. These perspectives have, of course, changed irrevocably. As his contribution to the great destabilization, Saussure began to ask not just what, but how, things mean. With Charles Peirce's work on the interpretation and classification of signs, linguists and philosophers began to apply Saussure's innovations to all arenas of communication, or, in Peirce's phrase, to all "sign systems."[63]

The result of these investigations was to call forever into question the idea that language and languages are innocent, our servants, that things are necessarily the way they appear. In both direct and indirect ways, the people we have been discussing grappled with these issues, particularly as they related to the sign systems of music.

In the first chapter we discussed how, up to the present, musical discourse has stayed somewhat clear of these semiotic currents. Questions about musical identity have taken precedence over thinking of music in social spheres, and in social communication. And although attention to technology, microtonal composition, chance operations, and the problems of inaccessibility are all very important issues, their priorities reflect a real resistance to semiotic inquiry.[64]

This is not mere stubborn reaction, however; as with the *Deserter* example, we have seen some of the complications that have arisen in relation to music and meaning. The fact is that music resists semiotic elaboration more than most modes of communication. In music the link between signifier and signified is not direct or causal, as in many other systems. *T-a-b-l-e* may be a completely arbitrary sign for the object it represents, but long usage and the immemorial naming functions of human language make the sign comprehensible. But the image, the kind of table these letters bring to mind suddenly opens up a great space. This being the case with such a concrete concept, the vastness of, say, a C-major triad, becomes quite daunting. This is not to say that music is not a signifying system. Western musical notation is a rational, comprehensible system of signs, whether one can read the music or not. But grafted onto this denotative plane is a whole complex of referential meanings, which enormously complicate the notion of what and how music means. Parallelism, or the perpendicular? A waltz is a piece of music in 3/4 time, but its rhythm also suggests certain social constructs, a certain period, key composers, and all this whether everyone recognizes the waltz rhythm or not. The polyrhythms of "world music" bespeak multiculturalism, or new colonialism, profound cultural interchange, or dabbling dilettantism, an overdue acknowledgment of discounted expressions or a dubious favor done in the name of political correctness. After the first instance, when one pauses to ponder, the connections and disjunctions proliferate.

Of course musicians and musical commentators have also grappled with these problems, and in many different ways. The first established theories of musical meaning were imitation and expression.[65] These have substantial use and merit, but they are not systems of signification. Although it sounds like a storm in Beethoven's Sixth, and Debussy's *Prélude a l'Après-Midi d'Un Faun* evokes languor and *La Mer* has a certain spray surrounding it, these pieces are finally impressions and approximations. Though these are musical sketches that evoke the objects sketched, "impressionism" for music is only a simile, and it falls short of our experience. Language, to be a language, must communicate comprehensibly to all those who use it. The fact is, not everyone will hear the water or be stirred by the storm. This is a kind of musical onomatopoeia, but sounding like something is not the same as utilizing an array of linguistic signs to communicate an idea which lies outside the materiality of those signs. Although languages are full of imitative harmony, of words that sound like things, these words are finally special cases that differ from the mainstreams of language.

As for music's ability to express an idea or articulate some sensation, Raymond Monelle expresses a common view that is difficult to refute, that "music is a presentation of feeling rather than a direct expression," and so we seem to have a standoff.[66] Overtonal complications, Pudovkin's practice, music theory, all affirm the great difficulty of suggesting clear meaning, of affecting intellectual montage through music.

But here is where source music, particularly classical music, provides a solution. Early in this chapter we discussed the problems of musical parallelism, and the withering correspondences that it relied upon. I wish to point out, however, that inadequate execution does not necessarily invalidate the idea behind that execution. Béla Balasz identifies a simple, essential truth, allowing for the *musical* communication and proliferation of meaning.

> Asynchronous sound has no need to be natural. Its effect is symbolic and it is linked with the things it accompanies through its significance, in the sphere of the mind, not of reality. . . . The similarity of certain sounds may invite comparisons and evoke associations of ideas.[67]

This relates to much more than Beethoven's thunder or Debussy's salt smell. Hans Keller makes a simple point that helps us to understand oppositional "counterpoint," and the way music actually can signify: "Musical irony has to work on established material."[68] Similarly, Michel Chion observes that "audiovisual counterpoint will be noticed only if it sets up an opposition between sound and image on a precise point of meaning."[69] As Balasz suggests, after the conceptual collision, the moment of montage, the associations begin to flow.

How does this work? When film music steps up from the paralleling, subservient role so often prescribed for it, it suddenly starts to signify. David Raksin recalls that for *Laura* (1944), "Darryl Zanuck had wanted to throw out about 50 percent of that apartment scene, which is the crucial scene in the picture." This is understandable, since viewed without Raksin's music this famous sequence is not even half finished, or even half comprehensible. The detective investigating the apparent murder appears to be wandering very aimlessly and nearly endlessly through the dead woman's apartment.

Raksin makes good on his promise to "make clear what the detective is feeling," but it is only through music that that clarity, that meaning is achieved.[70] And how? Through a motif. Tempo and color suggest what music has always successfully suggested: a feeling. But the *association* of the melody with the person anchors that feeling to a referent and context. That tune *equals* Laura, and it is by association, not to mention the collision with the images, that the music is brought out of the subconscious haze into the realm of the rational.

Music in film can speak to us, can have meaning for us. It does so in a straightforward and multiply effective way, though that way is still too generally discounted or decried. Irene Atkins speaks of the fortuitousness of an *unfamiliar* piece of source music. The reason: "the performance of a well-known piece would have carried with it *too many* built-in connotations."[71] But it is precisely through connotation, whether specific to an individual film—Raksin's theme comes to signify "Laura"—or more general, that film music has meaning. As we will see in upcoming chapters, "too many" is precisely the advantage, and even the nature of musical meaning.

Bob Last, a pioneer in the use of precomposed music in motion pictures, notes that usual ways of using and thinking about film music fall short of the actual ways it functions. It doesn't just accompany, it means, and ambiguously.

> Film resists single responses, and of course music does too. Within the visual domain it's difficult to be multivalent, but music inherently works that way. But it works underneath, subconsciously. You can theorize about the way music means, but ultimately it's intuitive. Even lyrics don't quite make music concrete. It doesn't exist as a sign system. It retains its ineffable qualities.

Which music means most, or best? Last feels that source music is most valuable because of its previous exposure, and the dense associations it brings. "After the mundane reasons—the director liked the song—enter the intangible emotional ones, and specific historical references, or a combination of the two. Source music crosses all genres, and brings them together too."[72]

Accounts that speak of music as simply congruent or contrasting artificially limit its real effects. For and against are only the most obvious ways that film music works. We will develop the idea of how music works on points of meaning, moving away from the problematic, insistent reality that in practice and discussion the point of meaning is almost invariably reduced to binary logic, to a one-way interpretation. We will counter this by asserting and illustrating the fact that after discord, or concord, comes *conceptual* counterpoint, in which the various implications and possibilities, both tonal and discordant, both parallel and perpendicular, start to sustain and echo and resonate in the spectator's mind.

Sound montage, then, works best when the music emerges as a disturbing detail, when its familiarity and cultural specificity brings history and association into play. As I have demonstrated, however, and as the next chapters will amplify, that play is not reducible to strict montage geometries. It is not true that a sound plus an image will always equal *one* interpretation. The overdetermination of classical music, not to mention the range of knowledge and feeling in film artists/artisans and spectators, insures that the most reliable, helpful synthesis lies between the reductions of both subservient music and overconfident opposition.

NOTES

1. In Wollen, 1982. For discussion of "avant-garde" vs. "classical" art see Burger, 1984, 70.
2. Cf. Adorno, 1973.
3. Wollen, 1982, 95.
4. On the cinema worker see Petric, 1987.
5. See Eisler, 1947, 23–27 for examples.
6. I see these conflicts not so much as weaknesses as signs of the humanity and sincere grappling behind the work. My emphasis on Soviet theory here is intended to more clearly delineate terms and possibilities, and also to suggest how clear delineations, in this and other cases, have sometimes obscured and complicated both the application and the understanding of theory.
7. In Adorno, 1972, 125–26. Characteristically, Horkheimer and Adorno find that the detail, "a vehicle of protest against the organization" which operated from Romanticism through Expressionism, can no longer function under the totality of the culture industry.
8. Brecht, 1964, 37–38; 1976, 281–82. See Adorno, 1972, 124 for Adorno and Horkheimer's dire characterization of modern artistic integration in television.
9. Brecht, 1976, xxix.
10. Ibid., xxx.
11. Brecht, 1964, 38. The most famous part of this essay, later anthologized as "The Modern Theatre is the Epic Theatre," is the grid placing conventional "dramatic theatre" against the new "epic theatre." In this grid numerous elements of narrative theater were similarly opposed to reveal their old dramatic and new epic functions. For a

strictly musical demonstration of disturbing detail consider the work of *Les Six*, including their incorporation, as in a collage, of popular idioms, pastiches, and quotations in their compositions. A number of this circle (Auric, Milhaud, Honegger) went on to compose for films. Thomson, 1966, 52–72; Brown, 1988, 174.

12. "Of course such innovations also demand a new attitude on the part of the audiences who frequent opera houses." Ibid., 39. Dziga Vertov, preceding the better-known Brecht, articulately represents the cinematic applications of many of these ideas. See Vertov, 1984.

13. As suggested in my first chapter, film music has only recently taken up some of these issues again. See, for instance, Brown's writerly prescriptions (1994, 1, 22) against Thomas's traditionally integrated suggestions (1973, 16). Generations of film musical romanticism (which I do not wish to reject uncategorically) have combined to obscure the points so well made some seventy years ago.

14. Atkins, 1983, 21. The elided word is "source."

15. "Film music did not become film music until the music began to coordinate with the action." Brown, 1988, 169.

16. Lang/West, 1920, 13.

17. Ibid., 54.

18. Rapée, 1924, iii.

19. Rapée, 1925, 11.

20. Quoted in Berg, 1976, 91. Using a similar range of sources, George suggests to the accompanist that "anything associated with the production should be looked for." George, 1912, 18.

21. Kracauer, 1960, 141.

22. Burch, 1990, 234–36.

23. I.e., Ervine, 1934.

24. See Rapée, 1925, 14.

25. Gorbman calls Rapée's "the definitive lexicon." (1987, 85.)

26. Rapée, 1925, 31.

27. It is important of course not to assume that lexicon usage was monolithic, or universal. Virgil Thomson (1966, 32) says that he never used provided cue sheets for his silent film accompaniments. A contemporary Dutch film journal advised theater management not to use the scores provided with the films, as they required too much extra outlay for musicians. (In Van Houten, 1992, 24.) Gaylord Carter did not find Rapée very useful, and suggests that the collections were basically for nonmusicians (Carter, personal communication, 1994).

28. Eisenstein, 1949, p. 258, emphasis in original.

29. See Pudovkin, 1949, 140, for the famous experiment with the actor Mozhukin that illustrated this claim.

30. Taylor and Christie, 1988, 73. See also "The Origins of Montage," an interview with Lev Kuleshov in Schnitzer et al., 1973, 66–76.

31. See Brown, 1988, 165 on similarities between musical composition and montage.

32. Apel, 1972, 208.

33. Eisenstein, 1949, 30. This great breadth of reference and comparison contains not only the enthusiasm and even joy of montage discourse, but some of its confusions as well.

34. Ibid., 1949, 28–44.

35. See "Methods of Montage," in Eisenstein, 1949, 72–83, especially 81. I will return shortly to the other methods.

36. See Burger, 1984, 80–81 on constructedness and the uses of shock.

37. Soviet cinema has many well-known and effective examples of intellectual montage. See, for instance, the slaughter in Eisenstein's *Strike* (1924), titles and the tribunal, spring thaw and revolution in Pudovkin's *Mother* (1926), candles and clouds in Eisenstein's *Old and New* (1929), bovines and bourgeois in Dovzhenko's *Earth* (1930), etc.

38. For one example, compare Eisenstein, 1982, 26, to the procession sequence in *Old and New*.

39. A. Kraszna-Krausz, writing in 1931 and quoted in Leyda, 1960, 251.

40. They do that too, as the hagiographic *Three Songs of Lenin* (1934) shows. My position is that they are too full, too fecund to do only that.

41. Prendergast, 1992, 26.

42. Pudovkin, 1949, 157. See 155–65.

43. Balasz, 1952, 216, 218.

44. Quoted in Huntley, 1947, 158. "The term *counterpoint* [designates the] notion of the sound film's ideal state as a cinema free of redundancy where sound and image would constitute two parallel and loosely connected tracks, neither dependent on the other." Chion, 1994, 35–36.

45. Quoted in Steiner, 1989, 93. Emphasis in original.

46. Eisler, 1947, 70. Similarly, for Kracauer counterpoint in film consists of having music oppose the image to create a concept. Kracauer, 1960, 139–42.

47. Thompson, 1980, 117.

48. Ibid., 127, 133.

49. Randel, 1986, 205.

50. Chion, 1994, 36–37 (see 35–39).

51. Metaphors do not and need not meet every circumstance. Wagner

said he used his operatic leitmotifs like symphonic motives, but acknowledged that the simile is inexact. Both leitmotif and metaphor are as much dramatic as musical/structural. Still they can be expressive and illuminating. Warrack, John, "Leitmotif," in Sadie, 1980, X, 645. For different kinds of musical contrapuntal analogy see Kolker, 1983, 41, on Renoir's *Rules of the Game* (1939), Louis Jacobs on intertwining stories in Griffith's *Judith of Bethulia* (1913). Jacobs, 1969, 56.

52. For the sad story see Marshall, 1983.

53. For the first statement see "Montage of attractions" in Eisenstein, 1942, 230–33. Also, in another translation, in Taylor and Christie, 1988, 87–89.

54. Eisenstein, 1949, 79.

55. Ibid., 66. Emphasis in original.

56. See ibid., 80–81.

57. See "A Course in Treatment," in Eisenstein, 1949, 84–107 (esp. 104–5), for a virtuosic rendering of the related literary device of inner speech (cf. Joyce's *Ulysses*). Also see Eisenstein, 1942, appendix 4 and 5, for actual film treatments incorporating and suggestive of these ideas.

58. For more on this in-between space see my fifth chapter.

59. In Eisenstein, 1949, 81. Emphasis added.

60. Pudovkin, 1949, 162–65. Playing against the picture was not entirely new. Ido Eyl speaks of oppositional scoring as a matter of course during the early silent period in the Netherlands. In Van Houten, 1992, 45–46.

61. See Pudovkin, 1949, 165.

62. Kracauer, 1960, 142.

63. For a semiotic summary see Silverman, 1983.

64. See Kerman 1985; Said, 1991.

65. Monelle, 1992, 1.

66. Ibid., 5.

67. Balazs, 1952, 219, 217.

68. Keller in *Music Review*, XVII, 1956, 338.

69. Chion, 1994, 38. See Brown, 1988, 172–74, 198–99 for some examples.

70. Quoted in Brown, 1994, 283.

71. Atkins, 1983, 45. Emphasis added.

72. Last, personal communication, 1995.

4

Narration, Program, and Narrative

I HAVE DISCUSSED two very separately motivated rejections of musical subordination in the classical Hollywood score, as well as of the musical parallelism that in many ways preceded its development. That subordination was seen, at least in part, to exist in the trite and vulgar appropriation of source music, and of the standard repertoire in particular. Although negative reactions are not wholly invalid, I have suggested that the polar responses of aesthetic music critics and the Soviet montage artists respectively also contain inadequacies. Isolation and plain opposition can be as unhelpful and even crude as that which they are meant to counter. By following up the musical implications of counterpoint I have proposed a solution which lies, in a kind of overtonally dialectical synthesis, in between the extremes.

In this synthesis, collisions between image and music often and most effectively turn on points of reference and association. Previous rejections and ignorings notwithstanding, because of the way it multiplies these points, source music is a particularly interesting and important montage element. In this chapter I will propose a context, through a second film-music analogy, that will help clarify the ways that classical music works in films. This context resides as well in a second film-music synthesis, the product of the collision between the aesthetic and the political avant-garde.

Suspicions concerning the use of source music in film actually descend from a much older tradition, even more dependent on a premusical source. In his 1946 book, *Music and Society*, Wilfred Mellers noted that pre-Purcellian English music did not generally suffer from hierarchical divisions, that it was open to and participated in by all. He states that in this early period "intense human feeling finds complete realization in terms of music, rather than working by mental association, as does so much of the music of the nineteenth century (in this sense, of course, *any* great music is impersonal)."[1]

Mellers sets up an opposition between great music and that which works by association (from a source), and so locates the fall from musical egalitarianism in the programmatic forms of the nineteenth century. Mellers agrees with critics already cited when he states that an "appalling level of taste absorbed both people and artists more or less impartially" in that century.[2] As we have seen, Mellers's contribution to the 1954 *Grove's Dictionary* entry on film music confirms his feeling that that direness continued into his present, and is still evident in, for instance, film.

Whether or not one agrees with this take or its tone, it is certainly true that far from Mellers's early-music plenitude, between the extremes of Adorno/Keller elitism and Sovietlike political engagement, lies program music. Program music is in some ways a literary/musical hybrid, and many observers have found that the mixture ill serves both components. As I hope to demonstrate, however, far from being a poor servant of either master, program, or principles related to it, can effectively mediate seemingly irreconcilable positions. It brings opposites together and suggests a substantial way to understand and appreciate all music, and other cultural phenomena as well.

Just as the counterpoint analogy has been both confusing and extremely liberating for film studies, so too does program music have somewhat perilous, but also very important, literal and figurative uses. These uses are the focus of this chapter. Speaking literally, program has some clear and illuminating similarities to film music. Speaking figuratively, with regard to the broader contexts and various predispositions with which we come to film, film music, and especially classical music in film, program applies to and enriches every instance.

ADAPTING PROGRAM TO THE PRESENT

I will presently define and discuss program music in the dictionary sense, but I wish to note at the outset that in the end my use of program is a decided appropriation, involving a transposition of the original expressions to current conditions. In this current sense, program extends far beyond Hector Berlioz and Franz Liszt. As appropriated and transformed here, program traditions suggest that music always has reference to some kind of narrative, artistic or cultural, beyond it. As I will demonstrate, this referentiality exists as a quality of the music itself, as well as being a property of musical interpretation.[3] Also, consistent with the musicalness or even indeterminacy of conceptual counterpoint, I will take the liberty of grafting on ideas that polite parallels or perpendiculars would not normally admit.

The first of these grafts will serve to ground the discussion here of program, and I will return to it in the final chapter as I summarize the implications of this study.

In the last chapter I discussed the ideas of Bertolt Brecht and how they opened up and defined a political, progressive space for musical action. Those ideas were consistent with, and in some ways led to, some fairly strict Marxist prescriptions. I have questioned these, but I wish now to point out that Brecht's work not only contains the seeds for my critique, but also an apt rebuttal to it.

Today there may be an excessive solemnity to discussions of Brecht, connected with his presumed progressiveness and seriousness of purpose. The grave sound of "epic theatre" and the predominance of terms like "alienation effect" have distanced us from the sense of fun and play in Brecht.[4] More to the point, though vulgar Marxism may use him with a dialectical severity, close attention to both the work and its method reveals an important sense of contingency, even chaos.

In their introduction to the collected works, Ralph Mannheim and John Willett discuss Brecht's "contempt for 'originality.'" This contempt was repeatedly revealed in the way that Brecht borrowed, without attribution, from other sources, in the way he took credit for the work of a collective, or, conversely, did not take credit for some of his own substantial collaborative contributions.[5]

In the end, Mannheim and Willett conclude that Brecht was a "piecemeal writer."

These works were patched together from a variety of sources, then taken apart and restitched, sometimes with loose threads dangling; their eventual length and shape was never all that clearly determined.[6]

The significance of Brecht's method lies in part in its similarities to the scramblings of Hollywood composers and the musical appropriations of other sources in narrative films. Here, as in Brecht's work, depth and insight might well be found if we've a mind to look for it.

More than that, Brecht's approach is analogous to the figurative workings of program I am proposing here. Clear and neat are not always accurate, or even necessary. Sources, appropriations, and determinants are multifarious, complex, not always acknowledged or even realized. The unpredictablity of history, the vagaries of musical meaning, and the ebbs and flows of literal counterpoint all suggest how complicated, confounding, and revelatory the mixing of media and disciplines can be.

PROGRAM MUSIC AND THE FUNCTION OF THE LITERARY TEXT

Before developing these ideas, I will discuss program music in its original setting and definition. Program music was current from the second half of the nineteenth century and into the early part of the twentieth.[7] It emerged in earnest with Beethoven's Sixth Symphony (1808) and Berlioz' *Symphonie Fantastique* (1830).[8] Beethoven's composition, in addition to its not unconventional musical or symphonic structure, has a narrative component. The music is anchored to this extramusical narrative by means of evocative movement titles as well as by imitative orchestral effects and other associative devices. Through these devices the symphony relates a kind of country day-in-the-life, which includes the musical suggestions of flowing water, birds, peasant dances, a summer storm, and a horn call.

Berlioz takes Beethoven's mix of narration and music a step further. Instead of the usual movement titles that give instructions for tempo, dynamics, and expression (*allegro con brio*, for example), Berlioz essentially names his movements for their dramatic content. "Reveries—Passions," "A Ball," "Scene in the

Country," "March to the Scaffold," and "Dream of a Witches' Sabbath" all signal an important change: a story is as important as the music being used to support it. Berlioz made this reversal explicit by publishing a program with his symphony, to be read before listening, in which the events of his musical narrative were made very explicit.

These compositions were original, as were the narratives attached to them. Another kind of programmatic musical narrative would adapt preexisting texts (play, poem, legend, even landscape) to new musical settings. [9] In this regard symphonic overtures, particularly some by Beethoven, are directly antecedent to later programmatic forms. It is important to remember in the context of this study that this music's expressivity was directly related to the theatrical works (Goethe's *Egmont*, Shakespeare's *Coriolanus*) which it supported.

This interdependence is not without precedent, and I will presently demonstrate the pattern's recurrence in film culture.[10] As for program music itself, the dictionary account by Roger Scruton is that it evoked dramatic events while maintaining musical self-sufficiency.[11] Beethoven and Berlioz both composed overtures that were related to literary sources (Scott's *Waverly*, and *Rob Roy*), but which were performed separate from any other kind of literary or theatrical setting. But I wish to emphasize that although the degree of literary preeminence varied, in much serious music the communication of musical meanings was at first anchored to and made possible by narrative and literary forms, by text.

Franz Liszt is the central figure in the development and codification of the symphonic poem and of program music, both of which terms he coined. Liszt's early piano pieces from the 1830s contain descriptive passages, and though he largely avoided a too literal rendering of the motivating literary or historical sources, through imitation and word painting, he nevertheless sought to evoke the external by musical means. Later he composed a series of twelve symphonic poems (1848–58) that elaborated this external strategy. Examples of the kind of subjects that interested Liszt include a rendering of nature's immensity (*Ce pu'on entend sur la montagne*, 1848–49, after Hugo), a description of a fifth-century battle (*Hunnenschlacht*, 1857, inspired by a painting), a work suggestive of the characters of Hamlet and Ophelia (*Hamlet*, 1858), homages to the suffering of creative genius (*Prometheus*, 1850) and the uplifting power of art (*Orpheus*, 1853–54). Liszt also wrote full-scale symphonic works based on *Faust* and the *Inferno*, with passages suggestive of specific episodes from both works.

The next major elaborations of the symphonic poem depended in different ways, but just as surely, on elements emerging from outside the music. Czech and Russian composers wedded descriptive impulses to national and nationalistic subjects, again through recourse to historical narratives and attempted descriptions of native landscapes. Examples include Glinka's uncompleted *Taras Bulba*, Mussorgsky's *St. John's Night on the Bare Mountain* (1867), Tchaikovsky's *Romeo and Juliet* (1869), Smetana's *Ma Vlast* (1872–79), and a great many more, reaching up to and past the generally acknowledged close of the programmatic cycle in the 1920s. All of these compositions were dependent upon a familiarity with source material. Where such familiarity was absent, or where the work's title did not anchor the music to some specific association, its communicability remained open to question and its intent at least was not fully fulfilled.

Scruton points out that there has been much difficulty rising out of the connections and differences between "narrative" and "emotional" depictions, and to what program music actually is. He emphasizes that Liszt did not want to describe objects or events through music. The music put listeners in the "same frame of mind as could the objects (or theme, idea) themselves."[12] Scruton maintains that Liszt's desire was to evoke or suggest. This approach allows for programmatic anchoring, but also, if one is not aware of the anchor, a more intrinsically musical experience.[13]

In his dictionary account, Scruton stresses the musical self-sufficiency of program music. His entry affirms the possibilities and validities of the form. But it should be noted that some of Liszt's actual comments about program music contradict Scruton's take on it, and these contradictions suggest some of the reasons that in different circles program has been so generally discounted, and even derided.

> In programme music . . . the return, change, modification, and
> modulation of the motifs are conditioned by their relation to a
> poetic idea. . . . All exclusively musical considerations, though
> they should not be neglected, have to be subordinated to the action
> of a given subject.[14]

Program music was subservient to the external subject. It followed a theme, or related to a story or character. Liszt saw that
there had been no real place for narrative in symphonic music.
In opening up such a place, he prescribed from the beginning
that the music should be understood through its program, or in
other words through its literary referent. And it was the referent
that was most important.

Not only did the subordinate position of the music cause discomfort for musical purists, but the use of that music could be
troubling in another sense. Liszt defined a program as a

> preface added to a piece of instrumental music, by means of which
> the composer intends to guard the listener against *a wrong poetical
> interpretation*, and to direct his attention to the poetical idea of the
> whole or to a particular part of it.[15]

The symphonic poem declined as modernism challenged these
very ideas. We have already considered how the aesthetic musical avant-garde rejected the subordination of music to narrative,
opting instead for the notion of music's abstraction and independence. The same is true of the political and ideological critics
who rejected the rigid parallelism of correct poetical interpretations. We see then how extramusical determinants contributed to
the eclipse of program music, which coincided not only with the
rise of the Vienna school, but also with modernist decenterings
and deconstructions of meaning. More moderate critics too may
have felt that it was finally impossible to merge the formal requirements of the two forms. "The natural architecture of music
was not that of poetry."[16]

The dilemmas of program music in the twentieth century take
on a special interest and pertinence to this study, since it shares
the very incompatibilities and compromises engendered by using
music underneath film images—underneath being the standard
position of film music in commercial narrative contexts. Is there
a solution?

Once again, here is the present standoff. Musical avant-gardes, and other voices too, resist subordinate forms and parallelism, while conventional film community discourse protests too much their validity.[17, 18] However, my feeling is that both constituencies could do with a shift, the specifics of which are suggested in some of the ways that program music relates to film. We will see that, whatever music's inherent significance, it is in combination with other contexts and considerations that it most vividly and directly comes to participate in the exchange of meaning, and feeling as well.

PROGRAM AND FILM MUSIC: FORMAL AND IDEOLOGICAL PARALLELS

There are striking parallels between program music and the conventions of classical film scoring. At first the similarities, as well as the dominant reactions to them, appear to be negative. After this section I will return to the question of whether they must be so considered. Again, Liszt said that a program was

> any preface in intelligible language added to a piece of instrumental music, by means of which the composer intends to guard the listener against a wrong poetical interpretation, and to direct his attention to the poetical idea of the whole or to a particular part of it.

Liszt's preface seems to be analogous to a film script, a directorial concept, the expectation of a producer, or of a targeted audience. These are possible "programs" that precede and contain the composition. In another sense we might add that film music itself also acts as a sort of program. As has been mentioned many times, guarding against wrong poetical interpretations is precisely the mandate of the classical film score.

The way program music guards against these wrong interpretations is also a striking echo of standard film music mandates.

> In programme [*or film*] music . . . the return, change, modification, and modulation of the motifs are conditioned by their relation to a [*narrative*] idea. . . . All exclusively musical considerations, though they should not be neglected, have to be subordinated to the action of a given subject.

Chapter two's aesthetes note that both these forms of subordination ultimately diminish the music, as well as its setting, all resulting in a fatal underdetermination. The results are a closing off of musical meaning and musical feeling, all through an excess of concrete reference. According to this view program and film would be a nefarious binding of the worst in nineteenth- and twentieth-century musical practice.

I would like to propose a contrary view, which is that music, especially placed narratively, can also resist the restrictions of musical muzzlings and excessive subordination. It was not in prescribing programs, but in seeking to limit their effects that Liszt was unduly timid. Music, even, especially with some extra-musical prologue, is automatically overdetermined. This overde-termination may imperil the dictionary definition of program, but it opens up rich metaphorical possibilities.

Summarizing to this point, program music is *like* film music. As with film and counterpoint, this statement has both literal and figurative meaning. First, as with Beethoven's, Berlioz's or Liszt's original compositions, specially composed film music requires narrative elements external to it to be fully comprehensible. Second, appropriated compositions—source music—bring with them programmatic information, relating not only to specific pieces and their composers, but also to entire historical settings, institutions, and ideologies.

Was Rachmaninov responding to the extramarital affair of a London doctor and a suburban housewife when he wrote his Second Piano Concerto?[19] Certainly not, but the core of this analogy is that program is contained not only in what is intended, but also by what is apprehended. Regardless of what the composer was thinking, or even what motivated the filmmakers, the juxtaposition of source music and the motion picture creates overtones of ideology and history and effects a multiplication of meaning.

Program music's inexact, semimetaphorical relation and similarity to film music illuminates a great number of film music contexts. Some of these are literal, practical ones.

Since music that suggested an emotional mood, created atmosphere, or imitated a natural sound was prized by the film musician, program music of one sort or another was the standard accompaniment for the silent film.[20]

Film appropriations of program music were conscious, though the use of Liszt's language might not have been. Regardless, the following echo is dramatic.

Charles Berg observes that "as discontent with *inappropriate accompaniments* mounted, the central question asked by film musicians was how to realize an *appropriate, dramatically relevant score.*"[21] Liszt spoke similarly; film music's parallelism directly descends from programmatic ideals of appropriateness and relevance.[22] And as the following quotation suggests, the film narrative as it relates to musical accompaniment is very similar to negative takes on musical programs.

> In seeking to have the music cleave as closely as possible to the pictures, to action, expressions, sentiments, etc., the aim, long before the introduction of the optical track, was already the mechanistic subordination of sound to picture . . . [A] sound should never be anything but the consequence of the movement of a picture.[23]

In both musical and cinematic settings, looking at it from a certain perspective, the result was a kind of crippling correlation, a shotgun accompaniment by music of things external to it. This is the double context of parallelism. Giuseppe Becce's 1919 *Kinothek*, which Kurt London identifies as the first illustrative compilation, is full of programmatic selections which are used to correspond with narrative moods and emotions. Becce's collection

> contained, if we follow the romantic conception of programme music, all the moods of men and the elements, every kind of reaction to human destiny, musical drawings of nature and animals, of peoples and countries: in short every sphere of life, well and clearly arranged under headings.[24]

A few years earlier W. Tyacke George had described this very range.

> We may have alarm, abhorrence, ardour, curiosity, dreaming, distrust, fear, faith, happiness, danger, death, doubt, hope, hatred, excitement, grief, sorrow, pain, foreboding, joy, jealousy, humour, suffering, sorrow, resignation, ridicule, listening, laughter, tears, salvation, resentment, reserve, meditation, prayer, surprise, longing, pining, wishing, triumph, and all the various phases that go to

make up the gamut of human emotions, each of which is capable of individual musical illustration.[25]

As in Becce's guide, and Rapée's too, George goes on to list both serious and popular compositions that accomplish this illustration.

We have considered two film-era responses to this apparently smothering excess of concrete reference. But even before these aesthetic and political responses, more mainstream musical culture also hewed to other alternatives. I will now look more closely at a romantic response to program music. The response is negative, but I hope to show that between this and the continued rejections of ideological critics, there exists a helpful synthesis of the two approaches. As with musical film counterpoint, a valid film-program strategy is already contained within apparently opposed critical factions.

Turn-of-the-twentieth-century musical commentator Philip Goepp consistently celebrates "[musical] meaning in pure tones," but generally devalues the notion of program music. Speaking of Beethoven, Goepp says that "on the whole, the untitled symphonies are much to be preferred."[26] "As soon as the mind occupies itself with the details of an imaginative picture, the musical attention flags."[27]

> In a very large degree, programme music is . . . a pretty, intellectual game, a subtle flattery, a mental feat, a guess at conundrums. Generally, there is a real loss in the apparent gain. If the emotional is the true attitude, it can be seen how the title, by absorbing attention, prevents a pure enjoyment and the test by natural perception.
>
> Creating a false interest, the label withdraws the normal, unbiased attention from the music itself, preconceiving the mind to an *a priori*, arbitrary connection or significance. In one way, entitled music is like the clever juggler who tricks by diverting attention from the real to a pretended act; in another, it is like the poor painter who holds the witless mind by the strength, not of his art, but of the printed label.[28]

Goepp's contention was that music had enough inherent narrative already, and that externals used to tie it down were superfluous, even vulgar.

For his part Elie Siegmeister, a Marxist music critic writing here in the 1930s, found that program music, and ultimately all of late Romanticism, and its alleged connections to the world outside finally insulated the listener from the most pressing externals, alienating him from the issues that should have most concerned all, and that were art's proper purview.

> Later romantic music became at once an emotional compensation and a spiritual salve for the commercial middle class audience. . . . It became the fashion for the artist to be isolated from "ugly" reality and to deal only with supernal, grandiloquent exaltation, grand sorrow; either the most thrilling ecstasy or the most abysmal despair. Nothing in between would do . . . Relishing melodrama and big doses of emotion for their money, the bourgeois audience came to the concert hall to be ecstatically exalted and furiously depressed, so that the tedium and spiritual emptiness of the day-to-day commercial grind could be forgotten.[29]

Siegmeister identifies the traditional social uses of music, how it has from antiquity been used as an aid to labor. In modern times, and especially through late Romantic music, ancient usages are now subsumed in and by the culture industry. If we were to apply this strictly materialist view to Hollywood and its factory-produced films, we would indeed find that film music is used to

> energize, to lighten the monotony, to set the rhythm for repeated labour movements . . . [and] to regulate the pace . . . of large groups of workers, as well as to stimulate and help workers spur one another on in the performance of tedious and protracted tasks.[30]

This striking description applies on the level of the composers, whose idealistic and romantic view of the artist consoles them in their indentured circumstances and distracts them from the anesthetizing use to which their music is put; it works especially at the point of audience reception and use, as the glosses of melodrama and post/sub-nineteenth-century music mask the standardized nature of the product and the underlining ideologies it carries.

Siegmeister's description can effectively be transposed to the level of music's ceremonial or ritual functions.[31] Now, instead of helping the listener/participant understand his society and his or her place in it, late Romantic music, as well as the film romanticism that grew from it, smooths over and hides the various gaps (cuts, ideologies, etc.) that were part of the cinematic and societal artifice. In either case the music's emphatic and overdetermined nature worked insidiously upon the audiences. Individual difference and individual discontent were elided, contributing to the creation of a community of undifferentiated, passive subjects who were then delivered over to a variety of ideological and commercial hailings.

This at least is the simplified Marxist rendering of the effects of music in the above-mentioned settings. Here, in nineteenth-century Europe and in twentieth-century Hollywood, is music produced for profit and not for use: the romantic idiom, in its programmatic manifestations, from Liszt to Mahler and Richard Strauss, makes one forget and is good for business.

The last chapter questioned the effectiveness of these simple oppositions. The question remains: Are Berlioz or Liszt, or at least the conventions they developed, the most egregious examples of dangerous ideological effacement? Could it be that, with regard to a materialist critique, forgetting, hailing, and subject obliteration are all more native to the discourse of musical absolutism, to nonprogrammatic music? From a certain perspective it might be argued that the validated musical forms were potentially more dire than the underappreciated ones.[32]

As we have seen, Horkheimer and Adorno discussed the once liberating possibilities of the "detail," the art element that makes itself seen, heard, or felt. Siegmeister's criticisms of late-nineteenth-century music can be countered when we consider the possible awareness of process that can be gained through program. As we will see, program music, and film's appropriation of it did not have to smother, and by no means did it always do so.

PROGRAM, FILM MUSIC, AND MULTIVALENT MEANING

The film community and those sympathetic to program music have had their own consistent response to the fairly constant undervaluing and even derision that we have been tracing. In 1910

Ernest Newman contended that "the desire to write programme music is rooted in humanity from the very beginning."[33] In other words, films were not the first to subordinate music to external narrative. Film composer Elmer Bernstein: "the concept of using music as an adjunct to what is basically a mixed medium is ancient. . . . Music in its inception was really adjunctive. . . . Its emergence as pure entertainment was relatively late in history."[34] If film music was suspect for its supportive functions, then it was in good company.

Roy Prendergast says that appeals to program precedents are not mere self-justification; Wagner, Puccini, Verdi, and Strauss faced and solved the exact same kind of dramatic problems the film composers had. Prendergast makes a point of quoting "distinguished music historian" Donald Jay Grout. "For Wagner, [too] the function of music was to serve the ends of dramatic expression."[35]

Are these self-justifications, or valid connections? Both perhaps, but the real similarities should not be ignored. Parallels between program music and the conventions of classical film scoring are especially evident in Liszt's career and compositional practice. For a period he collaborated with orchestrators to help him with his scores.[36] With some resemblance to the later film practice of writing variations to familiar external airs (including classical ones), we find Liszt denying Mephistopheles his own theme in the third movement of his *Faust* symphony. Instead he simply parodies the first movement's Faust theme.[37] Also in regard to apparent appropriations of outside material, Liszt also freely, and sometimes modestly, composed on themes by other composers.[38] Finally, his technique of "transformation of themes" uncannily prefigures the conventions of Hollywood scoring, as well as providing an alternative to Eislerian claims that serious music needs space and time to properly develop musical material.[39]

One may not like these connections, but they are not as strained or artificial as they have been made out to be. For example, in their film music primer Lang and West cite grand opera as an ideal model for appropriate film accompaniment.[40] At the time cultured film-haters may well have bristled at the presumption.

But unlike later writings, these early primers do not have to reach so far back for respectable models. Here is an essential point.

In 1920 Puccini, and program music too, are still more or less contemporaneous. If this music was not quite cutting edge, it still maintained a high level of respectability, as well as a considerable popular currency. We have seen how film used classical music to garner respectability, but we may also allow that, as suggested in our introduction, much of this respectable music was also simply familiar.[41] Elmer Bernstein and Roy Prendergast, and the silent period figures too may have been rationalizing slightly, but their points are also true.

Why is this important? Because it means that film music appropriations were not only mere appropriations. Film musicians and later composers too, as well as the audiences who heard them, were using materials to which they had valid relations. It also means that when outside music was brought into cinematic settings, the culture and conditions and associations of that outside music were also brought in.

As an example, film organist Gaylord Carter matter-of-factly says that "my score [for *The Thief of Baghdad*] consists of a theme for 'The Thief' character that I composed, material from [Rimsky-Korsakov's] *Scheherazade* of course. . . ."[42] "Of course;" for Carter, Ali Baba and *Scheherazade* just go together. They, along with their literary and musical and cinematic expressions, simply belong. In a similar sense Carter also used the *Dies Irae* from Berlioz's *Symphonie Fantastique* for the unmasking scene in *The Phantom of the Opera* (1925), feeling that he had merely, and quite justifiably, transposed one generation's macabre to another's.[43]

So, while film music figures worked to justify themselves and overcome musical prejudices, they also just acted naturally, or at least continued to do what others had done before. George Antheil, writing in 1936:

> Picture music is more closely allied to the dramatic forms than to the symphonic. By its very nature it must be loose in form and style. It is, quite simply, a kind of modern opera. And operatic music must certainly follow the emotional content of its drama and its accompanying poetry. Unless it does so, it will seem totally beside the point. This is just as true with picture music.[44]

As stated by Antheil, the dramatic form, "a kind of modern opera" text, is just another program, or something external to the music—drama and poetry—which sets and contextualizes that music.

With regard to film appropriations of source music, this suggests an intriguing musical mutability. Compositions were inflected by the original source as well as the present cinematic context. The result could contradict or confuse, but a certain cavalierness notwithstanding, it could also overcome a perceived limitation lying at program's core. Multiple musical elaborations meant that Liszt's "wrong poetical interpretation" ceased to be such a problem. Programs could carry their original sense as well as being transposed to other settings and tailored to other narratives.

Dictionary objections may arise at this point. As already mentioned, Roger Scruton warns against a common misapprehension. Music with "a narrative or descriptive meaning," for example, music that purports to depict a scene or a story, is validly programmatic. However, Scruton feels that to refer to all music with extramusical reference, to events, personalities, or feelings as programmatic is impossibly broad, reductive, even useless.[45]

But the fact is that, though Scruton quite properly points out some of the dangers of over-generalizing the program, generalization can still be appropriate. Other institutional statements allow for a broader application of the principle.

> Recent scholars argue that the dichotomy between absolute and program music is false, that the best program music can be appreciated without knowledge of the program. . . . Furthermore, some of the finest absolute works (eg. the symphonies of Haydn) are rich in references to dance rhythms and other stylistic conventions that a listener must recognize in order to follow the composer's thought fully.[46]

I would take this statement even further. Given the models of multivalent meaning already presented, given multifarious networks of intention and reception and indeterminacy and connection, I contend that *all* music has a program, even several programs. Literally, intentionally, this means that our understanding of a composition by Franz Liszt is enhanced when we understand *his* intended, explicit pretext to that composition. This means that our understanding of a composition by Franz Josef Haydn is enhanced when we understand the implicit, mostly masked, but still relevant pretext to *his* composition. This is program music. Speaking figuratively, and receptively, with regard to "program music" that goes beyond the official Grovean definitions, the program multiplies when we graft Liszt onto a text by Max Ophuls, such as *Letter from an Unknown Woman*, 1949, or when we add Haydn to a text by Louis Malle in *Lift to the Scaffold*, 1957. It multiplies even more when we apprehend the combination.[47]

Program music has not heretofore been applied, at least in the present sense, to discussions about film music specifically, and cinematic intertextuality in general. Clearly, after my own appropriation and application of the term and its related principles, further discussion is required to more firmly situate it. But in this preliminary sense I deem it valid, and valuable, to urge the connection. Outside narratives and context inflect all musical experience. This is especially true of appropriated film music. The limitations of the program are not in any smothering it is supposed to do, but in not taking the concept far enough.

PROGRAM EVERYWHERE

[Some] have so broadened [programme's] application as to use the term for all music that contains an extra-musical reference, whether to objective events or subjective feelings . . . [This application] is . . . so wide as to be virtually meaningless.[48]

As with the counterpoint analogy, literal and figurative programs may differ. In dictionary terms, Scruton is arguably correct, but we are looking at the way that external musical, and film/musical context is *like* a program. We are looking at the way that programmatic elements, references, and allusions, with the associations and connotations connected to them, become the elements of contrapuntal and montage equations.[49] In these applications, the generalization works and we are on firm ground. There is ample support for this idea. This section will demonstrate how even, especially from a music community point of view, program is everywhere.

Anthony Newcomb (1984) points out how even nonprogrammatic orchestral music from the nineteenth century would quite frequently, and quite casually, be written and heard as connected to and as expressions of larger literary forms, or of prevailing ideas and themes beyond specific literary works. To understand these works, Newcomb says, we must look beyond formal properties and musical architecture. Other questions pertain. What were people thinking and feeling as they wrote, and received, music? How did words process and transform the pure musical experience?

Through the period we find that even notions of musical absolutes depend more on language, on externals than it may have seemed. E. T. A. Hoffman holds forth on the notion of how Beethoven's *absolute* music brings us to "the spirit realm," to the place of highest human expression and meaning, though what that meaning might be remains unarticulated.[50] Similarly Philip Goepp makes a point of rejecting the musical crutches of liturgical or literary texts as he privileges pure music.[51] Then, paradoxically, in that pure, unprogrammatic place he finds musical meaning all over.

> The first melody for instrument alone had to atone for the new lack of words, avoid the danger of "mere vacant beauty." Here begins the stir for a definite language of pure tones. And this is significant, too: none of the older forms were the achievement of music itself, its self-found utterance. They are foreign; they belonged to poetry, like the song, or to the dance, like the minuet. See, therefore, how this new sonata form is actually the first proper mode of expression of the pure art of music. *It says something in mere tones.*[52]

And what does music say? Harmony, orchestration, all further musical development was a symptom of a need to talk about the tune, in which musical talk would reside meaning. Ultimately, all musical means would combine to express "one homogeneous expression of a great emotional idea."[53]

Goepp's expression is potentially opaque, the idea potentially vague. How can we understand what music is saying to us?

Goepp surmounts such challenges with a remarkable bit of musical anthropomorphizing.

> And now the [musical] story really begins: the characters are described; now they act and talk; the several musical ideas are discussed, singly or together, to new surprises of climax and beauty; they take on the guise often of new melodies, or melodies of kindred beauty are suggested.
>
> Thus . . . the themes pass from the mere phase of lyric utterance to that of epic narrative, not without strong dramatic power.[54]

Musical ideas come together to express more than the sum of their parts. Here is some of that epic narrative.

> Somehow, there is a little more [in Beethoven's musical descriptions] than mere chance imagery; for there is real truth in the symbolism of the moral strife of individual, of debate and dispute, drawing truth from the dregs, rising to final enlightenment. Every phase of life is here idealized . . . Beauty, strength, each have their figures. The moral, not the external life of man finds in music its full play and mirror. The true essence of life is in its emotions, and these play in tones as do fish in the waters. The highest problems are ethical, emotional, of experience; science is but a lesser helpmeet. In music their utterance is so real that they seem to be there themselves in the life of the tonal stream.
>
> Given the type of pleading, of defiance, of plaint, of dim foreboding akin to objective omen, of prayerful trust, of triumphant joy,—given all these, together with the full play of dispute and strife,—and you have all the resources, unconscious and therefore the more genuine and convincing, for the utterance of man's most vital thought. So you have in the Fifth Symphony actually as stirring a refrain of the same high truth as in the book of Job.[55]

This long quote demonstrates the intricate musical narration that to some extent prevailed in this period. By these descriptions we see that, however absolute the music may be, the act of describing, which has to be considered part of music's discourse, is very often plainly programmatic. Images are enlisted to explain, to contain the music, to bring it back to the realm of human comprehensibility. What the composer does not give—and in not giving he is valorized—the critic seems impelled to provide, however contradictory the provision to his absolute preferences.

Examples of this phenomenon appear repeatedly throughout the period.

> Haydn's . . . symphonies lead us into vast green woodlands, into a merry, gaily colored throng of happy mortals. Youths and maidens float past in a circling dance; laughing children, peering out from behind the trees, from behind the rose bushes, pelt one another playfully with flowers.

And again:

> Beethoven's instrumental music opens up to us also the realm of the monstrous and the immeasurable. Burning flashes of light shoot through the deep night of this realm, and we become aware of giant shadows that [move] back and forth, driving us into narrower and narrower confines until they destroy us. . . .[56]

Even Liszt, prior to valorizing the program, waxes rhapsodic in this purple paean to the metaphorical power of absolute music.

> On the towering, sounding waves of music, feeling lifts us up to heights that lie beyond the atmosphere of our earth and shows us cloud landscapes and world archipelagos that move about in ethereal space like singing swans . . . what is it that causes ideals to shimmer before us like the gilded spires of that submerged city, that recalls to us the indescribable recollections that surrounded our cradles, that conducts us through the reverberating workshops of the elements, that inspires us with all that ardor of thirsting after inexhaustible rapture which the blissful experience?[57]

Paul Bekker describes the theme in the closing pages of Beethoven's 32nd and final piano sonata as

> increasingly spiritualized, dematerialized. High notes call up a vision of ideal unapproachable heights, the accompanying rhythms flow along, sweeping, harp-like; high above all, a trill suggests the glitter of stars, while among them all runs the melody like a silver thread—the thread woven between earth and heaven by the aspiration of a great soul.[58]

And finally, Beethoven

> is above putting his own personality forward in any way, and all his endeavors are directed toward a single end—that all the wonderful enchanting pictures and apparitions that the composer has

sealed into his work with magic power may be called into active life, shining in a thousand colors, and that they may surround mankind in luminous sparkling circles and, enkindling its imagination, its innermost soul, may bear it in rapid flight into the faraway spirit realm of sound.[59]

These programmatic declarations by absolutist writers are challenging, certainly, and perhaps "impossibly broad." But they cannot be excluded from the programmatic equation. It might be added that the period music movement has to do not only with correct orchestration and authentic instruments, with original tone and tempo, but with a period's state of mind as well. This means that in the nineteenth century program was not limited to Liszt and Berlioz. Neither need it be now.

Royal Brown observes that a distinction between "film" and "serious" music "reflects a prejudice, common in the musical community, against programme music."[60] He goes on to suggest, as I have done, that even the most apparently absolute of pieces can hide some kind of program.

In the first instance program music was subservient to the external subject. However, as we have seen, all music can be said to have a program or some essential external consideration, whether relating to the circumstances of composition, or of apprehension. A way around the decried subordination of music to text is the alternative possibility that music, though it need not be secondary to externals, cannot be completely understood without them. Romantic and post-Romantic writers applied a kind of after-the-fact poetic program to music. Even more important is the application of history, and historical awareness.

Newcomb explains.

The sources of meaning brought to this interpretation [of Schumann's 2nd Symphony] would scarcely seem distant or daring to our colleagues in literary or art criticism. Yet we tend still to stay away from them in contemporary music criticism. Ludwig Finscher recently deplored . . . the habit, even in current musicological practice, of avoiding the interpretation of content by falling back on mere description of form, with a concomitant relegation of questions of content to the realm of the ineffable. Although the widespread timidity before the task of bringing into words the transmusical content of large, structurally demanding works is all too understandable after our experiences with common program-booklet hermeneutics . . . , this timidity can scarcely be allowed to define the considered behaviour of a historian toward his object of study, all the less so when the merest glance at the scores shows that formal and idiomatic peculiarities of the works cry out for an interpretation according to transmusical content.[61]

Distaste for extramusical consideration has been an excuse for dismissing the music for which such consideration is essential. This is an unfortunate state of affairs, and an unnecessary one, since far from closing down music's possibilities an expanded definition of program increases them.

To get beyond the problem of program music and "correct interpretations" we might consider "The Golden Years," an unproduced script by Emeric Pressburger on the last great purveyor of program music, Richard Strauss. The central conceit of Pressburger's script was to make Strauss the camera, and to see everything, literally, from his point of view. Different lenses and lighting would suggest how perceptions changed with the passage of time.[62] The subjectivity suggested here is intriguing, and it points to an essential and liberating fact: programmatic connections, especially contained within something as intractable as music, are inevitably personal and can't be contained by limiting notions of correctness.[63]

In program and "program" music, then, we are dealing not only with meaning but with the looser, more confounding, more musical term "signification," with all the slippage and subjectivity that goes with it. Contrary to the cautiousness of the *New Grove Dictionary*, some musicologists such as Newcomb, and film composers as well, agree that whatever its ineffable essence, in practice, music had meaning, even in the days of highest romanticism. It continues to do so, complexly, transformed in each context, and by each listener. The result need not be chaos, however. In fact there are powerful democratic implications. The resistance and even snobbery of some music scholars don't allow for another quite ancient and respectable musical function.

PROGRESSIVE PROGRAM: MUSIC AND EDUCATION

It is instructive to compare classical music as it is heard today—a serious thing for the concert hall, with how it was once used—

liturgically, theatrically, and domestically. It is the difference between the frame and the fresco; high art absorbed separately,
exaltedly versus an integrated, integral part of experience and the
praxis of life. Although we have heard claims that program music
is emblematic of the generally appalling level of taste in the nineteenth century, I would argue for additional interpretation. If
there were individual lapses in taste and execution, then it can
still justly be argued that in general program music bridged the
increasing distances between composers and listeners, between
creators and receivers. We will also see that it can still do so.

I have just mentioned program's democratic potential, and I
use that word in the traditional, documentary sense.[64] This is to
say that previously underheard, underattended voices (the British
working class, and so on) gain some access to the discussion,
and are even able to alter the terms of that discussion. Egalitarian
parallels in film/musical areas are numerous. In composition, the
Vienna school had attacked tonal hierarchies and the tyranny of
melody, which attack revolutionized twentieth-century musical
culture. There is also a clear paradox here; serial music, while
eliminating some elemental hierarchies, was also deemed to be
superlatively inaccessible and elitist. These would seem to be
irreconcilable accounts, and yet both interpretations clearly bear
truth.

This contradiction also informs my own opening characterization of musicology's mingled validity and elitism, or at least insularity. Debates over program are similarly split, and just as
susceptible to synthesis. "Democracy" enters this discussion as
hierarchical breakdown extends beyond musicological settings
into areas of reception and use. We have already discussed how
increased attention to music can help to break down the traditional hierarchy of film elements—the primacy of picture and
dialogue, and purposes—narrative first. Increased, disciplined
musical attention also contributes to the breakdown of the traditional, still powerful subordination of the spectator to the artist.

In the first chapter I spoke briefly of the work of Donald Tovey,
Leonard Meyer, and Deryck Cooke. They sought in their writings to make erudite musical matters accessible, a project that
was not appreciated by all musicians. For some of these musi-

cians, the desirability of access depended on what was being made accessible to whom, and at what cost.

Elie Siegmeister counts among music's ancient roles the pacifying of children, the making of magic, even the facilitating of reproduction.[65] These tasks all bespeak something primordial. Should not the music that soothes the savage breast distance itself from such elemental, precivilized contexts? Should it be so unrefined?

There is persistent musical attitude that suspects the popular, and the accessibility of things popular. Philip Goepp refers to "true leaders" from the classical past, and compares them with the "inevitable demagoguism" incident to democratic change.

> Men appealed over the heads of those who had the true, the saner intuition to the ruder mob to whom clear thought was naught, sensational amusement all. Democratic as we must be in government, there is no doubt that the bursts of popular will throughout the nineteenth century have had a sinister effect upon art. The lower instincts with the lower classes have broken away from the higher.[66]

This declaration might sound slightly fascistic, and it is decidedly defensive. It appears that Goepp actually fears the demagogic possibilities of program music. Given how he felt about literalism's besmirching effects, his preferred alternative comes as no surprise.

> Gradually . . . the truth is breaking, that, while the apparent purpose is that of mere delight, *the true essence of music is its unconscious subjective betrayal of a dominant feeling*, in contrast with the conscious, objective depiction in poetry and in the plastic arts.[67]

The excesses of program music portended seriously negative social consequences, and so there is a desire to keep music and musicians, and music lovers too, safe and separate.

But as with the case of Hans Keller or Theodor Adorno, this is not plain elitist isolationism.[68] Goepp speaks from the other, more inclusive side too, and in so doing suggests why he found *un*programmatic meaning everywhere. *Contra* the staunch absolutists, he felt that music must be involved in a search for moral quality. "Impossible . . . as it is to sum up in systematic philosophy, nothing is so clear to the persistent and open-minded listener [than] the good and the bad, the moral and unmoral."[69] Later Goepp elaborates on this quality.

> This [Schubert's] tenth symphony, is in every way typical, symbolic, directly eloquent of this greatest of heroic struggles, which ought to come to every man, whereby the artistic victory becomes an expression of the moral, and whereby the corresponding artwork has perhaps, as its greatest value, this stamp of ethical achievement.[70]

These were also the positive, empowering possibilities of program, especially in the more multivalent, modern use of the word. Against referentialism, its resultant oversimplifications and the philistinisms that followed, Goepp wished for music, and art in general, to make us better. And, though given many music critics' positions on program music, it may seem paradoxical, this was one of the original reasons for program music, too.

Although we may now think of Liszt as the arch virtuoso, and that his music is implicated by bourgeois or reactionary associations, the fact is that the music he developed was designed to reach out. Liszt himself wrote repeatedly about bringing music to the masses through subsidizing musicians, orchestras, and choruses made up of regular people, through cheap music editions, for example.[71] His wide-ranging piano transcriptions of symphonic works were not always a case of simply showing off. They brought inaccessible large-scale works into the parlor, some degree of high culture to those excluded from privilege. This was also the point of his programs: to bring all art and knowledge and experience into music.

> [Liszt felt] it his mission to heighten man's experience and at the same time embody it in all its manifestations—the quest for the spiritual . . . the ceaseless exploration in spite of loneliness and insecurity. . . . He felt that music should embrace the world, and he cast his net as wide as possible.[72]

Program is variously looked upon as bourgeois, as pandering, and as a denial of music's rightful place and function. It is also possible to see it as a progressive and democratic solution to the alienations of the emerging industrial age. The rise of narrative in classical music, through the agency of the nineteenth-century program, can be seen as an attempt to return text for and from the people to the art music that had, in being sundered from folk traditions, been taken away from them. Instead of refined aristocratic strains or heroic individualism, both of which were beyond common reach and outside of common experience, program was at least partly designed as something unspecialized, unprivileged, and accessible.[73]

It was one of the sentiments of the age that art, and in the present instance music, was for healing and education, truth and beauty.[74] But these were not to be vaguely edifying abstractions; what was required was that truth and beauty bear fruit in action or improvement. Why was the program important? Why does it remain so?

Hegel, in his *Aesthetics*, makes an essential point. The *connoisseur* is able to comprehend and appreciate music in a sophisticated and rarefied way. This kind of enjoyment is not available to the layman, but this does not mean that the layman should be left to and derided for his own musical devices. The laity has the right to its own enjoyment.

> So complete an absorption is seldom the privilege of the amateur, to whom there comes at once a desire to fill out this apparently meaningless outpour of sound and to find intellectual footholds for its progress and, in general, more definite ideas and a more precise content for that which penetrates into his soul. In this respect, music becomes symbolic for him, yet, in his attempts to overtake its meaning, he is confronted by abstruse problems, rapidly rushing by, which do not always lend themselves to solution and which are altogether capable of the most varied interpretations.[75]

The layman's solution? Program. Liszt affirms that communication is the job of art, which means that the assistance rendered by programmatic forms does not diminish artistry—it makes artistry possible. "A work which offers only clever manipulation of its materials will always lay claim to the interest of the immediately concerned—of the artist, student, *connoisseur*—but, despite this, it will be unable to cross the threshold of the artistic kingdom."[76] So Liszt, only partly rationalizing his chosen approach, derides musical professionals as cold formalists whose work is inaccessible to noninitiates, and lifeless to all.[77]

Tovey, Meyer, and Cooke are sympathetic, and in some degree criticism of their work, from elite corners anyway, might affirm its validity. Tovey was a composer and concert pianist, but felt at last that his most important role was as an educator. He disliked musicological aridities, and did not proclaim himself a scholar. His most noted writings (Tovey, 1937) were originally prepared as program notes for a long-standing, public prescription Edinburgh concert series. He felt that popularizing was precisely his duty.[78]

Leonard Meyer's M.A. was in music, but his Ph.D. studies were in the history of culture. As this would indicate, his interest has been in music contextualized and not isolated from the conditions of its creation and distribution. *Emotion and Meaning in Music* (1956) repeatedly, and not hierarchically, distinguishes between musician and lay experience, implying the essentialness of production *and* reception, whatever their nature.[79]

Cooke's *Language of Music* (1959) is remembered for suggesting that music is an indirect but real expression of a composer's emotions. Cooke posited equivalencies between words and musical phrases, and was not always clear about whether music meant conventionally or naturally, extrinsically or inherently. Though roundly criticized, Cooke's transgressions, and also the perceived shortcomings of these other writers, must be seen in the light of what they intended.[80]

For more than twenty years Cooke had responsibility in music presentation at the BBC. He can be seen as a vulgarizer, but given the range and reach of his educational activities, both as a broadcaster and as a presenter of popular classical concerts ("The Proms"), it seems more kind, and accurate besides, to call him a popularizer or better yet, a teacher.[81]

Leonard Bernstein speaks for the currency of all of these concepts. He talks about the relevance, the essentialness of discussing musical meaning.

> I as a musician feel that there has to be a way of speaking about music with intelligent but nonprofessional music lovers who don't know a stretto from a diminished fifth; and the best way I have found so far is by setting up a working analogy with language, since language is something everyone shares and uses and knows about.[82]

This was, and remains, the rationale behind program music. Bernstein uses words to preach the gospel of edifying music, thus bringing light to the musically darkened. In this sense program becomes an agent of equality, as it establishes common terms on which initiates and neophytes alike can meet.

As Goepp suggested, however, sometimes talk of democracy can merely signal the rising of the rabble. The perceived limitation of program was that it nailed down the ineffable by prosaic equivalencies. The process suggested a kind of dread medium crossing counterpoint. The prosaic mind, by means of the prosaic sentence, took the poetry of the musical phrase and, through literal means, translated it again into prose. Here, many felt, was a prescription for philistinism.

But that was just one view. Could not program also be seen as an Aristotelian transformation, by which the familiar was made fresh and new? And if the material is not familiar, then there is, at least, communication.

The significance of these ideas to classical music in film is obvious. The criticisms cited in my first three chapters are still important, but the receptive transformation I have just suggested also allows for a complete and salutary reversal of attitude.

> The borrowing or symbiotic exchange between the fine, popular, and folk arts has indeed been beneficial for American culture as a whole by broadening the exposure of every aesthetic level, encouraging many to seek out and experience the original forms, and making some headway in breaking down the class barriers that are inherent in the social predilection for stratifying art and culture.[83]

Exception was not always taken to accessible music. Schubert wrote music that his friends and he himself could play. Chopin's etudes, which have become the property of virtuosi, were written as studies for amateurs.[84] Before Paganini's rise in the 1820s, music was, allowing for certain social inaccessibilities, for all. The rise of the concert hall, and the end of patronage, and the necessity for the artist to make himself distinct and thus make his financial way, for example, took music out of amateur's hand.[85]

The record is not complete without this contextualization. In reaction to art's separating itself from the people came the rise of the concept of extrinsic meaning in music, of the program.

This meant ideally a continuation and expansion of listener engagement, and the possibility that not everyone would be shut out. However this need not have meant the takeover of the lowbrows. Practically all of Berlioz is connected to specific extramusical meaning, without an awareness of which, comprehension, and enjoyment, are incomplete. But there is still the possibility, the necessity of musical listening. Prosaic elements did not necessarily eliminate poetry.

In this connection it is too often forgotten that, while programs were expressed in nonmusical language, those language sources were very frequently poetic. Newman points out that preromantic composers were practically indentured servants, with little opportunity for extramusical accomplishment. In contrast, many nineteenth-century musical figures were extraordinarily cultured, intimately aware of the intellectual and artistic life of the time. They brought that awareness to their compositions, which were not only expressions of inner feeling but expressions of a desire to share and teach.[86]

If program music constituted a diminishing of musical feeling, then there were still great compensations. Music, though a handmaid, introduced listeners to varieties of great feeling from other discourses and contexts. In this way it actually countered the potential insularity—and certainly the later elitism—of absolute approaches. And, since preparation and synthesis were required to properly read the program, since the listener had to work, the possibility of progress and empowerment far exceeded the dangers of philistinism.[87]

This is the situation in the nineteenth century, or at least one possible rendering of the situation. Words, which mean and are understood, added to music, which expresses and stimulates our higher feelings, add up to edification and understanding and union.[88] This can still be true, and even more than was contemplated in the original discussions. The words in question are not just Liszt's authorized, authorizing ones. They are also critical, analytical, historical, theoretical, and instinctual. Music communicates, and we communicate about it.

In this summary the terms, possibilities, and complications seem to multiply. In the next chapter, then, I will apply the analogies of montage, counterpoint, and program to specific instances, through which we will see how these figurative notions can be practically and specifically applied to understanding and enjoying classical music in film.

NOTES

1. Mellers, 1946, 54.

2. Ibid., 103.

3. For elaboration on the idea of program as both creative and receptive, see discussions in my chapter five on intentionality, intertextuality, and phenomenology as relating to musical quotation in film.

4. In addition to the plays themselves, note the lightness found throughout the selections in Brecht, 1964. Brecht's famed "Short Organum for the Theatre" (ibid., 179–205) states that "entertainment" and "pleasure" are the first and the final necessities for any theatrical endeavor.

5. Brecht, 1976, xv–xvi, xx.

6. Ibid., xxxi–xxxii.

7. This discussion on program music draws upon materials in Scruton, 1980 and Randel, 1986, as well as other citations listed below.

8. See Newman, 1910, 108–9 and 125–32, Randel, 1986, 657–59 (sec. III) for details concerning partially programmatic practices from earlier periods of music history.

9. As in Mendelssohn's *Hebrides Overture* (or *Fingal's Cave*).

10. I.e., word painting, typified by but not limited to Monteverdi, where melodies and melodic accompaniments in some way followed the sense of a song's lyric. Later examples include, for instance, Schubert's "Gretchen at the Spinning Wheel," with its circular instrumental support, or *Erlkonig*, where the accompaniment suggests a galloping horse. See Randel, 1986, 935.

11. Scruton, 1980, 15: 283–86.

12. Scruton, 1980, 15: 284, 283. "If the music does achieve a real connexion, it will illustrate the subject; but you will get nothing out of the expectation that the subject will illustrate [the music]." "Study of the whole poem [Lenau's *Don Juan*] will be much more illuminating in the light of the music than study of the music in the light of the poem." Tovey, 1937, IV, 84, 156. It should be noted that Tovey was not necessarily a great lover of program music, or at least of the concepts behind it. Tovey, 1937, IV, 129, 133, 140, 149–55.

13. "All programme music must indeed be representative, but it must also be, in part, self-contained; that is, a given phrase must not

only be appropriate to the character of Hamlet or Dante, or suggestive of a certain external phenomenon such as the wind, or the fire, or the water, but it must also be interesting as music." Newman, 1910, 112. See also Tovey, 1937, IV, 1, 155. However, Newman does go on to argue against the "fallacy" that program music should be just as satisfying to the listener who is unaware of the program as to the initiated. Ibid., 147–57.

14. Liszt, quoted in Scruton, 1980, 15: 284. Tovey, in his discussion of Berlioz, points out how inadequate these subordinations could sometimes be. Though delighted with much of Berlioz's music, he found that it often fell far short of any substantial correspondence with the proclaimed program. Tovey, 1937, IV, 74–89. Others, observing the same gap, were not open to these delights. See Shaw, 1981, I, 214 for an amusing dig at the programmatic content in Liszt's *Inferno*.

15. Quoted in Scruton, 1980, 15: 283. Emphasis added. Also quoted in Berg, 1976, 86.

16. MacDonald, Hugh, 1980, "Symphonic poem," in Sadie, 1980, 18: 432.

17. Musical absolutism, which rejects the idea of extrinsic, referential musical meaning for the notion of inherent, purely musical significance, resists subordinate forms and parallelism. This idea has been articulated through different periods and in different contexts; for a classic romantic expression see Hanslick, 1963 and 1986.

18. On the other side are those advocating "invisible" film scores that are only sensed subconsciously.

19. Once again, the reference here is to the use of this concerto in Noel Coward's and David Lean's *Brief Encounter* (1945).

20. Berg, 1976, 84. For a critique of program music and its impulses in film, see Eisler, 1947, x, 13, 35, 57, 103.

21. Ibid., 99. Emphasis added.

22. See Wagner's criticism that Berlioz's compositions are not *musically* rational, because they are appropriate and relevant to *extramusical* imperative. In Newman, 1910, 143.

23. Burch, 1990, 236.

24. London, 1936, 55.

25. George, 1914 (2nd ed.), 15. See Hegel, 1979, 128, for a similar list of absolute music's expressive versatility.

26. Goepp, I, 38, 125. See also discussions throughout on Mendelssohn, some Beethoven (particularly the third, sixth, and ninth symphonies), Berlioz, Liszt, and Richard Strauss. Merits and charms notwithstanding, Goepp always finds that these programmatic symphonies fall short of absolute musical ideals.

27. Ibid., I, 174–75. See also II, 230–31.

28. Ibid., I, 126.

29. Siegmeister, 1938, 51.

30. Ibid., 22.

31. Ibid., 23.

32. Cf. the Soviets' later preference for serials and circuses over respectable theater and literature.

33. Newman, 1910, 114.

34. Quoted in Thomas, 1979, 160. One might add that music's emergence as feeling's pure expression, as suggested by Romantic absolutists, was also comparatively recent.

35. In Prendergast, 1994, 39–40.

36. Searle, 1985, 288.

37. Ibid., 297–98, 302. For similar variation or parody of classical themes, listen to Lou Forbes's musical direction in *Intermezzo* (1939), or Korngold's score for *Kings Row* (1941).

38. As in the 1855 *Prelude and Fugue*, with sections taken from a theme by Meyerbeer. Ibid., 302. Liszt's numerous transcriptions and adaptations are also related.

39. Built on a monothematic approach, Liszt's transformation of themes was "a process by which one or more short ideas are subjected to various techniques of alteration (change of mode; change of rhythm, meter or tempo; ornamentation; change of accompaniment, etc.) to form the thematic basis of an entire work." Searle, 1985, 260. Also Sadie, 1988, 130.

40. Lang and West, 1920, 6.

41. See Harlow Hare's discussion concerning a number of these issues (musical precedents for quotation, contemporary familiarity with nineteenth-century art music) in a review of J. C. Breil's *Birth of a Nation* score, in Brown, 1988, 171–73. See Anderson, 1988 for an account of how music helped make film respectable. The specific compositions Anderson cites as being used in the silent era are part of a musical culture much more diversified than is conventionally admitted. For more evidence of this diversification see Russell, 1987, Turner and Miall, 1972 and 1982.

42. Behlmer, 1989, 29.

43. Ibid., 54. Also see James, 1989, 63, on adapting Gounod's *Faust* for a modern screening of the silent "Phantom"; and Larson, 1987, 7, concerning how original "Phantom" composer Gustav Hinrichs composed from Gounod's work in the first place. Gaston Leroux's original novel also borrows freely from Goethe's text.

44. Quoted in Steiner, 1989, 90.

45. Scruton, 1980, 283.

46. "Program music," in Randel, 1986, 657. Anahid Kassabian's notion (2001, 2–9) of "affiliating identifications" also relates quite directly to the issues being considered here.

47. Or, in different ways, when we do not apprehend. Chapter five deals in detail with the range of creative and receptive possibilities across intertextual fields.

48. Scruton, 1980, 15: 284. Scruton also feels that this use contradicts Liszt's original intent, as well its conventional critical use since.

49. See Said, 1991, 90, as already referenced in my chapter one.

50. Hoffman, 1813. Also cf. Kerman, 1985, 65; Dahlhaus, 1989, 75. See Sadie, 1988, 78–80 on the dominance of metaphorical musical commentary in the nineteenth century.

51. Goepp, I, 24, 125, 174–75.

52. Ibid, I, 38. (Emphasis in original.) Note the similarity of Goepp's retrospective rationalizations to film's contemporaneous protesting too much about its own validity. Also here is the step that film theorists in France and the Soviet Union would soon take as they found validation in calls for and celebrations of medium specificity.

53. Ibid., 39.

54. Ibid., 40.

55. Goepp, II, xi–xii. Note Goepp's quite specific comments on the standard "meaning" of absolute symphonies. It is "an expression of a dominant feeling, from a subjective point of view, or, objectively, as a view of life, in four typical phases or moods, of which the first is of aspiring resolution, the second of pathos, the third of humor, the fourth of triumph." Goepp, I, 147; also I, 41.

56. Hoffmann, 1813, 36–37. See also 39 for Hoffman's very programmatic description of his experience with a Beethoven trio.

57. Liszt, 1855, 110.

58. Becker, 1925, 141.

59. Hoffman, 1813, 40–41.

60. Brown, 1994, 48.

61. Newcomb, 1984, 247–48. See also Abraham, 1985, 175–76 for Schumann's very frequent dependence on extramusical sources in numerous other compositions.

62. See MacDonald, 1994, 338, for a description of Pressburger's project.

63. It is well to point out that a "personal" reading is a complex notion, inevitably subject to external pressures, often predicated on collective perceptions and the nature of the interpretive communities to which the individual belongs. For elaboration on this idea see Altman,

1987, and Stefani, 1987, as well as my chapter five. I hold here to the notion of personal perception to ground the musico-cinematic interpretations that will follow, which are largely my own. Though I am obviously not above the influences of ideology and community myself, my approach to classical music in film does depart somewhat from views previously expressed in both film-musical, musicological, and film-theoretical communities.

64. This notion of democracy in and through the documentary film is most famously—though not uncontroversially—articulated in Grierson 1966.

65. Siegmeister, 1938, 23.

66. Goepp, I, 16–17.

67. Ibid., 18, emphasis in original. It is interesting to note the same attitudes relating to the developments of early film. See Burch, 1990, especially 43–79.

68. For the elitist, though not completely the isolationist, see Adorno on Schoenberg (1973).

69. Goepp, I, 21.

70. Ibid., 193. See also II, xvi–xviii.

71. Siegmeister, 1936, 48–49.

72. Searle, 1985, 320.

73. Cf. Merrick, 1987. Merrick traces the ways in which Liszt's programmers were far from mere fancy, but were always serious expressions of his beliefs and his involvement in the real world. In this light program music emerges as more than an irrelevant anomaly. It is allied in intent, and to a degree in result, with the democratizing musical impulses of Ralph Vaughan Williams (1934), Sabine Baring-Gould (1895–96), Cecil Sharp (1912–22), etc.

74. On links between literature and education see Matthew Arnold's "Democracy" (1861), *Culture and Anarchy* (1869), and "Equality" (1878), in Arnold, 1993.

75. In Liszt, 1855, 120. See Hegel, 1920, III, 424–25 for another, more convoluted translation.

76. Liszt, 1855, 121. Liszt undercuts his egalitarian declarations when he locates the program within the unusual sensibilities of "great hearts," which understand in a finer and more refined fashion than the "plain man." Ibid., 126.

77. Ibid., 130.

78. On Tovey see Sadie, 1980, 19: 102–3.

79. On Meyer see ibid., 12: 244–45.

80. Monelle, 1992.

81. Discussed thoroughly in Russell, 1987.

82. Bernstein, 1976, 53. There is a potential problem attached to this notion of art communicating, and Bernstein's implied equation of communication and verbalization. As Goepp suggests, egalitarian communication can become a diminished, even depraved thing. Not all communications, particularly when they are musical, are so easily reduced to the verbal. (i.e., the elusive musical narratives of Wagner, Strauss, Schoenberg, Berg; Scruton's valid concerns about reductive program discussions, and of music's resistance to reductive interpretation.) The mixing of media, the interpretations that accrue to this mixing, are inevitably problematic. For a discussion on this problematic, see my section on "indeterminacy" in chapter five.

83. Edgerton, 1988, 4.

84. Temperley, 1985, 18.

85. Cf. Subotnik, 1976.

86. Newman, 1905, 137–41. Hegel (1920, III 425), speaking of preromantic composers, says that although they may have shown a great musical gift at an early age, that otherwise they "remain their lifelong men of the poorest and most impoverished intellectual faculty in other directions." (See also Eisler, 1947, 46–47; also Bazelon, 1975, 20, on similar circumstances of Hollywood composers.) This situation is in marked contrast to Mendelssohn, who globe-trotted and was a friend of the cultured famous, to the voraciously literate Schumann (Abraham, 1985, 101) and the even more broadly cultured Liszt (Searle, 1985, 241). In fact, Liszt also developed a literary reputation, and one of his earliest subjects was the need for the artist to leave his "superior servant" status and be accepted as a respected member of the community. Ibid., 243. It could be said that Eisenstein and Vertov and the general progressive notion of the unalienated revolutionary artist descend directly from this programmatic place.

87. See Newman, 1910, 157–79, for a convincing discussion of program music's progressive potential.

88. For musical and musical dramatic expressions of these aspirations, see Beethoven's 9th Symphony, Wagner's *Die Meistersinger*, or *Parsifal*.

5

Interpreting Classical Music in Film

IN THE LAST CHAPTER I suggested that musical and extramusical programs are everywhere, whether explicit or effaced, whether intended or apprehended. Program extends far beyond Berlioz, if we are willing to expand our definition. In the first instance, program composers attached something external to the music which was to aid and direct experience and interpretation. But programs do not end at, nor are they limited to, authorial intent. We have discussed how this form can bring in the spectator. As the nineteenth-century Belgian composer and historian François Fétis observed: "the large audience . . . will never listen to a symphony, quartet, or other composition of this order without outlining a program *for itself* during the performance, according to the grandiose, lively, impetuous, serenely soothing, or melancholy character of the music."[1]

Fétis extends the site of programmatic creation, and this extension will be the focus of this chapter. I have suggested that meaning in music, not to mention feeling or affect, comes not through musical/verbal correspondence, in which a note *equals* a word and a phrase *equals* a phrase, but through series of multivalent and multifarious juxtapositions. Now I wish to develop the idea that these things come not only from the composer, but also through listener transformation of musical material into some verbal, conceptual, or even sensuous analogue. This is, if you will, intellectual, overtonal, even emotional montage. Nineteenth-century, and nineteenth-century-derived, absolutists resist the notion, but their transposition of music through criticism (and the imagery used therein) to words and responses testifies to the power and universality of the process.

This is how I wish to situate classical music in film. Liszt pointed out how program music can "by defining its subject draw new and undreamed of advantages from the approximation of certain ideas, the affinity of certain figures, the separation or combination, juxtaposition or fusion of certain poetic images and perorations."[2] Liszt's description, allowing for certain circumstantial adaptations or transpositions, really applies to all music. When music appears in films, and after we have adjusted the way in which we attend to it, the advantages become very apparent.

It is now time to set forth some practical applications of the ideas we have been discussing. How can we deal with an intellectual and overtonal montage based on the principles of musical counterpoint, always remembering that collisions and intertwinings are fueled and informed by broader programmatic contexts? What typology, or classification of uses, can we establish to help navigate through different montage equations?

The first question to arise is that of audience. Who apprehends the montage synthesis, plots contrapuntal relationships, sets or receives the programmatic setting? Who is watching, hearing, interpreting, even misreading? Janet Staiger, drawing on literary models, identifies a number of possible reading positions that relate to texts in general. In addition to plotting the positions of these readers along a continuum of communication, however, Staiger emphasizes the *quality* of that reading. Ideal, coherent, competent readers, even misreaders are all important in helping us understand a range of relationships between text and audience. (I will say something about authorship and reception in my discussions of intention and phenomenology.)

Staiger emphasizes the conventional nature of these definitions and of the implied readings behind them. An ideal reader, as defined by the likes of Johnson, Dryden, Coleridge, and Frye, is a useful conceit, a construct addressing how the theorist feels we should interact with a text. Staiger points out the implication behind the concept, which is that there are ideal *readings*, interpretations of and responses to a text that imply a kind of rationality and order not necessarily in critical fashion now. Similarly, coherent readers suggest that the text and response are, if not absolute, then at least containable, and subject to substantial agreements on meaning and implied action. Competence steps down a bit from amiable coherence, but in implying incompetence as its opposite it still affirms the existence of preferable readings. Misreading, which suggests plain error in an ideal setting, becomes much richer and more interesting in a postdeconstructive world.[3]

All of these positions suggest rich possibilities and deserve close attention. With regard to the present work, however, especially as it seeks to establish the terms of a largely new discussion, let it be clear that this is not a study of reception theory, and that I do not wish to establish the effects of classical music use in film on any particular class or community of spectators. The readings, which are set forth to suggest something of the range of possibility in both the use and understanding of this music, are my own. I do not claim any absolute authority for my responses, though they are hard-thought and aspire to a kind of coherence and all that it implies. At the same time I am open to the implications of slippage and the interest of misreading (see the brief discussion on "bracketing" in my phenomenology section). Though I intend no howling inaccuracies, they may well appear, doubtless illustrating certain helpful points, and requiring no apology. Regardless, it should be noted that I am the audience, and the site of an experiment on the points that I have posited. My work on this subject should justify and substantiate certain conclusions, while my shortcomings should provide helpful cautions in their own right.

Now, then, how should I proceed with this self-experiment? We have seen that one standard set of film music categories, that of parallelism and counterpoint (as traditionally defined), is not really adequate to the complexities of film music, especially when we consider programs incident to classical forms. Neither are traditional distinctions between diegetic and nondiegetic sound up to the elusive reality of much practice.

Ken Russell's 1968 "biopic" about Frederic Delius, *Song of Summer*, demonstrates some of the complexities of film-musical voice, as well as some of the difficulties, and perhaps irrelevancies of the diegetic/nondiegetic split. Young Mr. Fenby, the character through whom we witness the story, has just arrived in France to help the crippled Delius, and is introduced by Mrs. Delius to the household. "This is the music room, where Delius has written all his finest music." Music, a composition by Delius, now rises up on the sound track as the young man explores the room. What is its source and meaning?

There are several questions, and several possibilities: Is the music an echo emanating from the room's walls, representing Delius's work in the room, or is it an arbitrary external effluence added by the filmmakers for our benefit? Is the music from Fenby's aural point of view, or the wife's? Are they hearing it in their heads? On a gramophone? Does it represent Fenby's relation to the fame of its composer, or the new circumstances that are now inflecting that relation? Does this lyrical burst represent Mrs. Delius's perception of her husband's artistry, or given the complications of character and marital relations that are soon to be portrayed, is it an ironic statement about the gaps between talent and the lives of the talented, between ideals and the real? Each possibility is intriguing, and none eliminates any of the others. The film itself doesn't answer these questions, nor does it seem to have a need to.

As the discussions of Michel Chion and Claudia Gorbman have demonstrated, conventional diegetic discussions cannot really address film music's ability to permeate different narrative spaces, or account for the complexity of quotation. Nor can they account for musical motivation: the source of the musical interpolation, whether it be a character's action, an implied or explicit editorial from a narrator, or the author, and so on). Musical subjectivity and irony, especially in source music, are also beyond the reach of the standard terminology. I find Gorbman's metadiagetic formulation to be most useful, especially in this critical context. As she suggests, inside and outside, text and intertext, sound and picture, are mutually implicated, the result of that implication being a rich, swirling *"combinatoire* of expression."[4] As I proceed and interpret on a case-by-case, issue-by-issue basis, I will continue to be open to the permeable, multivalent nature of musical placement and signification.

Still, the task of scholarly inquiry is not just to admire impressionistic swirls, nor less to make them. It is rather to make at least some attempt at definition and understanding, and this can be accomplished in the area of film music's multifarious programs. Programmatic sites can be plotted along a kind of interpretive spectrum, where environments of intention and reception, author and audience, order and accident, are all acknowledged. Once again, Janet Staiger provides a helpful discussion of these receptive and interpretive settings. In her book *Interpreting Films*, Staiger enumerates the function and interrelationship of text, reader, and context-activated theories as applicable to films in general. What did the author intend in her creation of a text? What does the work contain that may not have been intended, but which nevertheless exists and must be accounted for? What is the experience of the person receiving the work, with all of his insights and blind spots? What are the contexts of history and society, which preexist and exceed the efforts of textual participants, and which form the ground upon which textual exchanges take place?[5] The structure of this chapter traces a similar trajectory, with adjustments made for musical conditions. Each of these factors inflect the musico-visual equation and will be investigated here.[6]

Here, it is hoped, are some clear categories with which we can proceed. In this last section of the book I will apply these general tools and sensibilities to specific contexts, and to specific texts. Here we will consider interpretation as it relates to creative intent and creative reception, not to mention unwitting creation and viewing. I will discuss the place of indeterminacy, and suggest how and when interpretation should give way to a kind of neoformalist explication.

This chapter summarizes and expands upon what I feel to be the most pertinent interpretive issues and settings relating to classical music in film. For the sake of clarity, I will include brief examples of film-music equations that illustrate those issues, though the illustrations are not intended to be exhaustive. As in my first chapter, when I surveyed a wide array of critical responses to this musical usage (pugilistic prescription, textual emphasis and neoformalism, historical description and aggressive interpretation, and finally a proving and holding of the most useful of all these alternatives), the scope here is broad; it is hoped that my survey, and even the small readings attached, will provide some tools that will facilitate others in the more detailed explorations that might follow.

INTERPRETIVE STRATEGIES: INTENTIONALITY

Irene Atkins writes that "the elements of a specific source-music sequence or scene having been determined, the historian or critic can then approach an analysis of the music and the scene in terms of the filmmaker's rationale and the ways in which he uses music to communicate with the audience."[7] Although our critical responses need not be predicated solely on artistic intent, Atkins is right in emphasizing the filmmaker's rationale, especially when his or her musical choices are clearly conscious. Valuable interpretations can derive from these understandings, and there are many examples of this kind.

In Sally Potter's remarkable *Thriller* (1979), Puccini's *La Bohème* is played, both narratively and musically, against Bernard Herrmann's music to Hitchcock's *Psycho*. The film's argument is set up, discursively, patiently, convincingly, on the disjunction between the music sources: romantic strains and jarring screeches are revealed as diverse expression of the same impulse, of doing violence to women.

In Jean-Luc Godard's *Scenario du Film Passion* (1982), he explains his use in *Passion* (also 1982) of some "magnificent romantic music, this little-known Dvorak piano concerto. Perhaps it will help me see, and say, that there is romance in labour." Godard confirms that, in at least some cases, musical selections are made for what they represent, and not just for accompaniment. In this case the cue is chosen because of its idiom. Dvorak aside, we don't understand part of the film if we don't identify that idiom.[8]

One of the powerful effects of idiomatic selection and identification is the kind of epochal conflations—the time of composition bound to the time of quotation—they effect. John Addison speaks of his score for *Tom Jones* (1963). "The film opened with a sequence in silent film style, for which I used the very simple device of a harpsichord to represent the eighteenth century and a slightly out of tune piano to denote the silent movie element."[9]

Here traditional forms, or forms associated with tradition, such as the harpsichord and the eighteenth century, support the film-modernist rendering of an iconoclastic narrative. "Though it was the eighteenth century which 'swung' on the screen, there was a dimension of audacity, style and high spirits relevant to the scene that was taking shape in contemporary London."[10] In this sense *Tom Jones*'s period elements become a kind of subversive disguise. Along with *Billy Liar*'s fantasies and *A Hard Day's Night*'s release in youth and rock culture, Tony Richardson and John Osborne's film provides an escape from the dead end of kitchen sink dreariness, to the brief hip utopia of new moralities, swinging London, and the free 1960s. And all this is signaled by a simple baroque pastiche at the film's opening.

What we have observed is all in the film, but is that all there is? To stop here with our *Tom Jones* reading, as many have, is to stop too soon. The film's formal alienations—direct address, jarring shifts in tone, the ironic and distancing narration—are unusual for its time, but they actually correspond to the formal strategies of Fielding's original novel, and of the period of its publication. In this period the enclosed, contained conventions of the nineteenth-century novel were not yet codified, and a reading of any Dickens novel problematizes the generalizations and delimitations that such a construct implies. John Addison's reference to eighteenth-century/silent film music suggests an important, related feature of the film. One of its most striking accomplishments is that it brings us into contact with other discourses and other discursive strategies of the originating period, effecting a kind of interdisciplinary unity, including literature, music, and film, not to mention Hogarth and other influences of the era. A similar unity also accrues beyond the texts, as apparatus-revealing techniques underline connections between life and the human condition in both 1749 and 1963. Since the arts, in addition to providing critical insight and fostering debate, also illuminate things we hold dear and have in common, then Addison's musical conflation reveals more than just two Londons swinging. Comparing the two Tom Joneses together we see that not only naughtiness, but kindliness, not just transgression but reconciliation too, affirm cultural continuity and human nobility.[11] Again, in the film, it is the simple, elegant juxtaposition of musical idioms by which all this is accomplished.

These last cues and references are featured in the foreground, but it is also possible for conventionally effaced, mechanically functioning pieces, when carefully chosen, to resonate very dramatically. Early in John Schlesinger's *Sunday, Bloody Sunday* (1971) we see a wealthy physician played by Peter Finch, alone in his tasteful and well-appointed town house listening to Mozart. At this point the music simply suggests a certain level of culture and education. But as the film continues this first diegetic cue will continue nondiegetically, over and across a number of different situations, eventually not only covering the physical joins but also uniting seemingly irreconcilable narrative threads in the story.

The cue in question is the final trio, "*Soave sia il vento,*" from Act I of *Cosi Fan Tutte*. On the surface this opera is a comedy about female infidelity, as the male leads test and trick their fiancées into compromising themselves, or at least being willing to do so. The complications resolve in the end, but beneath the light tone of the farce lie darker currents; the sexual play carries a threat of ruined illusions and broken character. All, tricking and tricked, are chastened finally, aware of limitations and frailties, the strong imperatives of sexuality, and the need for mercy and reconciliation.

In Schlesinger's film it is not woman's infidelity but that of a bisexual man, played by Murray Head, who casually deceives and betrays both the Finch character and his rival, played by Glenda Jackson. For all the daring of this skewed triangle, and for the attention the film gained upon release, the point of the film would not seem to be plain provocation or gender bending. Rather it would affirm that there are universal challenges which, the film suggests—*cosi fan tutte* is roughly translated as "that's what they all do"—so surpass mere sexual preference as to make it irrelevant. As subordinate as the music might seem to be, it functions here in a way quite contrary to illusionistic, pacifying tradition. A disturbing detail, in the form of a familiar piece of source music, transforms a romantic melodrama into a political statement.

The Mozart seems at first to be associated with the Finch character, but as we hear it in relation to events concerning all three principles, and as it crosses scenic transitions between all three, it is clear that this is not merely a character *leitmotif*. It is not the doctor, but what he feels the music addresses. The act's farewell trio prays, "may the wind be gentle, may the sea be calm, and may the elements respond kindly to our wishes" (*"ai nostri desir"*). This is a sweet expression of romantic yearning, innocent and kindly, and occurring just before all manner of disillusioning complications in the story. And for all those following complications, it is the trio's sentiments that still prevail. It is so too in the film, where the musical trio's beauty is designed to unite the seemingly shocking, seemingly disparate narrative strands. Yearning, aching, shortcoming are shared by all, as well as the promise and hope for something better. *Cosi Fan Tutte* has a mixed history, and it is generally less admired than the other Mozart/Da Ponte operas. But its "failure to accord with the nineteenth century's heroic notions about ideal womanhood is not a flaw in the opera but a commentary on the limitations of those notions."[12] Beyond its mechanical and narrative functions on the sound track, Mozart's music brings those original issues to bear on the film and its contemporary reception.

The specificity of these cues, and the specificity of their identification are very important. They can cause us to interrogate our affective responses as they simultaneously engage our intellects and increase our knowledge, so that feeling and thought can profitably coexist. In clear examples such as these we see that intent is an important part of understanding some uses of classical music in film, but intent is often more difficult to ascribe than in these instances. In terms of what an artist means to communicate, there are a number of possibilities to consider.

It seems clear that some classical music choices are fairly casual, and the associations they are expected to summon are fairly rudimentary. For instance there are cues chosen not for the implications of the particular work, or of its composer, but simply to signify "classical" or serious music. Classical music has been offhandedly and shorthandedly used to evoke class, culture, accomplishment, and a multitude of relations to them. In many cases articulation beyond that is neither intended nor expected.[13]

Royal Brown suggests that the use of music in relation to a narrative is not usually specific, or specifically meaningful, but rather mythical.[14] In Alfred Hitchcock's *Vertigo* (1958) a cue generally identified as being composed by Mozart and written in the script as being by Vivaldi, is in fact an obscure sinfonia by J. C. Bach. Johann Christian may be, as Brown says, "the very embodiment of a rationalized art,"[15] but in terms of the film Bach and his rationalism are probably beyond the mark, at least as set by whoever chose the music. It is more likely just a classical period counter to the roiling psychoses of the narrative and the dark postromanticisms of Bernard Herrmann's score.

Another kind of shorthand is not keyed on a particular idiom, but on a specific composer, or on a specific piece. For example, just as in many films the Twenty-third Psalm has been used to suggest a kind of general plain piety, so too has the music of J. S. Bach appeared as an echo of past devotions, and of the assurances that justified them.[16] Occasionally the quote will have very specific connotations, as when in *Dr. Jekyll and Mr. Hyde* (1932) we are introduced to the virtuous Doctor as he plays a chorale tune on the organ.[17] To suggest the victorious alter ego, as well as the more dominant, horrific associations that the story evokes in the viewer, the opening and closing titles offer as counter the secular tones of Bach's *Toccata and Fugue in D minor*.[18] Similarly, it is the religious nature of the *St. Matthew's Passion* that allows its closing chorale to frame and then (apparently) redeem the naturalisms of Pasolini's *Accatone* (1961) and Scorsese's *Casino* (1995).[19]

More frequently the outlines are rough and general. Ingmar Bergman doesn't distinguish between the secular and sacred Bach, as the entire *oeuvre* signifies for him an unalienated plenitude.[20] A great many films have used Bach's *Air* from the third orchestral suite to suggest precisely this loose and sometimes sloppy musical religiosity.[21]

In these instances it seems that, rather than discussing what an individual artist meant to have happen, it would be more advantageous to discuss some of the following points. How does classical music function as part of a cultural shorthand? How do intercontinental and cross-temporal connections or disjunctions affect musical appropriations? What are some of the levels of musical engagement and choice in industrial filmmaking contexts? How can the actual instance of musical use sometimes exceed intent or anticipated effect?

Twenty-third Psalm-quoters may not have any particular familiarity with or sympathy for the pious sentiments they plug into, nor do a great number of classical music cues hold a very studied or substantial relation to their borrowed culture. There is a *Hooked-on-Classics* cynicism and superficiality in many instances as, like the immemorial Hollywood movie, the music is reduced, contained, vacuumed, and packaged for the undiscerning masses.[22]

Still, intended and/or not, wonderful and artful things still emerge from seeming superficiality. In Michael Powell and Emeric Pressburger's *A Canterbury Tale* (1944), the climax occurs as one of the characters, a bitter cinema organist, plays Bach's D-minor *Toccata and Fugue* in the Canterbury cathedral. This piece and its formal structure have no liturgical function, but again as Bach has come to mean holiness, even the Toccata becomes a signifier of grace.[23] That grace is here expressed through the most famous composition in the organ repertoire. Though the choice of the familiar piece sacrifices elegance for lay comprehensibility, it still provides apt and meaningful accompaniment for the series of semisecular, beautifully cinematic miracles that it accompanies.

Many classical quotes then are quite casually motivated, and still quite if casually meaningful. However, this is not always so. We have seen how many have held that any familiar composition is cinematically unassimilable, and is therefore bad film music. The general argument is that the tune takes over the whole, and does not make much sense in doing so. It is perhaps for this reason that references to source music frequently neglect to name the actual source, either composer, or actual title and opus number. This is not so serious with regard to the generalist quotations just cited, but as we consider artists' motives we should remember that there are instances where cues are very carefully chosen for specific connotative purposes. In these cases it is only through identification that the connotations properly resonate.

Again, examples abound. Mussorgsky's *Night on Bald Mountain* reinforces macabre elements in MGM's *Wizard of Oz* (1939). Mendelssohn's *Midsummer Night's Dream* material, not to mention the credited Delius, enrich and expand the pictorialist raptures of *The Yearling* (1948). Mahler's Fifth Symphony *Adagietto* from Luchino Visconti's *Death in Venice* formally underpins the cutting and treatment of the sequences in which it is heard, but it also confirms the connection between Thomas

Mann's protagonist Aschenbach and Mahler—star Dirk Bogarde is made up to resemble the composer. It is thus that Visconti deepens and marks the story's connections with Romanticism's apotheosis and demise, with an obsessive and sickly beauty on the brink of the twentieth century.

Elsewhere, very specific choices have very specific and far-reaching ramifications. In Visconti's *Ossessione* (1942) the adulterous protagonists have a chance reunion at a fair; they, along with the wronged husband, enter into a singing contest where a soprano sings the *Habañera* from the first act of Bizet's *Carmen*. In the opera this is the piece by which we are introduced to the fickle, headstrong Carmen. In the film this quote bespeaks carnality, abandon and, if we will, tragedy.

Following the Bizet selection the cuckolded husband rises, and sings a baritone aria from *La Traviata*.[24] In the opera this aria is sung by Germont, the father of the rather headstrong, headlong Alfredo. He asks where his son's customary joy has gone, assures him that present imbalances will pass and that contentment will return. Does this selection not subtly shift the story? At first glance we have seen, or because of narrative stereotypes we think we have seen, a brutish oblivious husband and his bruised flower of a wife, who very naturally and properly craves more tender attention. But with further listening we must now factor in the provocative declarations from an infamous hussy, countered by the well-meaning appeal of a firm but loving older man who feels kindly toward youth, wishing only to help it avert its follies. In this setting intertextuality, if we attend to it, generates sympathy for the older generation, which may not fully understand or remember youthful passion, but which is suddenly not all bad.

Visconti's quotes signify beyond the narrative itself. Sweaty, boorish, uneducated Signor Bragana's familiarity with Verdi's high-culture text at least problematizes the universality of the notion that serious music is the property of privilege.[25] Or it might become a point of convergence where the auteur's aristocratic background and socialist inclinations meet, where is contained the paradox of the opera director/neorealist. It also explains Visconti's not-so-strange interest in this apparently American pulp fiction—*Ossessione* was notoriously cribbed from James Cain's *The Postman Always Rings Twice*—an idiom much like that other font of raging passion and melodramatic excess, Italian opera.[26]

These then are authorial programs, specific choices that lead to important chains of association. The level of specificity is important. A loose idiomatic identification—that sounds like classical music—will lead to a particular response; the more particular the identification, the more complex and interesting the effects that can be traced.[27]

AFTER INTENTION: PRAGMATISM, OBSCURITY, INADEQUACY

Work-specific considerations can, of course, have elitist implications, as a certain amount of experience and sophistication are required to negotiate these intertextual byways. This is one reason that artist-first interpretive approaches are not always sufficient. Furthermore, as we move from the artist's program to that surrounding a spectator's interpretation and experience, we encounter instances where authorial autonomy breaks down, and where his or her intent becomes less important. Proper appreciation of musical uses in these instances depends on an awareness of purely practical motivations, very personal and even idiosyncratic or incommunicable musical choices, and the possibility of unconscious, accidental, or even inept selection.

Musical quotation often has fairly mundane motivations, and in these cases it is not so much creativity as the plainly practical that leads to certain musical uses. This circumstance applies to specific films, and even to dominant patterns of use during certain periods.

The use of classical music in the silent cinema illustrates this latter point. A 1917 decision in the U.S. Supreme Court granted composers royalties for public performances. Charles Berg suggests that this decision led to a further dependence on public-domain compositions from the standard repertoire. Since public performance of compositions by living composers would now force studios and theaters to pay for the privilege, the classics now emerged as the most economical business option. Whatever serendipitous meanings might arise from the silent period juxtaposition of a film and a particular piece of music, at least as important is the fact that the latter was free.[28]

At present conditions are reversed. In contemporary filmmaking classical cues may be used less frequently for copyright and contractual reasons. To use them can be too expensive.[29] Film music scholarship has often privileged aesthetic and formal issues, but in this instance we see that social and economic determinants are just as important in motivating use and nonuse.

On a related note, I have argued that the early consensus in Hollywood against using classical music can be seen as the result of music community solidarity.[30] This is still true today; use of recordings means fewer jobs for composers and musicians. For this reason recent Musician's Union pacts, as well as American Federation of Musicians agreements, throw up logistical disincentives to the use of classical music in films (having to pay every session musician royalties, and so on).[31] These are some of the reasons why there was once a great deal of classical music usage, and why this usage has now dropped off somewhat.

Such practical considerations can even put traditional concerns about source music in an interesting new light. Max Steiner defends original film music, on the assumption that familiar material draws undue attention to itself. "While the American people are more musically minded than any other nation in the world, they are still not entirely familiar with all the old and new masters' works and would thereby be prone to 'guessing' and distraction."[32]

This may at times be true, but although it can be the case that a familiar piece of music will overturn the traditional narrative hierarchies and call undue attention to itself—and I have already suggested that this is not necessarily bad—the fact is that much of the repertory is not that familiar. Silent film organist Dennis James tells of his efforts to reconstruct the original score for *Don Juan* (1926). Pieces were missing from the manuscript, and had to be transcribed from the sound track. James, a musician with a fairly substantial knowledge of the repertory, later found out that the cues were directly from Massenet and Wagner, and that he was just not familiar with them.[33] As with latter-day reconstructions, so in the original instances the idiomatic appositeness of late-Romantic music did not only provide a model for original composition, but it was very possible for the model music itself to blend in, seamlessly and, figuratively speaking, silently.

Gino Stefani suggests that "in a minimal sense, competence at opus or work level is the trivial fact of recognizing a piece."[34] Similarly, film composer David Raksin speaks of the oxymoronic "esoteric howler," of a predominant kind of musical joke that requires the *Grove* musical dictionary to understand it.[35] Just as this kind of joke may not quite reach the cheap seats—nor is it guaranteed comprehension by the initiates—so too it is with the use of apparently familiar music: much of it will remain unrecognized, and will thus be unable to distract.

In addition to the likelihood of unfamiliarity, utilitarian practices in the past reveal for us the possibilities of familiarity. Richard Bush points out how often music composed for one thing can be quite aptly used for something else.[36] His discussion of recycled music from serial pictures pertains to a strictly industrial setting, with strictly practical motivations: reusing music was cheap and fast. What applies in this instance also pertains to classical cues we recognize, and music's circumstantial transposability is that much more true in other settings where quotations are more rational and responses more studied.

If practical motivations are an important factor in dealing with musical quotation, so too are impractical motivations. In other words, we are sometimes at a loss to understand exactly what a filmmaker or musician is doing. Silent film organist Gaylord Carter holds that "the key of D flat has a rich brown velour feeling, like lush drapes."[37] This seems a valid enough observation, but it points to the complicated fact that an artist's mind has its own reasons, and they are not always communicated clearly to the outside. Godard's *Pierrot le Fou* (1965), *Two or Three Things I Know About Her* (1966), and *Tour/Detour* (1978), Pasolini's *Uccellacci e Uccellini* (1966) and *Oedipus Rex* (1967), and Bresson's *L'Argent* (1983) are a few examples of films in which classical quotation seems careful and at least semirational, but where substantial opaqueness makes comprehension difficult for the viewer.

What, then, of the mandates of communication outlined in the last chapter? Our misunderstandings, whether derived from a flaw of authorial execution, a gap in our own perceptions, or a difficulty in verbalizing either, point up again a basic reality of contrapuntal interactions. They tend to exceed, bypass, and confound categorizations, intentions, and expectations.

It is often true that obscure, elite, even arcane motivations keep quoted film music from communicating clearly, if in fact clear communication is even intended. I have mentioned how it is important to identify the work being quoted, but knowing what it is does not necessarily help us with what it is doing, or with what it means.

For example, Jean-Luc Godard uses the second movement of Beethoven's C major quartet (op. 59, no. 3) throughout his film *Prénom, Carmen* (1983). It took me some time to identify the piece, which seemed necessary in order to ascertain symbolic intent and import. But finding, and then researching, the piece itself didn't much help me. Beethoven certainly means a great many things, as does this particular composition. Of all filmmakers, Godard would be aware of these meanings, but I was unable to find which of these motivated him. Which is relevant to my own response? Was he quoting his own past music uses, from films I'd not seen, or not listened to with sufficient care? Did he just like the sound of it?[38]

These examples suggest one reason to move away from author-based interpretation. Ascribing artistic intent without full awareness of the artist's motivations can be a perilous undertaking. Did Luchino Visconti mean all the things that I observed earlier, or are these interpretations simply examples of my own critical excess? The latter is certainly possible, and excess is one of the causes for the kind of neoformalist, against-interpretation strategies already discussed.[39] But I will argue that hearing something that an artist is not aware of having said is not necessarily a problem; meaning can be reaped whether or not an author is aware of having planted the seed. Cues and their connotations are as important, but in these cases it is not the motive of the artist so much as the listener/critic's cultural awareness that flushes out connections and informs the interpretation. Martin Nordern makes a helpful related distinction in discussing "clear-cut influences, likely influences and coincidental but still noteworthy similarities" in films' interactions with the other arts. [40] As with the arts generally, so too it is with music; the point is that the creative critical reception of a text is valid, and that such reception should not and need not justify itself by ascribing a creative interpretation to the artist.

There is another reason to move away from authors and from artist-first criticism/interpretation. An audience may not fully grasp an artist's intentions; these may be circumvented by purely practical pressures. Or, similar to the overreaching critic, it may be that the artist's intentions/executions are not completely coherent or justified. Our Romantic predilections notwithstanding, the creator is not always in full control of his or her materials, or aware of the ways they reinforce or undercut the apparent, or the intended, message.

In his discussion of sound montage Pudovkin said the following:

> Always there exist two rhythms, the rhythmic course of the objective world and the tempo and rhythm with which man observes this world. The world is a whole rhythm, while man receives only partial impressions of this world through his eyes and ears and to a lesser extent through his very skin.[41]
>
> This is obviously as true for the producer as it is for the receiver, for the filmmaker as much as the film viewer. Impressions are partial, conclusions drawn from them are incomplete, and our expressions inadequate.

Much use of classical music in film is simply unaccountable. In the 1943 British release *San Demetrio, London*, a crippled tanker appears to be sinking, at which time there is heard a brief snatch of melody from the first movement of Rimsky-Korsakov's *Scheherezade*. Why? To suggest the romance of wartime transport? To link a modest piece of Ealing Studios propaganda with ancient and noble storytelling traditions? Or, as is more likely, for no reason at all?[42]

Music critics have often strenuously objected to this kind of loose and unmotivated quotation. Hans Keller, writing in *Music Review* about George Auric's score for *The Titfield Thunderbolt* (1953), derides "a twice used D maj. parody of *Eine Kleine Nachtmusik* . . . (it) is formally bad, dramatically obscure, and not funny enough to be musically justified."[43] Keller objects here to a brief quote, but apparent miscues can also be much bigger, and more interesting.

What does one make of a juxtaposition like the one in John Woo's *The Killer* (1989)? The eponymous assassin and his admiring policeman foil are united in the final shoot-out, which takes place in a church, where the men are defending themselves and the blinded heroine from a horde of villains. At a climactic moment said bad guys' perfidy reaches a breaking point, which point is demonstrated when they machine-gun a statue of the Virgin Mary. It shatters in slow motion, and at that moment the sound track strikes up the strains of the sinfonia from Handel's *Messiah*. Woo's montage fireworks and operatic melodrama literally explode from this point, and although the combination of music with image and story could be seen as having sacrilegious implications—consider the figure summoned by this particular music, the nature of this sacrifice, and the merit of the cinematic savior—to take it as such seems a touch oversensitive.

Having bypassed offense, confusion still remains. What motivates this quotation? Does it refer to the killer's sacrifice? The virginal ideal represented by the blinded singer? Is it all pure sensation, with intertextual correspondences being purely unwitting? Given such proliferations it is easy to take note of Woo's breathlessly exhilarating yet absurd enactment, enumerate the elements contributing to it, shrug one's shoulders and move on.[44]

Shrugging aside, this is the course recommended by the formalist schools mentioned in the first chapter. Where we don't know, or don't acknowledge the importance of intent, where the results are aboundingly complex, it is a good course. This is especially true when we think of the many unconsidered and underconsidered uses of this music throughout film history.

Still critical elaborations can be appropriate when we see clearly how clumsy cues have exceeded the filmmaker's intent and expectation, leaving us with unwitting but still substantial insights. *Chapayev* (1934), by Georgi and Sergei Vasiliev, was one of the most celebrated successes of Soviet socialist realism. Its aims were to celebrate the revolution and to condemn the reactionary forms and factions that opposed it. In one scene a hulking peasant soldier, adjutant to the sinister White Russian General, appears to be dancing in stolid fashion to the first movement of Beethoven's *Moonlight Sonata* (no. 14). His commander—dressed and groomed, incidentally, like Erich von

Stroheim's sinister Prussian—is playing the piece, and intercutting reveals that the soldier is actually polishing the floor, with his bare foot in some kind of brush contraption. The music provides a bizarre accompaniment to the lowly task, which the soldier is forced to perform in humiliating fashion. As the sequence continues, intercutting combines with the use of heavy and heavy-handed strings which fatten the piano score, increasing tension and suggesting a worm about to turn.

The intent of this curious montage is doubtless to associate the bourgeois militarist with the reactionary values of individualistic romanticism, as symbolized by Beethoven, and/or the kind of man who would be playing his music. What looks like cultured enjoyment is revealed to closer attention as exploitation, and culture being a poor consolation for the starving, the dance is suddenly not so enjoyable.

This view of classical music is enhanced when contrasted with another use in Cecil B. de Mille's *The Buccaneer* (1938). Soon after being introduced to the story's rough and attractive pirate/hero Jean Lafitte (Frederic March) we hear a lovely air played on a violin. "Beautiful," says our hero. "What is it?" "Handel's Largo," replies an anomalously musical pirate who stands alongside. The point of this rather protruding incident is to suggest, by classical music, that Lafitte is subject to improvement and culture. This incident occurs immediately before Lafitte catches some rogue mutineers and initiates said self-improvement. (Later, to reinforce the music's civilizing effects and how they are threatened by the brutes of the world, the violinist is killed and in a brief pointed shot some savage steps on his violin.) And what shape does it take? Patriotic pro-American action, of course. It is precisely this kind of connection that informs contradictory pictures like that of the Vasilievs.

De Mille's entertaining film is another entry in the group of movies where a rough-hewn character, an apparent cad, is really just an as yet unfinished heroic individualist, who needs only the influence of a good woman and the call of country to end his rakish adolescence and assume his proper nobility. For other examples, see for instance *The Sea Hawk* (1940), *The Black Swan* (1942)—and *Chapayev*. The actual effect of the latter's Beethoven sequence is not so straightforward as it might first sound or appear. The montage equation leaves considerable remainders. The use of strings brings Beethoven, for instance, into the realm of high Hollywood melodramatic manipulation, while the piece itself, and the associations connected to its composer, most suggest the individualistic romanticism of the character of Chapayev himself. In the end it is the film as much as the reactionary commander that buys partially into the bourgeois values and techniques it seeks to oppose. Apart from the national allegiances *Chapayev* and *The Buccaneer* are much the same, and ideological distinctions, when considered with their cinematic renderings, are not as great as we might think.

One important reality, then, is to acknowledge when and how the artist falls short, though I am not simply advocating conventional evaluative criticism. As I hope the brief discussion of *Chapayev* demonstrates, shortfall is natural, and interesting. Lewis Carroll had this to say when asked about hidden meaning in the "Alice" books. "I have but one answer. I don't know! Still, you know, words mean more than we mean to express when we use them, so a whole book ought to mean a great deal more than the writer meant."[45] In the same way that parallel/counterpoint geometries have caused some to underestimate the complex workings of music and meaning in film, an overemphasis on the artist can distract us from other fundamental parts of the equation. Proper perspectives about artist intent and artist autonomy lead us to the other part of artistic exchange, to reception and phenomenology. And a proper understanding about the giver and the receiver gives us a clearer view of the "message" in their midst, without which music and meaning in film cannot be comprehended.

INTERPRETIVE STRATEGIES: PHENOMENOLOGY

I will now address audience, the other interpretive element, the other program-providing entity that enables us to understand uses of classical music in film. In art music attention is generally paid to the production and not the reception of music. This fact coincides with prejudices about film music, and about film. This prejudice holds that expressiveness originates at the creative

source, which does not allow for the possibility of creative reception. "Considered as an art, music has two distinct branches, the
art of the composer and the art of the executant."[46] And the listener? With regard to film, the viewer?

When Dudley Andrew wrote in 1978 of the "neglected tradition of phenomenology in film studies," he was speaking in a
climate of what might be termed structuralist fatigue. Film theory had elaborately traced the ways in which semiotic, psychoan-
alytic, and ideological determinations construct us as individuals
and as viewing subjects. But for Andrew these theoretical models
had not been adequate to the *experience* of textual and aesthetic
elements of film. The work of signification, the cinematic apparatus, and classification could never account for the "quality of
experience," and the "surplus of meaning" that experience with
films gives us.[47]

Andrew's opposition of phenomenology to prevailing strands
of structuralism and the poststructural synthesis is just one instance of a long line of dialectical negotiations in the history of
this philosophical movement. Founded by Edmund Husserl at the
beginning of the twentieth century, phenomenology countered
positivist and materialist thought by attending to the mechanisms
of perception. Phenomenologists say that meaning is not strictly
held in a material object or ideal essence of form, but in the
individual experience. Although there are essential elements to
objects that exist, objectively and in fact, our experience is to
perceive in part and from a certain perspective. In the end we
must concentrate not on what something absolutely means or un-
equivocally is, but what it is in individual perception and respon-
siveness.

Husserl distinguished between the physical reality of things of
which we are conscious, and the actual act or experience of that
consciousness. Inner experience and awareness are primary. Phenomenology deals with mental objects, suspending the judgment
of ultimate, essential things, for the things that one sees, and the
way one sees them. Importantly, this emphasis allows, through
the concept of bracketing, even for "inappropriate" or "incorrect" perceptions. An illustration: it may be that source music
use in John Woo's *The Killer* is not a shoulder-shrugging mystery, but rather a parable for Hong Kong 1997, with Handel

roughly representing a British Asia menaced by an uncertain future. But phenomenology, without denying that this may be a true and authoritative interpretation, brackets such objective possibilities and considers the object or phenomenon as presented to and perceived by the individual. In other words, on first seeing and working through that particular sequence of Woo's film, this was all I was able to come up with.[48]

This is not to say that a phenomenological reading can justify indulgence or sloppiness, but it does mean that these readings are perceptual, perspectival, and do not claim completeness. As we consider individual acts of perception, we are aware that they are transitory and contingent, and that they are also valid and important.

When Andrew reintroduced these terms to film debates, the body of theory was perhaps not particularly amenable to them.[49] This was Andrew's point; discussions of ideology, after Benjamin and Althusser, and of subject formation through and by language, through Lacan and Baudry, though dominant in authority and influence, had brought the field to a joyless impasse. There was for Andrew too much systematizing, too much ideological and/or psychological determinism. These things of course deserved attention, but Andrew held that this attention came at the expense of the human, the precious and poignant considerations which are finally the reason and justification for scholarly pursuit. "If life and reality lie beyond human experience or our consciousness of it, as certain recent structuralists have avowed, then let's forget it anyway."[50]

Since Andrew's writing, however, there have been numerous developments along the more human lines that he advocated. The rise of spectator studies in film allowed for an investigation, by quantitative means and otherwise, of the place of the individual receiver in the whole equation. Since individuals also reside within larger social groups, as well as parts of subcommunities within those larger groups, spectator studies also considered how a plurality of meaning in texts could speak polyglossically to those various constituencies.[51] Reception theory emphasized the spectator as the active site of meaning, and not just a passive or neutral husk.[52] In support, theorists like Mikhail Bakhtin were appropriated to demonstrate the multiplicity of the processes of communication and meaning construction. For Bakhtin, the heteroglossic or many-voiced text invites a reader to participate dialogically, which exchange accounts much more accurately and joyfully for the process than previous hailing and inoculating accounts had done.

Phenomenology too was absorbed into this discussion, and proved particularly suited to addressing its questions. Vivian Sobchack's 1992 book, *The Address of the Eye*, discusses both the interior and the exterior of the film experience, suggesting again that to psychoanalysis and ideology and the other staples of poststructuralism must be added consciousness and an awareness of its transformative possibilities.[53] Such meetings and transformations are, of course, the project of phenomenology.

How do we create a reliable grounding amidst these acknowledged multiplicities? Sobchack develops the titular idea of the address of the eye, which occurs at the nexus of inside and outside, which partakes of social construction, but which also contains an element of individual choice. Film cannot be separated from our experience of film.

> Phenomenological description and interpretation have revealed the cinematic subject (both film and spectator) as at once introverted and extroverted, as existing in the world as both subject and object. Thus . . . the film and the spectator are never experienced as completely self-possessed.[54]

For Sobchack there exists between the cinematic text and its receiver a kind of mechano-biological complex, a multiple site of mutual creation.

> The camera its perceptive organ, the projector its expressive organ, the screen its discrete and material occupation of worldly space, the cinema exists as a visible performance of the perceptive and expressive structure of lived-body experience. Viewing, re-viewing, revising vision as easily and transparently as one mechanically operates and the other biologically breathes, each film and each spectator separately live the advent of vision.[55]

All of this means, in relation to the present study, that the workings of classical music in film, for all the proscriptions of composers and critics, for all the avowed intentions of those utilizing it, must finally be calculated and articulated in the way that a viewer sees and a listener hears. In connection, Dudley Andrew once again offers a helpful formulation.

In his 1983 book *Concepts of Film Theory*, Andrew surveys some of the theoretical approaches with which his first phenomenology article had taken at least implicit issue. Without rejecting these constructs out of hand, he also concludes that none, nor even all of them together, are ultimately sufficient.

> The inclination to invoke philosophy, psychoanalysis, linguistics, logic or ideological theory in undertaking film study suggests not so much that film is ruled by other disciplines as the fact that films are the site of myriad problematics, involving multiple aspects of culture.[56]

As for the problem of fusing all of these multiple and interdependent demands, Andrew comes at the end to hermeneutics, to cycles of interpretation and the final human factor as we account for our film experience. Texts call to us in ways that are, in the end, fundamentally human. And our responses, however analytical or informed by ostensibly objective theoretical models, are likewise "cries" of human aspiration.

> What we do with [film expressions and models of cinematic interpretation] is as varied as the variety of interpreters and theories of interpretation. Yet doing anything with them whatsoever shows the interdependence of mind and body, of thought and voice, of meaning and expression. Certainly this is not an untroubled interdependence, but it is one that gives to viewing, reading, and writing a place in human life different from philosophy, analysis, or sheer behavior. This border zone of reading is the life of the imagination. It is worth as much as we imagine it to be.[57]

Andrew's border zone, and film phenomenology generally, is built on the emphasis on text and on viewer, and on the notion that it is at the borders between the two where meaning resides, and it is in the meeting between the two that it multiplies. It is also built on the affirmation that this subjective and variable site is valid, and valuable.

I will now discuss the historical grounding, as well as the theoretical implications, of phenomenology as it applies to classical music. To do so I will briefly return to the aims of Soviet montage cinema, especially as it related to its intended audience. I will show how, although the audience was ostensibly the whole key and point to montage aesthetics, that audience's real nature and real rights were largely misunderstood, or even ignored. My chapter three suggested how the misunderstandings continue. By revisiting a movement away from strict montage geometries we will see, in an interpretive sense, how the audience can take its place in the cluster of montage, contrapuntal, and programmatic equations existing within film source music.

We know that Soviet film discourse is responsible for many "counterpoint" confusions. Significantly, artist/audience confusions are also contained in that same discourse. The polemical period of the first Soviet republic was characterized by vigorous debates over artistic issues, with the film front being perhaps the most furiously disputed. Along with the familiar formalist manifestos about increasing the expressiveness and fulfilling the high destiny of film art, 1920s debates also considered formalism in terms of social responsibility, the propagandizing of the proletariat, and the very serious problem of the popular inaccessibility of montage products.

Although we properly celebrate and concentrate on the standard milestones of early Soviet cinema, they don't give us all of the pertinent details. As had been the case during the silent period, in the early Soviet sound period the imports and potboilers, the more conventional narrative films, were simply more popular with the cinema audiences. Though its relevance remains, in terms of mainstream effect, the influence of the avant-garde has been considerably overestimated.[58]

There were important sound experiments, such as *Enthusiasm* (1930) and *Deserter,* but as with the earlier period of apparent plenitude, there was a feeling, and likely a valid one, that the filmmakers were using the situation as testing ground for their own erudite and inaccessible theorizing instead of for addressing the needs of the mostly illiterate people. The Communist Party's push at this time for "mass intelligibility" aimed, quite legitimately, given its avowed priority to indoctrinate the citizenry, to shift from an avant-garde more appreciated abroad to things the people and the state needed and could understand at home. In addition to pure villainy,[59] many Soviet film officials were independently inspired to consider how to more effectively reach the people, and thereby to demonstrate the social consciousness that was, avowedly, a universal subscription.

The incomprehensibility of much montage cinema contradicts the intentions of its original development, which were, if we are to very carefully take Eisenstein's formulation of intellectual montage as being at least partly typical, to communicate through juxtaposition certain ideas to the audience.[60] And although the fact may be effaced by auteurist celebrations of the Soviet avant-garde, the audience was always theorized as the key to and the reason for montage.

Here is an excerpt from Eisenstein's earliest statement on the subject, "The Montage of Attractions," written in 1923.

> Theatre's basic material derives from the audience: the moulding of the audience in a desired direction [or mood] is the task of every utilitarian theatre. . . . *An attraction* [in our diagnosis of theatre] *is any aggressive moment in theatre, i.e. any element of it that subjects the audience to emotional or psychological influence, verified by experience and mathematically calculated to produce specific emotional shocks in the spectator in their proper order within the whole. These shocks provide the only opportunity of perceiving the ideological aspect of what is being shown, the final ideological conclusion.*[61]

"Attraction" presupposes audience involvement. Individual shots, as attractions, are a stimulation by which the spectator senses similarity or contrast, which are then joined as appropriate.

It is in this notion of the appropriate that montage aesthetics become vulnerable, however. Propaganda was the means by which the regime communicated the articles of its faith, and in order for it to be successful, that communication was supposed to be accessible. A consistent inaccessibility was seen as an important failing and was certainly a complicating tension in much montage cinema. The avant-garde, in Soviet practice and in general, seems by very nature prone to opaqueness.

Beyond a not insignificant failure in reaching or serving a large lay audience, difficulty does not necessarily invalidate the work of this, or any other, period. The real problem may actually lie in the propagandistic impulse, or at least the Soviet articulation thereof. There is in the discourse of the period a tone, and thus an implied conception about the viewer, that says much about the inadequacy, or at least the incompleteness of the Soviet montage model. "The spectator *is made* to traverse the road of creation the author traversed in creating the image."[62] All through these early statements we find that which has made postmodernity so suspicious of totalities from John Knox to Karl Marx. Everywhere is coercion and inevitability, the idea of audiences forced down certain paths to the only correct conclusions. Pudovkin speaks similarly:

One must always remember that the film, by the very nature of its construction (the rapid alternation of successive pieces of celluloid), requires of the spectator an exceptional concentration of attention. The director, and consequently the scenarist also, *leads despotically* along with him the attention of the spectator. The latter sees only that which the director shows him; for reflection, for doubt, for criticism, there is neither room nor time, and consequently the smallest error in clearness or vividness of construction will be apprehended as an unpleasant confusion or as a simple, ineffective blank.[63]

Beyond the discomfort of this despotism, of "*forcing* the spectator to compare the two actions all the time," there is here a problematic picture of a passive and helpless audience.[64] This may or may not have been true of Russia's rural cine-illiterates, but when Pudovkin speaks of Pavlovian attempts to create certain emotional states through, it would seem, intrinsically expressive camera techniques, through things that invariably mean certain other things, then this totality trembles.[65] The underconsidered agent in the montage equation was the individual receiver.

Emphasizing reception may jeopardize the author's authority. It also destabilizes an author's message, but there are salutary effects to this destabilization. Too often the struggle for comprehension leads automatically to the assumption that comprehension can be, or must be, obtained. Godard counters, saying of his *Two or Three Things I Know About Her* that "basically what I am doing is making the spectator share the arbitrary nature of my choices, and the quest for general rules which *might* justify a particular choice."[66]

Alternatively, those rules might *not* justify the choice. Jean Vigo wrote of Luis Buñuel and Salvador Dalí's *Un Chien Andalou* (1928).

> I have met M. Luis Buñuel only once and then only for 10 minutes, and our meeting in no way touched upon *Un Chien Andalou*. This enables me to discuss it with that much greater liberty. Obviously my comments are entirely personal. Possibly I will get near, without doubt I will commit some howlers.[67]

Howlers are possible, if that means differing from an author's intent. But if the reader is an author as well, especially with a work as provocatively open-ended as Buñuel's, or Godard's, film, then "mistake" comes to mean something altogether different, if it means anything at all.

Gino Stefani reminds us that

> musicians and musicologists have a tendency to neglect or even to deny the semantic thickness of techniques; thus they consider music essentially as the production of objects and events. But for our society as a whole, for its general competence in music, music is always the production of signs. It is therefore particularly important here to consider *ordinary people*, what they think and feel about musical "language", and what they do with it.[68]

Jean Jacques Nattiez begins his discussion of musical sound and noise by subdividing it, distinguishing between "poietic" (composer choice), "neutral" (physical realities, sound waves, etc.) and "esthetic" (perceptive judgment) categories.[69] In Nattiez's model experiences with and analyses of music shift according to the level, though of course all the levels operate and interrelate simultaneously. Against general assumptions in the musical community, there is no hierarchy implied here.

This is an essential point, as the experience of the hearer is especially important in the experience and understanding of classical music in film. To an important degree, what the audience viewer thinks and feels when music meets image is the correct interpretation.

Just as Marx's prescriptions and predictions were not equal to his difficult-to-deny descriptions of the class struggle, so too

does the montage aesthetic fall short, at least in its earliest ac-
counting of the effects and affects it was likely to have. In art and
experience, collision is everywhere, but what may result proves
difficult to foresee. The inadequacy of social and cinematic dialectics lies in the fact that struggles, collisions, and reactions simply do not end precisely or predictably. This is especially true
when the collisions and chemical reactions take place inside of
the spectator's head.

Eisenstein:

> For us, to know is to participate. For this we value the biblical
> term—"and Abraham *knew* his wife Sarah"—by no means mean-
> ing that he became acquainted with her.
>   Perceiving is building. The perceiving of life—indissolubly—is
> the construction of life—the *rebuilding* of it.[70]

The genetic metaphor is an apt one. Wim Wenders asks: "At
what moment is a film born? Or perhaps it would be better to say
conceived?"[71] The phenomenological element is an essential part
of the montage equation; as with any coupling, the realities of
genetics, of dominant and recessive genes, not to mention envi-
ronmental determinations, make the outcome of the meeting impossible to predict.

> Films have no existence other than through our eyes. In fact, they
> are always seen twice: first by a director with the help of his writer,
> cameraman, actors and a few other people, and second by every-
> one in 'the audience'. Everybody sees and creates his/her own
> film, the reviewer, too. Like anyone else he is guided by the film
> on the screen adding (or subtracting) his own emotions, memories,
> opinions, sense of humour, openness, colours and so on.[72]

The original notion of the cinema of attraction was not neutral.
It had a decided hierarchy, with the artist at the top. Though it
presupposed audience involvement, its ultimate flaw was that it
did not sufficiently account for the viewer.[73]

But it is not sufficient simply to affirm audience rights while
offhandedly acknowledging that that audience is pretty diverse.
What is the nature of that diversity?

Dziga Vertov wrote in 1923 that "a ballet audience haphaz-
ardly follows first the ensemble of the groups of dancers, then
random individuals, then somebody's feet: a series of incoherent

impressions that are different for every member of the audience."[74] The complexity is daunting, and with a form featuring concrete visual moorings. Music is even more difficult.

E. M. Forster characterizes the personality of an audience as follows:

> There is no such person as the average concert-goer, and no one can speak in his name. Not only does our enjoyment of music differ, but our attention wanders from it in different directions, and returns to it at different angles; so that if the soul of an audience could be photographed it would resemble a flight of scattering dipping birds, who belong neither to the air nor the water nor the earth. In theory the audience is a solid slab, provided with a single pair of enormous ears, which listen, and with a pair of hands, which clap. Actually it is that elusive scattering flight of winged creatures, darting around, and spending much of its time where it shouldn't, thinking now 'how lovely!', now 'my foot's gone to sleep', and passing in the beat of a bar from there's Beethoven back in C minor again!' to 'did I turn the gas off?' or 'I do think he might have shaved'.[75]

Each response is different, as is each receptive program: the extracinematic frames of reference and experience that the viewer brings to the equation. We have seen the place of connotation and association in the complex ways that music means. Leonard Meyer suggests that susceptibility to musical connotation depends on the individual.

> Whether a piece of music arouses connotations depends to a great extent upon the disposition and training of the individual listener and upon the presence of cues, either musical or extramusical, which tend to activate connotative responses.[76]

The diffuseness of response here characterized points again to the difficulty of establishing any kind of rational semiotic system in relation to musical meaning. Frames of reference do not sufficiently coincide. This state of affairs need not be troubling, however, as possibilities of enrichment outstrip the challenges. For this we allow the idea of program to proliferate. Stefani observes that "speaking and understanding a language is different from studying its written grammar and theory."[77] This is true, especially in music/film music, where language, let alone theory and grammar, is so tenuous. But it still communicates.

John Cage:

I said that since the sounds were sounds this gave people hearing them the chance to be people, centred within themselves where they actually are, not artificially in the distance as they are accustomed to be trying to figure out what is being said by some artist by means of sound.[78]

Roland Barthes talks of the writerly approach to reading, where "the goal of the literary work (of literature as work) is to make the reader no longer a consumer, but a producer of the text."[79] The point here is that there is an artist and there is a receiver, or vice versa. Cage tells of a conductor for one of his compositions that doesn't have a score, but only his own part. "Though he affects the other performers, he does not control them."[80]

I have presented programs as elements of montage equations, the points of reference upon which collisions and counterpoints meet and turn. Eisenstein fully acknowledged and understood that things were not as simple as his original formulations had suggested. We have discussed overtonal montage, a method which bears revisiting in this context. In "Film Form: New Problems" Eisenstein takes from Jean Piaget the idea of inner speech, a preconscious, preverbal jumble of stimuli which clash and overlap. Speech, and other things (film theory, for instance), organize this jumble. But in addition to this organizing, other viabilities began to emerge. As mentioned earlier, Joyce's *Ulysses* became for Eisenstein a major inspiration, where another form of inner speech, one which remains unrationalized, emerges as exemplary. It is individual, subjective, and undomesticated. It is just this kind of inner speech which becomes, in the present instance and in relation to the processing of musico-cinematic information, a model of reception and apprehension.[81]

Eisenstein used musical metaphors, discussing montage overtones which are only sensed subconsciously, but are still there. Dominants conventionally command most of our attention, but here opens the possibility of the other tones being considered with equal care and given equal importance. Eisenstein's well-known admiration for Kabuki theater was largely a response to that form's neutralization of the narrative, the bringing of all elements onto an equal level. In "The Filmic Fourth Dimension" Eisenstein calls for just such neutralization, for an acknowledgment of the "secondary vibrations" beyond the "central stimulus."[82]

Neutralization is one place where the *cinematic* counterpoint that we have discussed does work. Overtones, though not necessarily what and how Eisenstein foresaw, ring off the apparent struck note; and it's in phenomenology that they do so.

Eisenstein came to advocate consideration and validation of the totality, and in doing so found himself moving from the conceptual oppositions of original cinematic counterpoint to true polyphony, luxuriating thereby in the resulting overdeterminations and overabundances of meaning.

The implications? Conceivably, chaos. Dudley Andrew says that the great flaw of Eisenstein's theory is the mountain of arcane data that constantly clutters and obscures it.[83] But this clutter contains a powerful truth, and the ultimate consistency of all of Eisenstein's multifarious investigations: everything is integrally connected, everything fits, even the remainders left at the end of the equations. In fact, without remainders, the equation has not been honestly worked out.[84]

Given all this, Eisenstein's first thoughts about intellectual montage are not so much invalidated as multiplied. Theses and antitheses create syntheses, but they are richer (and more difficult to contain) than he at first suspected. This remains true, even given, especially given the failure of the dialectical experiment with the historical Soviet audience. Its misperceptions and unresolved contradictions simply point up the need for a more complex phenomenological and overtonal model. As with the trajectory of Eisenstein's montage aesthetics—perception, emotion, cognition—so now emerges a neutralization based on a broader definition of cinema, one properly providing for the receiver.[85] To use Nattiez's terms we must move through every signifying space, from poietic through neutral to esthetic.

INDETERMINACY

In this chapter we have moved from the artist's plan to the audience's experience, considering how each is important to the understanding of classical music in film. To conclude I wish to briefly discuss how a certain indeterminacy, or perhaps an unpredictable multiplicity, aids that understanding.

I have argued that it is between strict parallelism and traditional figurative counterpoint that musical meaning is actually found, and that collisions, and syntheses too, are predicated on programs. Similarly I would like to suggest that the tentative space between the artist's intention and the receiver's apprehension is where this meaning can be contextualized. Though certainties may be professed on either side, classical music as appropriated and heard is, to a great degree, indeterminate.

In his compositions and other presentations John Cage relinquished authorial control, at least in its conventional sense.[86] There were also receptive, listener implications stemming from this relinquishment. The combined result was indeterminacy, which is to say, with all the points of address and apprehension, reference, and subjectivity, anything can happen.

There are critical applications for this broad generalization. There are specifically musical sites for the sender/receiver/context topography that Janet Staiger describes, and that I cited at the beginning of this chapter. In his *The American Film Musical*, Rick Altman suggests a useful model to account for the construction and communication of meaning, in film and elsewhere.

> Meaning, as I will define it, is never something that words or texts have but always something that is made in a four-party meaning-situation. An *author* (understood in the widest possible sense: individual, group, industry, etc.) circulates a *text* (which may vary from a single word, image, or gestures to multiple volumes) to an *audience* (singular or plural, present or removed) whose perception is partly dependent on the *interpretive community* to which its members belong. . . . The model I am proposing has no message, that is no specific meaning that may be permanently ascribed to a given text. Instead, a text turns into a message (or different messages) only in the context of a specific audience in a specific interpretive community. . . . The interpretive community may thus be defined in part as a *context* in which the text is to be interpreted; the interpretive community names the *intertexts* that will control the interpretation of a given text.[87]

The phenomenological parallels of this statement are clear. With regard to the sender/receiver axis, Altman refers to two lev-

els of language. One of these allows somewhat for authorial intent, but it still preexists and exceeds anything an author can
consciously intend. The second language level, emerging out of
vast history and histories, proliferates at the level of reception,
and beyond anything the receiver can comprehend.[88]

In the field of musical semiotics, Gino Stefani proposes what
he calls a "Model of Musical Competence." This model proposes five codes by which music is experienced, and by which
musical experience is comprehended. General codes, pertaining
to all experience; social practice, institutions and interactions
within particular societies; musical techniques, theories and techniques specific to musical practice; style, connected with periods,
genres, composers; and opus, the individual work or performance; all interact in complex ways. The complexities increase
with the model providing for general and specialized musical
competencies, for popular and highbrow practice and reception.
The issues informing musical experience change drastically according to the experiences and motivations of those participating
in that experience.[89]

The result of all these interactions cannot be predicted exactly,
but in that potentially frustrating fact lies the validity of it all.
When film music is used and heard and processed, multiplica-
tions result.

In conclusion, and contrary to conventional parallel doctrines,
film music resonates, and in its resonance its "appropriateness"
is multiplied. Ralph Vaughan Williams:

> You must not be horrified, if you find that a passage which you
> intended to portray the villain's mad revenge has been used by the
> musical director to illustrate the cats being driven out of the dairy.
> The truth is, that within limits, any music can be made to fit any
> situation.[90]

Around the same time as Vaughan Williams's statement,
Deems Taylor wrote the following of Walt Disney's *Fantasia*, on
which Taylor collaborated:

> The interpretations of the music in *Fantasia* are not the ordinarily
> accepted ones. The divergence from tradition is deliberate. Music
> is the most fluid of all the arts; and like any fluid, music, even
> program music, assumes the shape of its container. Granted that

the container [or] program is not too grossly inappropriate, a given piece of music may fit two or three other stories just as well as those originally assigned to it.[91]

This notion of fluids and containers is a striking one. Though the publication is in part promotional, and Taylor would be expected to defend his own departures, the film, as well as its sequel sixty years later, largely confirms the accuracy of his sentiments.

John Cage tells a story of eating lunch in a restaurant. He sees through the window a pond with swimmers. "Inside the restaurant was a jukebox. Somebody put a dime in. I noticed that the music that came out accompanied the swimmers, though they didn't hear it."[92] As with containers and accidentally synchronized swimmers, classical music is transformed in its film settings, where it can work in wonderful ways. Indeterminate confusions may frustrate an absolutist musical elite, but it opens up the music and can provide the layman with an accessible and valid point of entry.

Twentieth-century aesthetics, in film and around it, are full of investigations into randomness and what it portends.[93] In light of these we see that not only Cage's random musics, but music in general, in whatever setting, becomes sensical. "No matter what we do, it ends by being melodic."[94]

NOTES

1. Quoted in Liszt, 1855, 128. Emphasis added.
2. Liszt, 1855, 124.
3. Staiger, 1992, 24–34.
4. In Gorbman, 1987, 15–16, 20–26.
5. See Staiger, 1992, 34–48.
6. For a helpful discussion on "program" (pretext, context) in another setting, see Plett, 1991, which provides a set of tools and terms in the area of literary quotation. Plett considers the quality (surface structure giving way to deep structure), distribution (textual placement, whether temporal or spatial), frequency, interference (alienating incongruity) and marking (explicit isolation) of quotations. His discussion of perceptual modes and stages is also analogous to the concepts in ques-

tion in my own study. I am indebted to Donna Poulton for introducing me to Plett's valuable work.

7. Atkins, 1983, 26.

8. Irvin Bazelon raises an idiomatic concern as he considers what he feels to be the unequal partnership between the concert piece and the film in which it appears. "With this conjugal arrangement, the piece itself loses importance: only the music's ability to convey a mood or an association has any validity. The result is that distinct, individual pieces become pastiches, 'Bachlike or Chopinesque,' with distinctions simply disappearing." Here Bazelon suggests that idiom only has meaning *through* its individual expressions. Bazelon, 1975, 134–35.

9. Thomas, 1979, 204.

10. In Walker, 1974, 145.

11. Another noted example of this kind of effect occurs in Laurence Olivier's conflating version of *Henry V* (1944).

12. Sadie, Stanley, from the program notes for the London *L'Oiseau-Lyre* recording. 1985, 414 316–12 OH3, p. 22.

13. Still, that further articulation can still be justified and valuable. See following section on phenomenology.

14. Brown, 1994, 9.

15. Ibid., 82.

16. For instance, Psalm 23 is used in The Kordas' *Rembrandt* (1937), *How Green Was My Valley* (1941), even Luis Buñuel's *The Adventures of Robinson Crusoe* (1953).

17. *Ich ruf zu dir, Herr Jesu Christ*, BWV 639.

18. Cf. *The Black Cat* (Edgar G. Ulmer, 1934).

19. Scorsese's use of Bach is clearly an homage to the earlier film, as well as an effective device to import wholesale its various themes and associations. Note also the use of the same piece at the conclusion of George Lucas's *THX 1138* (1971).

20. Bergman frequently quotes the legendarily single-minded Bach, who means devotion regardless of musical form and context, and who stands in contrast to the author's modern(ist) fragmentation and alienation. See Bergman, 1988, 43, 281–82. Two striking uses among many are in *Persona* (1966), *Cries and Whispers* (1973). For the superlative work-specific use of Bach see Straub/Huillet's *The Chronicle of Anna Magdalena Bach* (1968).

21. Cf. the last moment of order before the descent into the absurd in Martin Scorsese's *After Hours* (1986), or an easy irony achieved amidst the urban squalor of *Seven* (1995).

22. Cf. musical compilations like *Opera Goes to the Movies*, etc.

23. See Westermeyer, 1985, 291–94.

24. *Di Provenza il mar, il suol*, from *La Traviata*, act 2, scene 1.

25. In Visconti's *La Terra Trema* (1947), a group of drunken and unemployed barflies dance through the streets of a backward Sicilian village, while one of their number plays Chopin's E major *Etude* (opus 10) on a harmonica.

26. See and hear also the use of very specific Wagner compositions in Claude Chabrol's *Les Cousins* (1959). Attentive viewers can ascertain not only character relationships, but the conclusion of the story from identifying and connecting the cues. Substantial significations are not limited to the international art cinema, or to the activities of its *auteurs*. In MGM's *The Picture of Dorian Gray* (1945) Gray has deflowered a young singer and driven her to despair. After hearing of her suicide he attends a performance of Mozart's *Don Giovanni*. Soon after he casually whistles the tune from the "seduction duet" between Don Giovanni and Zerlina. Dorian's virtuous painter friend counters by playing on the piano a simple song associated with the dead girl. Here, through classical quotation, is an indication of Dorian's character and motivation, as well as a foreshadowing of his end. In the film we have, as in Wilde's book and Mozart/Da Ponte's opera, a cruelly carefree character who misses the foreboding in the apparently bright tones that surround him. For another significant, intentional use of this same duet, see Gabriel Axel's adaptation of Isak Dinesen's *Babette's Feast* (1986).

27. Atkins lists under "Concert ('Classical' or 'Serious') Music" the following: large orchestral works, chamber music, virtuoso solo instrumental works, choral music, opera, ballet, art songs and lieder. (1983, 26.) She leaves it at that, but in fact each category has its own specific periods, its received culture and celebrated proponents, its own associations and repercussions, all of which substantially alter the contexts (cinematic, in this case) in which they occur. One might profitably trace the cinematic appropriations and significations in each of these very specific musical areas. Of course it is also true that this work is not always done, and that there can be elitist implications to opus-level identifications. (Cf. Stefani, 1987.) The following sections investigate these implications, and some alternatives.

28. Berg, 1976, 80, 124–25.

29. Brown, 1988, 209, note 26; Last, personal communication, 1995.

30. See chapter one.

31. Brown, 1994, 65.

32. Quoted in Flinn, 1992, 37. Keller (1946–47, *Sight and Sound*, volume 15, number 60, 26) discusses the distracting potential of familiarity, and the related difficulties of self-satisfied snobbery in the listener who can identify the cue.

33. See James, 1989, 75.

34. Stefani, 1987, 15.

35. Raksin, 1943, 253.

36. Bush (1989, 147) discusses the use of Heinz Roemheld's score to *The Black Cat* (1934) in the first series of Flash Gordon serials, the many resurrections of Franz Waxman's *Bride of Frankenstein* (1935) score in subsequent horrors, and the delight of horror afficionados in recognizing the echoes.

37. Personal communication, September 1994.

38. This quartet also appears, and more clearly, in Godard's *Two or Three Things I Know About Her* (1966). Similarly, I erected a huge interpretive elaboration around Pasolini's use of later Beethoven in *Oedipus Re* (1967), only to find that it was in fact a particularly dissonant quartet by Mozart, (K465). An alternative elaboration replaced my first one, but the interpretive ice upon which I stood was clearly very thin.

39. For some critical overreaching, see Christopher Palmer on *2001: A Space Odyssey* (1968), quoted in Larson, 1985, 351. An interesting refutation of this interpretation is found in ibid., 274, 311–12, 349–51.

40. See Nordern, 1988, 10, 17–45.

41. Pudovkin, 1948, 158.

42. Or perhaps not: one of the episodes in the symphonic poem's last movement is entitled "The Ship Goes to Pieces on a Rock Surmounted by a Bronze Warrior (Shipwreck)."

43. Keller, 1952, *Music Review*, XIII, 222–24.

44. Such confusions point to phenomenological possibilities; see brief discussion on bracketing to follow. With regard to semicoherent/overabundant intertextual collisions, consider also the work-specific implications of Wagner in Chaplin's *The Great Dictator* (1940).

45. Quoted in Lewis, Peter, 1994, 5.

46. *Oxford English Dictionary*, 1961. Claudia Gorbman (plenary session, *Screen* conference, Glasgow, July 6, 1995) also discusses the resistance to and the validity of this notion of creative reception.

47. Andrew, 1978, 630–31.

48. On bracketing see Husserl, 1962, 96–101.

49. After the temporary eclipse of phenomenological film theorists like André Bazin and V. F. Perkins.

50. Andrew, 1978, 632.

51. For a clear retrospective summary of this shift see Leo Braudy and Marshall Cohen's introduction to the fourth edition of their anthology, revised from early editions coedited by Gerald Mast, Braudy and Cohen, 1992, x.

52. See Christian Metz's blending of Lacanian psychoanalysis and semiotics with the idea of a more active viewing subject in Metz, 1982.

53. Sobchack, 1992, xiii–xix.

54. Ibid., 298.

55. Ibid., 299.

56. Andrew, 1983, 189.

57. Ibid., 190.

58. See Taylor and Christie, 1988, 3–10.

59. Shumyatsky's "The Film *Bezhin Meadow*" at least would seem to validate his reputation as a sinister bureaucrat. Op. cit. 378–81. See also Eisenstein, 1968, 28 for a chilling account of things to come.

60. It is perilous to cite any single statement of Eisenstein's, as his investigations were so broad and his theory so constantly developing that each citation is sure to be quite contradicted by another. Still, there were constants, and each period can be characterized by certain preoccupations that remain valid within that period. With that in mind, one proceeds, though cautiously.

61. From Taylor and Christie translation, 1988, 87. Emphasis in original. Eisenstein refers to the theater, but the issues remain relevant to film, which would soon become his focus.

62. Eisenstein, 1942, 32. Emphasis added.

63. Pudovkin, 1948, 6. Emphasis added. Of course it was this very reflection, doubt and criticism, and the "errors" they generated, that brought Stalin into the montage mix. Directors were eventually forced in the same ways they thought to force their audiences.

64. Ibid., 48. Emphasis added.

65. Cf. *The Mechanics of the Brain* (1925), Pudovkin's first film which dealt with the "progress in knowledge of conditioned reflexes attained by workers in Professor Pavlov's laboratory." Ibid., 126–27.

66. Godard, 1972, 239. Emphasis added.

67. Buñuel, 1971, 75.

68. Stefani, 1987, 12–13. Emphasis added.

69. Nattiez, 1990, 47. As previously discussed, see also Chion, 1994, 25–34.

70. Eisenstein, 1968, 41. Emphasis in original.

71. Wenders, 1991, 86–87.

72. Wenders, 1989, viii.

73. Pudovkin, and early Eisenstein, may also have been hindered by a reductive notion of single meanings and one-to-one correspondence between sign and signification. Music, and especially source music's fecundity in producing meaning is an effective counter to such underdeterminations.

74. Taylor and Christie, 1988, 93. The multivalence of Vertovian cinema (as experienced; Vertov's polemical writings could be as prescrip-

tive as those of his contemporaries), like the musical concepts in the present discussion, counter most manipulative mandates in film. The countering applies not only to Pudovkin/Eisenstein, but also to the guiding of audiences central to and inherent in Hollywood's Industrial Mode of Representation.

75. Forster, E. M., 1944, "From the audience," in *National gallery concerts, 10th October, 1939–10th October, 1944,* London, printed for the trustees.

76. Meyer, 1956, 264.

77. Stefani, 1987, 13. Film music may not reflect any rational semiotic system, but it can still communicate generally, through codes that attentive film listeners come to recognize, and which inattentive listeners may still sense. So it is that accordions can take us to France, electronic music, in *Forbidden Planet* and elsewhere, effectively denote outer space, while discord, from *Wozzeck* on, suggests madness. Note, however, that the very constraining conventionality of these codes suggests the value of the more open, even confounding model being discussed here. See Plett on "stagnation," in Plett, 1991, 16.

78. In Cage and Tudor, 1959, side 1.

79. Barthes, 1974, 4.

80. In Cage and Tudor, op. cit.

81. I will not take the time here to thoroughly explore synaesthesia (Joyce representing a synaesthetic ideal for Eisenstein), but I should note that there are negative elements to things I am putting in a positive light. Douglas Kahn points out that the sonic elements of synaesthesia have been habitually reduced to elements of human agency (speech and music), and that this reduction of sound possibilities is symptomatic of a general constraint on the kind of phenomenological and writerly freedom that I am here presenting, in a somewhat idealized form. Indeed, my emphasis on music could well be seen as being exemplary of this sonic subjugation. (See Kahn's "Introduction: Histories of Sound Once Removed" in Kahn and Whitehead, 1992, 1–29, especially 14–17.) However, having acknowledged this potential oversight, I still take the concentration on musical issues to be completely valid.

82. Eisenstein, 1949, 66.

83. Andrew, 1976, 42–43.

84. Cf. Andrew, 1978, 1984.

85. Andrew, 1976, 42–75.

86. See Cage, 1961, 35–40. Of course from a certain perspective relinquishment was not complete. Though random operations were part of Cage's performances, his careful control of the score/script insured some substantial determination.

87. Altman, 1987, 2, 4.

88. Ibid., 3. This state insures not only an opening for more open apprehension, but also the continuation of the kind of misperceptions and contradictions already discussed in connection with Soviet montage experiments, and their affects—or not—on audiences.

89. Stefani, 1987, esp. 9–10.

90. Quoted in Huntley, 1947, 179. Michel Chion recommends an exercise called "forced marriage," where a film sequence is submitted to several diverse musical settings. He reports that when this is done there is an abundance of different correspondences, all according to the listener's point of view, or point of audition. Chion, 1994, 188–89.

91. Taylor, 1940, 16. See Brown, 1988, 166–67 on the transmutability of music in terms of meaning and feeling. Also ibid., 203 on Jean Cocteau's cue shifting "accidental synchronism," and 209, note 23, on the same in the work of Bernard Herrmann. The opposite effect can also take place, where the film becomes the fluid and the music contains it. In *Vivre sa Vie* (1962) Godard used only the first measures of only two of the eleven variations on a theme composed by Michel Legrand. Uncharacteristic of the usual film composer attitude, Legrand was approving. "(Godard) repeated it throughout the whole film. It's a great idea, and it works very, very well." Quoted in Brown, 1994, 189.

92. Cage, 1959, side 1. Keller provides a salutary alternative view. "In *Gone With the Wind* . . . [Max] Steiner drenches the sound track in a rather indiscriminate fashion; in places the music has somewhat less relation to the visual than the band's music at Lyon's Corner House has to your table talk." Keller, 1946–48, 16, no. 64, 169.

93. There are numerous examples. Dada advocated the breaking of all conventional connections. Luis Buñuel discusses the automatic writing that led to *Un Chien Andalou*, as well as the provocative alternating of "Argentinian tangos with *Tristan und Isolde*" at its Paris premiere. Buñuel, 1983, 104, 106. Surrealist André Breton randomly entered and exited Paris cinemas to enjoy the indeterminate juxtapositions that resulted. Jean Cocteau's "accidental synchronism" showed how effective a cue composed for one sequence could be when used in the "wrong" one. See Brown, 1994, 71–74.

94. Cage, 1959, side 1.

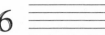

6

Summary, Conclusions, and Implications

To END THIS STUDY I will briefly summarize some of its main points, as well as suggest some of their broader, extracinematic significance.

JUSTIFICATION FOR FILM MUSIC, AND FOR FILM-MUSICAL QUOTATION

Roy Prendergast says that the "problem" with 1940s Hollywood films dealing with concert artists was that they used "what was essentially concert music. In order to bring some of the famous concert works in line with the dramatic needs of the story, great works of musical art had to be severely cut."[1] We have seen how certain music critics had deep reasons for resisting film's free use of the concert repertory. For them cutting and quoting were emblematic of and even contributors to a very serious, quite general social malaise. There was justification in this view, and the ubiquity of the culture industry is now, if anything, more marked than it was then. Yet, as we have also seen, when taken to extremes this alarmist attitude can lead to excessive compartmentalization and mutual exclusivity. What applies to quotation, to concert music used in film, can also apply to any intertextual exchange; adaptation from one context to another may cause discomfort, and yet it may be this very discomfort that generates new light and insight.

Adaptation is not only related to a specific work; it can also involve a more general phenomenon, or the conditions that gave rise to it. Changes in circumstance, the passage of time, new knowledge, and broader perspectives can all call for an adaptation of previously resistant attitudes.

If this is true then prescription and proscription might give way to observation and explication, with conditions not so much condemned or defended, as explained and understood. This shift allows us to adapt our way out of ossified attitudes toward, among other things, musical quotation in film.

Thus we would see that adjunctive, even subservient music has a valid history and a viable place.

> Film music takes second place to the story, the cast, the visuals of the medium, but that need not bother us. Bach's music was secondary to the celebration of the Holy Mass, Mozart's to the Court social functions and Rossini's to the splendour of the stage and the singing. Great music can still emerge in competition with other forms of artistic expression; film music can do just this.[2]

Here are both apology and defiance, but while straining to justify film music, Huntley also finds honorable precedent for extramusical dependence.

We have seen how the use of classical music in film creates a musicological tension. In most tonal classical music, formal architecture requires the playing of the complete work, as each part is inextricably bound up with the rest.[3] Considering this architecture, fragmentation means ruination, and so later film music practice (where musical cuts are taken for granted) is musically ruinous.

For the political avant-garde, however, not to mention musical archeologists, ruins are also instructive, and a true reflection of some historical/theoretical reality. To confound musicological expectations is potentially a way to uncover apparatuses. To disturb the integrity of a composition is also to upset the security of its exalted status. It is possible that when mystique is removed, knowledge follows, perhaps even another, broader exaltation.

Film music's gleeful disregard for preexisting texts has understandably caused alarm, but that is not the only possible response. "If you happen to have a scenic moving in one atmosphere lasting about six minutes and you choose a [musical] selection which only lasts five minutes do not hesitate in cutting the weakest parts of your scenic picture to suit the length of the music. . . ."[4] Rapée's guides were lightning rods of musical opprobrium, but as this quotation points out, his scissors could cut both ways. Perhaps on the one hand he is cavalier, but on the other? Adaptability? Praxis? Music as really experienced?

What has always been required of film composers is flexibility. The same might be enjoined by the film music listener, especially if he or she leans to the music side of the equation. Leslie Perkoff wrote the following in 1937.

> Music in its most profound use in the cinema must be in its role as an integral part of the cinematic scheme, in creating atmosphere and in developing emotional content. The success of this depends chiefly on the composer's willingness and initiative to throw overboard many of his orthodox methods of composition in the same way that the novelist-turned-scenarist might have to give up lengthy polemics and descriptive embellishments for the economic tempo of film.[5]

Even the *New Grove Dictionary* makes some allowance for a more flexible approach. Christopher Palmer notes that André Previn left Tchaikovsky's music practically unaltered in Ken Russell's *The Music Lovers* (1970). While this has always been the preferred course, Palmer also refers positively to Dmitri Tiomkin's freely altered and adapted score for the Russian film *Tchaikovsky* (1971). "Because of the kinship between [Tiomkin's] own musical language and Tchaikovsky's there is little stylistic disparity, and most of the paraphrases are appropriate for their dramatic contexts."[6]

Once again, I am not rejecting isolationist musical critiques of film music. But when Hans Keller allows that there is "definite if limited scope for the filming of unfilmic music," he is speaking as a film sympathizer whose allegiance is finally musical.[7] For the musician fidelity, and not collaboration, has been the only admissible treatment.[8]

Thus it is that Keller feels, for instance, that Carol Reed's *The Man Between* (1953)

> misuses an excellent recording . . . of a Salome . . . excerpt . . . for the purpose of prolonging the most vulgar kind of dramatic tension: the spectator is invited, *not to listen to the music*, but to be titillated by this dramatic suspension and to wait impatiently for the dramatic solution.[9]

But the fact is that the spectator does not accept the invitation so that he or she can merely to listen to the music. The spectator comes for the film; even the informed and musically erudite film fan is interested in a cinematic ensemble of elements, and not just the music.

Music critics of a certain period vigorously criticize film music, and for many good reasons. Hans Keller bemoans alienated listening states, their institutional proliferation and codification, and the distraction and "unbeauty" they imply. He fiercely criticizes the bad and just as fiercely defends the worthy individual film composer, stating finally that the music must be defended, and that mere functional use is offensive.[10]

Adorno decried fashion, thieving, rootless eclecticism, and found in these things emblems of twentieth-century alienation, insincerity, and artlessness. Here he was describing Stravinsky's "Magpie" period, condemning an acknowledged genius whose genius made his transgressions all the more egregious.[11] But Stravinsky's pastiches were at least confined to musical territory. Elsewhere popular music (for example, the Brill Building sound), and film music too were so hopelessly entangled in the deplorable conditions, and so without the talents and traditions that might have pulled them out, that they were pretty well beyond hope.

Edward Said reaffirms these regressions in modern contexts. Few amateur musicians remain, noise pollution dominates, mechanical reproduction creates a paradoxically obliterating musical ubiquity.[12] Said discusses the spectacle of the concert hall, and a transformation that has obtained in relation to it. "What competes with [concerts] is not the amateur's experience but other public displays of specialized skill (sports, circus, dance contests) that, at its worst and most vulgar, the concert may attempt to match."[13]

This shift in binaries is precisely what Wilfred Mellers so mourns. The professional-amateur axis becomes one of the professional and the professional transposed, while the humble, the human, is shut out. For Mellers, for all, modern music has cut out the amateur, and to pursue the implications etymologically, has eliminated love from the equation.[14]

Here is the oxymoron of industrial art making, the "regression to that pre-industrial stage of composition which, in Hollywood, is regarded as the basis of expertise."[15]

Grantable, and granted. But consider Robin Wood's—note, a *film* critic—insightful description of Stravinsky's *L'Histoire du Soldat*.

> Stravinsky uses the tango, the waltz, the march and ragtime, subjecting them to processes of extreme contrapuntal ingenuity and juxtaposing them without any hint of condescension and not at all in the spirit of parody; if he reduces these forms to basic clichés, it is not to mock the clichés but to validate them by investing them with his own intellectual and physical vitality.[16]

There is undoubtedly a great deal that is superficial and substandard in the age of sampling and generally rampant intertextuality. But surely it is evident, even amidst such proliferation, or even because of it, that Stravinsky can no longer be considered an exception that proves the rule. Eclecticism need not be rootless, and pastiche, or even parody, can both emerge out of and generate vitality.

In the same way Hollywood composition, and film scoring generally, are not just matters of filming unfilmic music, nor of the adaptation or utilization of substandard compositions. In terms of music in film it is transposition that is required; film and music are two different arts, their terminologies and fundamental principles distinct—counterpoint analogies notwithstanding. What applies to music in isolation is not necessarily the case when it occurs in film.

Ernest Newman describes the challenge.

> In a symphony or a fugue you have to consider nothing but the nature of absolute music; in the drama, you have to worry about no problems except those that lie in the nature of the drama. But as soon as you begin to work in a form that is a blend of the two, each of them wants to pull the other along its own road, and a compromise has to be arrived at.[17]

For an isolationist the problem is insurmountable, but a little flexibility, at points of production or reception, can provide a solution.

> We make allowances; we give up a little purely aesthetic pleasure in consideration of getting a great deal of another kind of pleasure—that of seeing a bigger picture of a more real life put on the

canvas. If we can only get the larger human quality . . . by giving up a little of the aesthetic gratification that comes from perfect form—well, being reasonable creatures, there are times when we will cheerfully accept the situation and make the compromise.[18]

Newman's compromise seems easy enough with regard to specific instances of use and response, but its portent is greater than it may at first appear. Increased openness to the advantages of medium hybridization imperils hierarchies of film narration and film expression—story above all, with picture and dialogue responsible for clear communication, hierarchies of high and low, and the rigid borders of disciplinary decorum and medium specificity.

Adorno observes that after Beethoven music left the social realm and became completely aesthetic.[19] This probably explains his defense of Schoenberg and a general tone of disappointment and isolationism.[20] But is that all there is? In response to Adorno we might offer Alan Merriam's oft-cited definition of ethnomusicology as "the study of music in culture."[21] After Adorno's terminal judgments came folk, rock, and for classical music—Stravinsky, and film—a new kind of slippage, ambiguity, flexibility. To a degree, when classical music suddenly appears in a film, the bets are off. As Martin Marks suggests, "the primary material of film music, both for the audience and the researcher, is not a recording or a score, but the film itself."[22]

Leonard Bernstein points out that "when . . . expectations are violated, you've got a variation. The violation is the variation."[23] Variation is essential to music, and if recontextualization in one sense is vulgar, in another it is fundamentally musical, a variation that can be, even should be, invigorating. Music, in ambiguous settings, might just become poetry. "All musical transformations lead to metaphorical results."[24] Or, if not always poetry—some appropriations *are* vulgar or inept—then certainly sociology, and history, and even humanity.

This fact has not always been acknowledged in film music discourse. Kurt London calls "the strong combination of picture with sound . . . a revolutionary novelty both in musical theory and in sound technique."[25] This is simply not true. There is not enough of the broad view in film music criticism, and much of it is plain wrongheaded. Film music uses have ample precedent, and if needed, justification in a great number of contexts.

MULTIVALENT MONTAGE

It is between pure parallelism and strict "counterpoint," between empathy and opposition that we find the great majority of picture-music equations, where we find multiplicity and multivalence. This notion jeopardizes a standard film music truism: "it is a peculiarity of film music that if it isn't just right, it can be very wrong."[26] "Wrong" could still be convincingly argued, but one could well add that the "right" is often wrong too. As I have argued, standard geometries are not sufficiently inclusive.

George Antheil wrote in 1938 about a better awareness and use of both alternatives.

> This does not mean that music must only play *with* a picture; it can also play against it; in fact I believe that very often indeed it should play against it. But this "against" should be a definite and intended contrast, heightening the drama and the effect of the picture instead of merely drawing attention to the queer non-matching music.[27]

Siegfried Kracauer felt similarly, that counterpoint must maintain contact with the narrative, that chaotic relations are pointless.[28] But Kracauer also reminisces about a certain drunken pianist in silent days whose accompaniments would wander from the apparent business at hand.

> The lack of relation between the musical themes and the action they were supposed to sustain seemed very delightful indeed to me, for it made me see the story in a new and unexpected light or, more important, challenged me to lose myself in an uncharted wilderness opened up by allusive shots.[29]

Kracauer here expresses some very contemporary-sounding sentiments, which implicitly suggest how timid our thinking has been. Walter Murch states the case more directly.

> In continuing to say that we "see" a film or a television program, we persist in ignoring how the soundtrack has modified perception.

At best, some people are content with an additive model, according to which witnessing an audiovisual spectacle basically consists of seeing images plus hearing sounds.[30]

Not only can music in film be much more, it usually already is. "The juxtaposition of the musical continuity with the spatial discontinuity of the editing creates a kind of extranarrative counterpoint that remains one of the largely untapped possibilities of the cinematic art."[31]

The terms "multivalent" and "indeterminate" appropriately suggest how tenuous and subjective musical connections and meanings can be. Classical intellectual montage posits oppositions and proclaims equivalencies—strutting peacocks and Alexander Kerensky, strumming balalaikas, and noodling Mensheviks—all of which result in social and cinematic syntheses. Alternatively, multivalent montage produces as many questions as answers. Where classical montage takes material fragmentation—the film material itself, as well as the social constructs it is rendering—and unites it in a new way, multivalent montage retains its cubist aspect, the differing and sometimes distorted perspectives characteristic of modernism and of modern life. It suggests possibilities of approaching a text, each of which will bring the viewer to a slightly, or even vastly different, place.[32]

Umberto Eco notes that some works are so packed that they are "open to a continuous generation of internal relations which the consumer must uncover and select in the act of perceiving the totality of incoming stimuli."[33] We find in most things not a single pattern, but a bunch of complex relations. As with packed works, so much more with packed traditions; David Bordwell has questioned the use of the musical analogy, but finally finds value in its very partialness, its inadequacy: it is not that it is, but that it is *like*.

Kracauer continues:

Precisely by disregarding the images on the screen, the old pianist caused them to yield many a secret. Yet his unawareness of their presence did not preclude improbable parallels: once in a while his music conformed to the dramatic events with an accuracy which struck me all the more as miraculous since it was entirely unintended. . . . And these random coincidences, along with the stimulating effects of the normal discrepancies, gave me the impression that there existed after all a relationship, however elusive, between the drunken pianist's soliloquies and the dramas before my eyes—a relationship which I considered perfect because of its accidental nature and its indeterminacy. I never heard a more fitting accompaniment.[34]

Gino Stefani lists fourteen possible ways for his five semiotic code levels to interact, to be heard. He emphasizes the importance of considering music-analytic, psychological, and sociological hearings. In stating that "semiotics of music is the discipline whose object is musical competence as we have defined it," he is implying that not meaning, or a way of meaning, but all those things multiplied are the proper objects of the discipline.[35]

As already noted, Rick Altman has said that "meaning . . . is never something that words or texts have, but always something that is *made* in a four-party meaning-situation. An *author* . . . circulates a *text* . . . to an *audience* . . . whose perception is partly dependent on the *interpretive community* to which its members belong."[36]

Interpretive communities can present a certain homogeneity, an inclination to dominant responses. Indeed, this is the source idea of, for instance, the Frankfurt School pessimism (Adorno et al.) that we have also considered. But I contend that communities are not inherently thus, and that it is precisely attention to the cracks and variables enumerated here that reveals the fact. Essentially, the community from which an individual reader comes will not be monolithic, just as that reader can never be an unconflicted, predictably reacting constant.

Altman discusses a first level of language and communication which operates with respect to the generator's intent, along with the many factors and determinants which inflect and deflect it. A second level, where what was formerly characterized as the message goes out to its receivers, increases geometrically.[37]

Milton Babbitt maintains that music is the same. Common musical practice (tonality) was just one set of rational choices out of an infinite domain of possibilities. His demanding music explores roads not taken, and draws as much upon mathematics as music, upon the permutations and possibilities of the form. The five points of Gino Stefani's "Model of Musical Competence" likewise allows for numerous permutations and, given the diversity of potential participants, quite vast and exciting possibility.[38] So it is with conventional montage geometries. Bordwell notes that the musical analogy was first used in a simple attempt to justify the medium, and then that Eisenstein's concept of the principle became decidedly, and often problematically, "roomy."[39] He points out the very distinct and ultimately incompatible ways that the analogy has been used.[40]

These things are all true. Musical analogies are inexact, but much of their power comes from the gaps and spaces; classical music in film explores these same infinities. Its presence and function is analogous to phenomenology, to cubist montage, to the multiple ways that multiple people deal with multiple works.

THE FIGURATIVE IMPLICATIONS OF *MUSICAL* COUNTERPOINT

One motivation for my revising of the counterpoint analogy is that I feel that much of prevailing film discourse continues to reflect the preinterpreted juxtapositions of classic intellectual montage, and the insufficiently nuanced oppositions of early montage theory. Range of reference is limited, as are the conclusions drawn. The result is that distortion, a lack of understanding, even of civility are still evident in theoretical discussions and uses of counterpoint.

> Mary Ann Doane has stressed the importance of synchronous sound as a means by which classical film staves off [the] threat [of opening up the image to its multiple meanings]; in routine production procedure, the editor 'marries' the sound track to the image track in order to domesticate sound's potentially disruptive effects.[41]

Doane and Flinn use loaded words to effectively describe the frequent domestication of sound in film. But by assuming oppressions in marrying and domesticity, not to mention film sound, they are dramatically underestimating the real complexity and possible progressiveness of these contexts.[42]

Royal Brown makes a similarly valuable point, with similar overemphasis.

> For if, on the one level, the cultural mythification via the merger of the music and visuals into the narrative can blind and deafen the viewer/listener to the existence of the filmic images as such within history while creating a pseudohistory with which the viewer/listener is encouraged to identify, the film/music interaction can . . . aesthetically create the presence of a broader, noncultural mythology that roundly negates the entire patriarchal belief in a scientific empiricism that holds physical space, chronological/linear time, and history/causality as absolute truths.[43]

By assuming "entire patriarchal beliefs" Brown is invoking the absolutes he condemns, and in doing so he diminishes his argument. "Audiovisual dissonance is merely the inverse of convention, and thus pays homage to it, imprisoning us in a binary logic that has only remotely to do with how cinema works."[44]

Must all be withering parallelism or revolutionary opposition? Staunch advocacy, as well as reading against the grain, are extremely important, but both have their dangers. Stuart Hall warns against the pendulum swing from naive assumptions of "necessary correspondence" to the equally totalizing "necessarily no correspondence," reminding us that one isn't any more helpful than the other, even if it is more fashionable.[45] Reading against the grain, with respect to film sound or family relations, should presuppose an awareness of the generating grain, as well as all the unexpected surfaces and depths that we don't see.

My point is that there is much more to film music, and to meaning in general, than simply parallelism and perpendicularity. If the former is congruent, and the latter at a ninety-degree angle to that congruent line, then musical counterpoint shifts from concord to opposition and back again, and covers the entire intervening space as well. If we use musical counterpoint as a figure for the way sound and music function in film, we must consider this in-between territory. Meaning in music is multifarious and difficult to pin down. This being the case, simple parallels and oppositions become nearly impossible, and not even particularly desirable.

Parallel and perpendicular, tonal concord and counterpoint

have not always been so polar. R. O. Morris speaks of rhythmic independence and tonal fluidity in sixteenth-century harmonic practice. To illustrate he uses the metaphor of several people, each standing for a melodic line, walking abreast; pace and distance may vary, but they are still out together. Wilfrid Mellers summarizes.

> Concord is the basis of 16th century harmony, discord is a momentary disturbance before the concord's repose; we can never consider any discord in isolation but only in relation to the context which it appears in, for it is not a self-contained entity but part of the progressive evolution of a number of equally important lines.[46]

Musical counterpoint does not oppose without coming together. Fugue is the superlatively contrapuntal musical form, in which an idea is followed by a counter-idea, the subject by counter-subjects. This terminology is most montagelike, and indeed classic montage principles would seem to be inscribed within fugal structure, at least as stated here.[47] But there are alternative views. And counterpoint in its traditional tonal setting is full of consonance.[48] Statements are followed by elaborations, but musical themes are returned to again and again, as without them the structure breaks down. Interestingly the tonal, affirmative parts of counterpoint are part of film, and classical film theory as well. We just do not hear as much about them. Eisenstein, writing well after the Statement, expressed his admiration for the "sound and sight consonance" in Disney's "wonderful" *Snow White*.[49] In addition to montage opposition, as well as the nonsynchronization of sound and image, Eisenstein would later find substantial spaces for concord, and even parallelism.[50]

Given some of Eisenstein's earlier polemical excesses, it seems surprising to hear him praise musical equivalencies. Equivalency and textual unity are not only or always repressive measures, however, and in fact the unity that informs the present study draws on the almost Blakeian transcendence of later Eisenstein. His many disappointments leaving him not just battered, but extremely philosophical, he seems to come in the end to a surprising and simple conclusion. No matter how far afield one's points of reference, everything is, in the end, connected.

Music, especially contrapuntal music, is not really reducible to

simple montage equations. It is not only that excessive correspondence between image and music ignores "undertones of
meaning"; the same is true when we excessively assume, in
"counterpoint," uncorrespondence.[51] "Too often homology
spells tautology, and contrast contradiction."[52]

The Twentieth/Twenty-first-Century Program

Edward Said:

> the study of music can be more, and not less, interesting if we
> situate music as taking place, so to speak, in a social and cultural
> setting. Another way of putting this is to say that the roles played
> by music in Western society are extraordinarily varied, and far
> exceed the antiseptic, cloistered, academic, professional aloofness
> it seems to have been accorded.[53]

The program analogy I have urged is linked to my models of
multivalent meaning and to the idea that greater inclusiveness
will illuminate our film-musical experience. In fact, the idea applies to culture and criticism in general; instead of Liszt's "correct interpretation" we have simultaneity and multiplicity,
referentiality, recontextualization, and recognition.

Classical music in film takes the tonality of the post-Romantic
film score—an effaced apparatus within an ideologically repressive apparatus—and disturbs it, jolts and awakens us by bringing
in the modernisms and postmodernisms of the twentieth and
twenty-first century. All this happens not in the music itself, but
in its context, where it appears, and what we make of that appearance. The result is a kind of movie version of Stravinskian pastiche, which lies in between the dead end of atonality
(Schoenberg as defended by Adorno), and the disavowal of a
Hollywood business-as-usual attitude. The possibility is of simultaneous challenge, social engagement, and beauty.[54]

Poetic power comes from incongruity, the most pregnant juxtapositions sometimes being the least expected ones. Consider
Stravinsky's quotation of Pergolesi in *Pulcinella*, the stringless
setting of the Latin text in the *Symphony of Psalms*.[55] Through
quotation and recontextualization composers, continents, whole

centuries are conflated, contrasted, renewed, and refreshed. And if we will, and if we pay attention and explicitly bring the making of meaning into the mix, Max Steiner's retreaded Romanticism, as well as most any quotation, can be as resonant as any of these more valorized forms of neoclassicism.

As we have seen throughout this study, classical quotations tend to outstrip the usual workaday functions of film music, leading to all kinds of unsuspected results. Thus, where in Aaron Copland's statement that "[film] music can be used to underline or create psychological refinements—the unspoken thoughts of a character or the unseen implications of a situation," classical music fulfils this function by taking individual, individualistic psychology and extending their "unseen implications," contextualizing them socially and historically.[56] As a result quotation does not celebrate unique sensibilities, with the resulting shadows of reaction or misapprehension, but the possibility of more rational, generalizable applications.[57] High romantic or high modernist impulses are seen in relief, reduced to human dimension, and they often become more powerful as a result.

Michel Chion says that the score communicates with all the times and spaces of a film, covering over gaps and smoothing rough edges.[58] Classical music in film, instead of communicating solely with the other cinematic elements, brings and binds vast portions of history, as well as the art and thought and life associated with them. The difference is that despite the fact, or perhaps because of the way that quotation has been so disturbing, the covering or smoothing is less effective, or may hardly work at all. And, perhaps paradoxically, the communication is greater as a result.

In summary, a program analogy applies to the use and understanding of source music in film, and to numerous other cultural subjects as well. Music and text, or music and some extramusical idea or association are always related, directly or by implication; in this sense, all music has always been programmatic. Opera only made this relation explicit, and the program composers only sought to tie it down. Roger Scruton says that titles in program music, such as "*Traumerei*/Dreaming," and "Wedding Day at Troldhaugen," only express emotion, rather than evoke a subject. But just as program was partly devised to better communicate with lay listeners, so it is the listener that makes and completes the program. Evocation takes place, and each listener's program is bound to be different.

Eisenstein describes Prokofiev conducting a film cue.

His lanky figure hidden to the waist by the sweeping movements of the musician's bows seemed to be swaying in the midst of rippling corn. He leaned over towards the musicians, listening intently to the interplay of the various instruments' motifs. *En passant*, he whispered to me, pointing first to one of the musicians and then to another, commenting: "That one is playing the light flickering across the waves . . . that one the billowing of the waves . . . that one the wide expanses of the ocean . . . and that one the mysteries of the deep. . . ."[59]

Lowbrow literalism? Maybe partly, but like Liszt, or Leonard Bernstein, Eisenstein is aware of one reason for the persistence of programmatic, extrinsic tendencies. "Like" and "as" may be seen as a harness restricting music's power and freedom, but they are also the first words of poetry, not to mention teaching. And Eisenstein's latter poetics, such as the stunningly operatic Prokofiev/Eisenstein collaborations, especially the "Ivan" films, remind us how expansive and multivalent "like" and "as" can be. As he says, "[music] is never merely illustrative."[60]

We have seen that program music is largely unappreciated because of the feeling that "the natural architecture of music was not that of poetry."[61] But that claim does not hold when we take poetry to be receptive or writerly, and allow that context—history, ideology, intention, reception—can be an architectural element. This is the foundation upon which music's poetic elaborations rest.

Gino Stefani suggests that "'musical genres' give us evidence of social practices in music."[62] Program music, and classical music in film, give this evidence in superlative fashion. Considering the same issues central to program and quotation debates, Stefani discusses high competence and popular competence in relation to musical understanding. He maintains that both are an essential part of the mix. Notwithstanding a nagging rift between musicological and sociological disciplines, should they not combine, to mutual advantage? While being aware of historical separations, as with nineteenth-century views about intrinsic and extrinsic meaning in music, high can relate to low, and cultural studies can approach and even inform erudite musicology.

Here is a program, a context for positive interdisciplinary exchange, for which film music is an ideal site. And classical music, that most directly appropriated from one discipline to the other, is especially apt.

NOTES

1. Prendergast, 1992, 70.
2. Huntley, 1947, 20.
3. Eisler, 1947, 38–39. Also Irving, 1954. Thus Eisler's advocacy for "new music" in film, because of its comparative brevity and motivic independence. To look at things in a different light, there is a strong suggestion (cf. Shaw, 1981, Russell, 1987), that the playing of the entire work had by no means been the general practice in the concert hall until the late nineteenth century.
4. Rapée, 1925, 10.
5. Quoted in Steiner, 1989, 96.
6. Palmer, 1980, 6: 553.
7. Keller, 1953 (*Music Review*, XIV), 311–12. The challenge for Keller, and the cause for the "limited scope" he refers to, as with the second use by Hitchcock of Arthur Benjamin's *Storm Clouds* in the second *The Man Who Knew Too Much*, is that the music is too good. In the presence of such "the musical person" will stop caring about the film. See Keller, 1956 (*Music Review*, XVII), 154.
8. This stand coincides with early notions of literary adaptation in film. Bela Balazs discusses (and then dismisses) the notion that poor novels provided the best film material, as story could be exploited without danger of besmirching a nonexistent artfulness. Balazs, 1952, 258–65. See discussion in Andrew, 1976, 87–88.
9. Keller, 1953 (*Music Review*, XIV), 312. Emphasis added.
10. See Hoffmann's composer (1819–21, 46) on the difficulty of musical/visual collaboration, on how such collaboration usually results in the hobbling of both music and verse in order to accommodate the opposing element.
11. Adorno, 1973, 135–217. Adorno's objection to Stravinsky's borrowings and to neoclassicism in general was that it was all an impossi-

ble, even disingenuous, conciliation, a doomed attempt to restore authenticity to an alienated, subjugated form.

12. Said, 1991, 96.

13. Ibid., 11.

14. Ironically the postwar, presound period in film and film music can be seen as a brief final moment of virtuous amateurism. Although media technologies would soon end the recreational dominance of the parlor piano, there was arguably a brief balance between entertainment that was homemade and that which was consumed elsewhere. In that brief period what is usually seen as bad film accompaniment was also evidence of a musical culture where valorized texts were accessible across the social scale. See Sadie, 1988, 63–68. Also cf. Russell, 1987.

15. Keller, 1958, (*Music Review*, XIX), 151.

16. Cameron, 1967, 88.

17. Newman, 1910, 145. See Tovey, 1937, 44–45 (on *Coriolanus* and *Egmont*), 104–6 (on Mendelssohn's incidental music to *A Midsummer Night's Dream*) for excellent examples of such compromise, both musical, and in terms of Tovey's own critical response to these works.

18. Ibid., 146. See Searle, 1985, for Liszt's unfussy willingness to adapt his musical material to the needs of extramusical sources.

19. See Subotnik, 1976, 251–53.

20. "Art that does not yield [to the cultural industry's flattening of aesthetic autonomy] is completely shut off from consumption and driven into isolation." And again, "the fear expressed in the dissonances of Schoenberg's most radical period far surpasses the measure of fear conceivable to the average middle class individual; it is a historical fear, a sense of impending doom." Eisler, 1947, x, 36.

21. Merriam, 1964, 6.

22. Quoted in Wright, H. Stephen, "The Materials of Film Music: Their Nature and Accessibility," in McCarty, 1989, 5.

23. Bernstein, 1976, 162.

24. Ibid., 153.

25. London, 1936, 14.

26. Thomas, 1979, 7.

27. Quoted in Steiner, 1989, 100–101.

28. Kracauer, 1960, 142.

29. Ibid., 137.

30. Chion, 1994, xxvi.

31. Brown, 1994, 69–70.

32. For a fine cinematic essay on musical multivalence, see Humphrey Jennings's underrated *The True Story of Lili Marlene* (1943). Also Richard Roud (1971, 65) on *The Chronicle of Anna Magdalena*

Bach (1968). For an application in a different context, consider Constantin Stanislavski's application of the idea of "if" to a role. The actor approaches a character from a number of possible perspectives, which, considered together, greatly expand, enrich, and complicate the presentation. Stanislavski, 1936, 46–71.

33. Quoted in Bordwell, 1980, 153.

34. Kracauer, 1960, 137–38.

35. Stefani, 1987, 21.

36. Altman, 1987, 2.

37. Ibid., 3.

38. Cf. Stefani, 1987.

39. Bordwell, 1980, 141, 148.

40. Wagnerianly (late Eisenstein) in terms of unity; in early Eisenstein, or Noel Burch, in opposition.

41. Flinn, 1993, 43.

42. Similarly, Flinn speaks of Ernest Bloch's interest in "mysticism, aesthetics and utopian thought," how Marxists are put off by such elements, how Bloch's relevance is endangered in discourse by the fact that his largest U.S. audience has been among theologians (ibid., 95). It is true that in many ways contemporary theoretical discourse and theology have (unfortunately) not had much to say to each other, but the assumption, which Flinn implicitly follows, that this is as it should, or must, be, is unfortunate.

43. Brown, 1994, 34.

44. Chion, 1994, 38.

45. Hall, Stuart, "Signification, representation, ideology: Althusser and the poststructuralist debates," in *Critical Studies in Mass Communication*, Vol. 2, # 2, 94.

46. In Mellers, 1946, 47–48. See also Brown, 1988, 170. Brown quotes composer Roger Sessions on individualist features in late-nineteenth-century musical practice, where dissonant detail takes precedence over lines, or the tonal and structural coherence of the whole. Sessions counters this to earlier dissonances (Bach, Mozart, etc.) which are rationalized within the whole.

47. I.e. "A dialectical approach to film form," "The cinematographic principle and the ideogram," and other such early expressions of enthusiastic prescription. See particularly Eisenstein, 1942, 1949.

48. Claude Levi-Strauss has said that fugue reunites sundered, oppositional elments in myth. Levi-Strauss, 1979, 50.

49. Eisenstein, 1968, 85.

50. See Eisenstein's monumental mickey-mousing with Prokofiev in 1938's *Alexander Nevsky*, in "Form and Content: Practice," in Eisenstein, 1942, 157–216.

51. Pudovkin, 1949, 163.

52. Keller, *Music Review,* vol. xvii, 154.

53. Said, 1991, xvi.

54. Godard's use of the standard repertoire is a rich and varied example.

55. Keller (1946–48, 16, no. 61, 30–31) gives what is probably his most enthusiastic praise for a piece of film music when reviewing Benjamin Britten's similar updating of an air by Purcell for Muir Mathieson's Crown film, *Instruments of the Orchestra* (1947). As might be said for *Pulcinella,* Britten's combination and conflation of periods and techniques both educates and edifies, providing beauty and even reconciliation.

56. In Prendergast, 1994, 216.

57. Cf. Kolker, 1983, 82–89, 163–65.

58. Chion, 1994, 81.

59. Eisenstein, "PRKV (on Prokofiev)," in Limbacher, 1974, 161.

60. Ibid.

61. In Sadie 1980, 18: 432.

62. Stefani, 1987, 12.

BIBLIOGRAPHY

Abraham, Gerald. 1985. "Robert Schumann." In Stanley Sadie, ed., 1985.

Adorno, Theodor. 1967. *Prisms*. Trans. Samuel Weber and Sherry Weber. Cambridge, Mass.: MIT Press.

———. 1973. *The Philosophy of Modern Music*. New York: Seabury Press.

———. 1991. *The Culture Industry: Selected Essays on Mass Culture*. J. M. Bernstein, ed. London: Routledge.

Adorno, Theodor, with Max Horkheimer. 1972. "The Culture Industry: Enlightenment as Mass Deception." In *Dialectic of Enlightenment*. Trans. John Cumming. New York: Herder and Herder.

Ali, Omer. 1995. "Music to Just Die For," *Sunday Times Scotland*, June 25, 2–3.

Altman, Rick. 1987. *The American Film Musical*. Bloomington: Indiana University Press.

Anderson, Gillian. 1988. *Music for Silent Films: 1894–1929*. Washington: Library of Congress.

Andrew, Dudley. 1976. *The Major Film Theories*. London: Oxford University Press.

———. 1978. "The Neglected Tradition of Phenomenology in Film Theory." In Bill Nichols, ed., *Movies and Methods*, vol. 2. Berkeley: University of California Press, 1985.

———. 1984. *Concepts in Film Theory*. New York: Oxford University Press.

Apel, Willi, ed. 1972. *The Harvard Dictionary of Music*. 2nd ed. Cambridge, Mass.: Harvard University Press.

Arnheim, Rudolf. 1957. *Film As Art*. Berkeley: University of California Press.

Arnold, Matthew. 1993. *Culture and Anarchy and Other Writings*. Stefan Collins, ed. Cambridge: Cambridge University Press.

Atkins, Irene Kahn. 1983. *Source Music in Motion Pictures.* London: Associated University Presses.

Balazs, Béla. 1952. *Theory of the Film: Character and Growth of a New Art*, trans. Edith Bone. New York: Dover Publications.

Baring-Gould, Sabine, ed. 1895–96. *English Minstrelsie: A National Monument of English Song.* 8 vols. Edinburgh: T. C. and E. C. Jack, Grange Publishing Works.

Barthes, Roland. 1974. *S/Z.* New York: Noonday Press.

Bazelon, Irwin. 1975. *Knowing the Score: Notes on Film Music.* New York: Van Nostrand.

Bazin, André. 1967. *What Is Cinema?* Hugh Gray, trans. and ed. Berkeley: University of California Press.

Becker, Paul. 1925. *Beethoven.* London: J. M. Dent and Sons.

Behlmer, Rudy. 1989. "'Tumult, Battle and Blaze': Looking Back on the 1920s—and Since—with Gaylord Carter, the Dean of Theatre Organists." In Clifford McCarty, ed., 1989, 19–59.

Berg, Charles Merrell. 1976. *An Investigation of the Motives for and Realization of Music to Accompany the American Silent Film, 1896–1927.* New York: Arno Press.

Bergman, Ingmar. 1988. *The Magic Lantern.* New York: Penguin.

Bernstein, Elmer. 1972. "Whatever Happened to Great Movie Music?" *High Fidelity*, July 1972, 55–58.

Bernstein, Leonard. 1976. *The Unanswered Question: Six Talks at Harvard.* Cambridge, Mass.: Harvard University Press.

Blom, Eric, ed. 1954. *Grove's Dictionary of Music and Musicians.* 5th ed. London: Macmillan.

Bordwell, David. 1980. "The Musical Analogy." *Yale French Studies* 60, 141–56.

———. 1981. *The Films of Carl-Theodor Dreyer.* Berkeley: University of California Press.

———. 1989. *Making Meaning.* Cambridge, Mass.: Harvard University Press.

Braudy, Leo, and Marshall Cohen, eds. 1992. *Film Theory and Criticism.* 4th ed. New York: Oxford University Press.

Brecht, Bertolt. 1964. "The Modern Theatre Is the Epic Theatre." In *Brecht on Theatre*. Trans. John Willett. London: Methuen, 33–42.

———. 1976. *Collected Plays*, vol. 2. Ralph Manheim and John Willett, eds. New York: Vintage.

Brown, Royal. 1988. "Film and Classical Music." In Gary Edgerton, ed., 1988.

———. 1994. *Overtones and Undertones: Reading Film Music*. Berkeley: University of California Press.

Buckley, P. Kevin. 1923. *The Orchestral and Cinema Organist*. London: Hawkes and Son.

Buñuel, Luis. 1983. *My Last Sigh*. New York: Vintage.

Burch, Noel. 1990. *Life to Those Shadows*. Berkeley: University of California Press.

Burger, Peter. 1984. *Theory of the Avant-Garde*. Minneapolis: University of Minnesota Press.

Busch, Eberhard. 1976. *Karl Barth: His Life from Letters and Autobiographical Texts*. Trans. John Bowden. London: SCM Press.

Bush, Richard H. 1989. "The Music of Flash Gordon and Buck Rogers." In Clifford McCarty, ed., 1989, 143–65.

Cage, John. 1959. *Indeterminacy: New Aspects of Form in Instrumental and Electronic Music*. Folkways, FT3704.

———. 1961. *Silence: Lectures and Writings*. Middletown, Conn.: Wesleyan University Press.

Calder-Marshall, Arthur. 1937. *The Changing Scene*. London: Chapman and Hall.

Cameron, Ian, ed. 1967. *The Films of Jean-Luc Godard*. London: Studio Vista.

Carringer, Robert L. 1993. *The Magnificent Ambersons: A Reconstruction*. Berkeley: University of California Press.

Chanan, Michael. 1995. *Repeated Takes: A Short History of Recording and Its Effects on Music*. London: Verso.

Chion, Michel. 1994. *Audio-Vision: Sound on Film*, trans. Claudia Gorbman. New York: Columbia University Press.

Christie, Ian. 1985. *Arrows of Desire: The Films of Michael Powell and Emeric Pressburger*. London: Waterstone.

Congreve, William. 1967. *The Complete Plays of William Congreve*. Herbert Davis, ed. Chicago: University of Chicago Press (see pp. 1, 2).

Cooke, Deryck. 1959. *The Language of Music*. London: Oxford University Press.

Cooke, Mervyn. 2001. "Film Music." In Stanley Sadie, ed., 2001, 8: 797–810.

Craig, Robert. N. D. *Glasgow Choral Union, 1843–1967: a Complete Catalogue of Choral Music Performed and Names of Artists*, 20 vols., unpublished manuscript. Mitchell Library, Glasgow, Scotland, donation #30942.

Dahlhaus, Carl. 1989. *Nineteenth-Century Music*. Berkeley: University of California Press.

Davie, C. T. No date. Sheet Music Archive. Mitchell Library, Glasgow, Scotland.

Deutch, Adolph. 1944. "Collaboration Between the Screen Writer and Composer." In Gustave Arlt, ed., *Writers Congress*. Berkeley: University of California Press.

Duckles, Vincent H. and Ida Reed, eds. 1988. *Music Reference and Research Materials: An Annotated Bibliography*. New York: Schirmer.

Dyer, Richard. 1993. *Brief Encounter*. London: British Film Institute.

Edgerton, Gary, ed. 1988. *Film and the Arts in Symbiosis: a Resource Guide*. New York: Greenwood Press.

Eisenstein, Sergei. 1942. *Film Sense*. Ed. and trans. Jay Leyda. New York: Harcourt Brace.

———. 1949. *Film Form*. Ed. and trans. Jay Leyda. New York: Harcourt Brace.

———. 1982. *Film Essays and a Lecture*. Ed. and trans. Jay Leyda. Princeton, N.J.: Princeton University Press.

———. 1983. *Immoral Memories*. Trans. Herbert Marshall. Boston: Houghton Mifflin.

Eisler, Hanns. 1947. *Composing for the Films*. London: Dennis Dobson.

Elvers, Rudolf, ed. 1986. *Felix Mendelssohn: A Life in Letters*. Trans. Craig Tomlinson. London: Cassell.

Ervine, St. John. 1934. *The Alleged Art of the Cinema*. London: The Union Society.

Faulkner, Robert R. 1971. *Hollywood Studio Musicians: Their Work and Careers in the Recording Industry*. Chicago: Aldine/Atherton.

Flinn, Caryl. 1993. *Strains of Utopia: Gender, Nostalgia and Hollywood Film Music*. Princeton, N.J.: Princeton University Press.

Foort, Reginald. 1932. *The Cinema Organ*. London: Sir Isaac Pitman and Sons.

George, W. Tyacke. 1912. *Playing to Pictures: A Guide for Pianists and Conductors of Motion Picture Theatres*. London: E. T. Heron and Co.

———. 1914. "Picture Theatre Music during 1913." In *Kinematograph Year Book, 1914*. London: E. T. Heron and Co.

Gill, A. A. 1994. "Suds' Law." *London Sunday Times*, November 13, sec. 10, p. 3.

Godard, Jean-Luc. 1972. *Godard on Godard*. New York: Da Capo Press.

Goepp, Philip H. 1897, 1902, 1913. *Symphonies and Their Meaning*, 3 volumes. Philadelphia: J. B. Lippincott.

Gorbman, Claudia. 1987. *Unheard Melodies: Narrative Film Music*. Bloomington: Indiana University Press.

Grierson, John. 1966. *Grierson on Documentary*. Rev. ed. Forsyth Hardy, ed. London: Faber and Faber.

Grove, George, Sir. 1927. *Grove's Dictionary of Music and Musicians*. 3rd ed. H. C. Colles, ed. London: Macmillan.

Hanslick, Eduard. 1963. *Music Criticisms: 1846–1899*. Henry Pleasants, ed. Baltimore: Penguin.

———. 1986. *On the Beautiful in Music*. Translation of an 1891 edition. Indianapolis: Hackett Publishing Co.

Hardy, Forsythe. 1990. *Scotland on Screen*. Edinburgh: Edinburgh University Press.

Hegel, G. W. F. 1920. "Music." In *The Philosophy of Fine Art*, vol. 3. Trans. F. P. B. Osmaston. London: G. Bell and Sons.

———. 1979. *On the Arts*. Abridged and trans. Henry Paolucci. New York: Frederick Ungar.

Hoffmann, E.T.A. 1813: "Beethoven's Instrumental Music." 1819–21: "The Poet and the Composer." Both in Oliver Strunk, ed., *Source Readings in Music History*, vol. 5, "The Romantic Era." New York: W. W. Norton.

Huntley, John. 1947. *British Film Music*. Reprint. New York: Arno Press and the *New York Times*, 1972.

Husserl, Edmund. 1969. *Ideas*. Trans. W. R. Boyce Gibson. New York: Humanities Press.

International Music Centre. 1962. *Films for Music Education and Opera Films: an International Selective Catalogue*. Paris: UNESCO.

Irving, Ernest. 1954. "History." In "Film Music," in Eric Blom, ed., 1954, 3: 93–98.

Jacobs, Louis. 1969. *The Emergence of Film Art*. New York: Hopkinson and Blake.

James, Dennis. 1989. "Performing with Silent Films." In Clifford McCarty, ed., 1989, 61–79.

Jaubert, Maurice. 1937. "Music on the Screen." In Charles Davey, ed., *Footnotes to the Film*. London: Oxford University Press.

Jennings, Mary-Lou, ed. 1982. *Humphrey Jennings: Filmmaker, Painter, Poet*. London: British Film Institute.

Kahn, Douglas, and Gregory Whitehead, eds. 1992. *Wireless Imagination: Sound, Radio and the Avant-Garde*. Cambridge, Mass.: MIT Press.

Kalinak, Kathryn. 1992. *Settling the Score: Music and the Classical Hollywood Film*. Madison: University of Wisconsin Press.

Kandinsky, Wassily. 1977. *Concerning the Spiritual in Art*. Trans. M. T. H. Sadler. New York: Dover Publications.

Kaplan, Sol. 1944. "The Obligations of Music." In Gustave Arlt, ed., *Writers Congress*. Berkeley: University of California Press.

Karlin, Fred. 1990. *On the Track: A Guide to Contemporary Film Scoring*. New York: Schirmer.

Kassabian, Anahid. 2001. *Hearing Film: Tracking Identifications in Contemporary Hollywood Film Music*. New York: Routledge.

Keller, Hans. 1946–48. In *Sight and Sound* 15, no. 60, and 16, nos. 61–64.

———. 1949. "Film music: the Question of Quotation." *Music Survey* 2, no. 1, 25–27.

———. 1947–1959. In Geoffrey Sharp, ed., *Music Review*, vols. 8–20 (1947–59). Cambridge: W. Heffer and Sons.

————. 1954. "British Music: Perspective." In "Film Music," in Eric Blom, ed., 1954.

Kerman, Joseph. 1985. *Contemplating Music: Challenges to Musicology*. Cambridge, Mass.: Harvard University Press.

King, Norman. 1984. "The Sound of Silents." In Richard Abel, ed., *Silent Film*. New Brunswick, N.J.: Rutgers University Press, 1996, 31–44.

Kolker, Robert Philip. 1983. *The Altering Eye: Contemporary International Cinema*. Oxford: Oxford University Press.

Kracauer, Siegfried. 1960. *Theory of Film: the Redemption of Physical Reality*. London: Oxford University Press.

Krummel, D. W. 1981. "A Landmark of Music Lexicography." *Choice,* 18, no. 6 (February), 762–66.

Kubik, Gail. 1944. "Music in the Documentary Film." In Gustave Arlt, ed., *Writers Congress*. Berkeley: University of California Press.

Lang, Edith, and George West. 1920. *Musical Accompaniment of Motion Pictures: A Practical Manual for Pianists and Organists*. Boston: Boston Music Co.

Larson, Randall. 1985. *Musique Fantastique: A Survey of Music in the Fantastic Cinema*. Metuchen, N.J.: Scarecrow.

Leroux, Gaston. 1986. *The Phantom of the Opera*. London: Virgin.

Levant, Oscar. 1940. *A Smattering of Ignorance*. New York: Doubleday, Doran and Co.

Lévi-Strauss, Claude. 1979. *Myth and Meaning*. New York: Schocken Books.

Lewis, C. S. 1961. *An Experiment in Criticism*. Cambridge: Cambridge University Press.

Lewis, Peter. 1994. "Inspiring the Alice Band." *London Times,* 6 November, *The Culture*, 5.

Leyda, Jay. 1960. *Kino: A History of the Russian and Soviet Film*. Princeton, N.J.: Princeton University Press.

Limbacher, James, ed. 1974. *Film Music: From Violins to Video*. Metuchen, N.J.: Scarecrow.

Lindsay, Vachel. 1916. "The Orchestra, Conversation, and the Censorship." In *The Art of the Moving Picture*. New York: Macmillan, 217–34.

Liszt, Franz. 1855. "From Berlioz and His 'Harold' Symphony."

In Oliver Strunk, ed., *Source Readings in Music History*, vol. 5, "The Romantic Era." New York: W. W. Norton.

London, Kurt. 1936. *Film Music*. Trans. Eric S. Bensinger. London: Faber and Faber.

MacDonald, Hugh. 1980. "Idée Fixe." In Stanley Sadie, ed., 1980, 9: 18.

MacDonald, Kevin. 1994. *Emeric Pressburger: The Life and Death of a Screenwriter*. London: Faber and Faber.

Manson, Eddy Lawrence. 1989. "The Film Composer in Concert and the Concert Composer in Film." In Clifford McCarty, ed., 255–70.

Marshall, Herbert. 1983. *Masters of the Soviet Cinema: Crippled Creative Biographies*. London: Routledge and Kegan Paul.

Mast, Gerald, Marshall Cohen, and Leo Braudy, eds. 1985. *Film Theory and Criticism: Introductory Readings*. New York: Oxford University Press.

McCarty, Clifford, ed. 1989. *Film Music I*. New York: Garland Publishing.

McGinn, Rob't E. 1979. "Stokowski and Bell Laboratories: Collaboration in the Development of High Fidelity Sound, 1930–1940." Unpublished paper presented at the annual meeting of the History of Science Society, New York City, Dec. 29, 1979.

Mellers, Wilfrid. 1946. *Music and Society: England and the European Tradition*. London: Dennis Dobson.

———. 1954. "The Musical Problem." In "Film Music," in Eric Blom, ed., 1954, 3: 103–9.

———. 1965. *Harmonious Meeting: A Study of the Relationship between English Music, Poetry and Theatre, c. 1600–1900*. London: Dennis Dobson.

———. 1973. *The Twilight of the Gods: The Beatles in Retrospect*. London: Faber and Faber.

Merrick, Paul. 1987. *Revolution and Religion in the Music of Liszt*. Cambridge: Cambridge University Press.

Merriam, Alan. 1964. *The Anthropology of Music*. Evanston, Ill.: Northwestern University Press.

Metz, Christian. 1982. *The Imaginary Signifier: Psychoanalysis and the Cinema*. Trans. Celia Britton et al. Bloomington: Indiana University Press.

Meyer, Leonard. 1956. *Emotion and Meaning in Music*. Chicago: University of Chicago Press.

Monelle, Raymond. 1992. *Linguistics and Semiotics in Music*. Reading, Mass.: Harwood Academic Publishers.

Nattiez, Jean-Jacques. 1990. *Music and Discourse: Toward a Semiology of Music*. Trans. Carolyn Abbate. Princeton, N.J.: Princeton University Press.

Newcombe, Anthony. 1984. "Once More 'Between Absolute and Program Music': Schumann's Second Symphony." *19th Century Music* 7, no. 3: 233–50.

Newman, Ernest. 1910. "Programme Music." In *Musical Studies*. London: John Lane, The Bodley Head.

Nordern, Martin. 1988. "Film and painting," in Edgerton, 1988.

Oxford English Dictionary. 1961. Vol. 6. London: Oxford University Press, 782–84.

Palmer, Christopher. 1980. "Film Music." In Stanley Sadie, ed., 1980, 549–53.

Pelikan, Jaroslav. 1986. *Bach Among the Theologians*. Philadelphia: Fortress Press.

Petric, Vladimir. 1987. *Constructivism in Film: The Man with the Movie Camera: a Cinematic Analysis*. New York: Cambridge University Press.

Plett, Heinrich, ed. 1991. *Intertextuality: Research in Text Theory*. Berlin: Walter de Gruyter and Co.

Powell, Michael. 1986. *A Life in Movies: An Autobiography*. London: Heinemann.

Prendergast, Roy M. 1992. *Film Music: A Neglected Art, a Critical Study of Music in Films*. 2nd ed. New York: W. W. Norton and Co.

Previn, André. 1991. *No Minor Chords: My Days in Hollywood*. New York: Doubleday.

Pudovkin, Vsevolod. 1949. *Film Technique and Film Acting*. Trans. Ivor Montagu. New York: Lear Publishers.

Pulling, Christopher. 1952. *They Were Singing, and What They Sang About*. London: George G. Harrap and Co.

Raksin, David. 1944. "Humor in Music." In Gustave Arlt, ed., *Writers Congress*. Berkeley: University of California Press.

———. 1989. "Holding a Nineteenth-Century Pedal at Twentieth-Century Fox." In Clifford McCarty, ed., 1989, 167–81.

Randel, Don, ed. 1986. *The New Harvard Dictionary of Music*. Cambridge, Mass.: Harvard University Press.

Rapée, Erno. 1924. *Motion Picture Moods for Pianists and Organists (Adapted to 52 Moods and Situations)*. New York: Schirmer.

———. 1925. *Encyclopedia of Music for Pictures*. New York: Arno Press.

Romney, Jonathon, and Adrian Wooton, eds. *The Celluloid Jukebox: Popular Music and the Movies Since the 1950s*. London: British Film Institute.

Rosen, Charles, and Henri Zerner. 1984. *Romanticism and Realism: The Mythology of Nineteenth-Century Art*. New York: Viking Press.

Rosin, Philip. 1980. "Adorno and Film Music." *Yale French Studies* 60, 157–82.

Roud, Richard. 1970. *Jean-Luc Godard*. 2nd ed. London: Thames and Hudson, British Film Institute.

———. 1971. *Jean-Marie Straub*. London: British Film Institute.

Russell, Dave. 1987. *Popular Music in England, 1840–1914: A Social History*. Manchester: Manchester University Press.

Sabaneev, Leonid. 1935. *Music for the Films: A Handbook for Composers and Conductors*. Trans. S. W. Pring. London: Pitman and Sons.

Sadie, Stanley, ed. 1980. *New Grove Dictionary of Music and Musicians*. London: Macmillan.

———. 1985. *The New Grove Early Romantic Masters I*. London: Macmillan.

———. 1988. *The New Grove Piano*. New York: W. W. Norton.

———. 2001. *New Grove Dictionary of Music and Musicians*. 2nd ed. New York: Grove.

Said, Edward. 1991. *Musical Elaborations*. New York: Columbia University Press.

Sandall, Robert. 1994. "You've Seen the Film . . ." *London Sunday Times*, October 23, sec. 10, p. 19.

Schnitzer, Luda, Jean Schnitzer, and Marcel Martin, eds. 1973. *Cinema in Revolution: The Heroic Era of the Soviet Film*. New York: Hill and Wang.

Scruton, Roger. 1980. "Programme Music." In Stanley Sadie, ed., 1980, 15: 283–86.

Searle, Humphrey. 1985. "Franz Liszt." In Stanley Sadie, ed., 1985. London: Macmillan.

Sharp, Cecil. 1912–22. *Country Dance Tunes.* London: Novello.

Shavin, Norman. 1954. "Them Days Is Gone Forever." *Music Journal* 12, no. 3, 13, 74–75.

Shaw, George Bernard. 1981. *Shaw's Music.* 3 vols. Dan H. Laurence, ed. London: Max Reinhardt, The Bodley Head.

Siegmeister, Elie. 1938. *Music and Society.* New York: Critics Group Press.

Silverman, Kaja. 1983. *The Subject of Semiotics.* New York: Oxford University Press.

Sitney, P. Adams. 1979. *Visionary Film: The American Avant-Garde, 1943–1978.* Oxford: Oxford University Press.

Smith, Jeff. *The Sounds of Commerce: Marketing Popular Film Music.* New York: Columbia University Press.

Sobchack, Vivian. 1992. *The Address of the Eye: A Phenomenology of Film Experience.* Princeton, N.J.: Princeton University Press.

Sontag, Susan. 1983. "Against Interpretation." In *A Susan Sontag Reader.* New York: Vintage.

Staiger, Janet. 1992. *Interpreting Films: Studies in the Historical Reception of American Cinema.* Princeton, N.J.: Princeton University Press.

Stanislavski, Constantin. 1936, *An Actor Prepares.* New York: Routledge.

Stefani, Gino. 1987. "A Theory of Musical Competence." *Semiotica* 66–1/3: 7–22.

Steiner, Fred. 1989. "What Were Musicians Saying about Movie Music during the First Decades of Sound? A Symposium of Selected Writings." In Clifford McCarty, ed., 1989, 81–107.

Steiner, Max. ca. 1964. *Notes to You.* Unpublished manuscript, Steiner Collection, Arts and Communications Special Collections. Harold B. Lee library, Brigham Young University.

Sternfeld, Frederick W. 1960. "Music and Cinema." In Rollo H. Myers, ed., *Twentieth Century Music.* London: Calder and Boyars.

Stokowski, Leopold. 1943. "Music and Motion Pictures." In *Music for All of Us*. New York: Simon and Schuster.

Stothart, Herbert. 1938. "Film Music." In Stephen Watts, ed., 1938, *Behind the Screen: How Films Are Made*. London: Arthur Barker Ltd.

Stratton, Stephen S. 1901. *Mendelssohn*. London: J. M. Dent.

Subotnik, Rose. 1976. "Adorno's Diagnosis of Beethoven's Late Style: Early Symptoms of Fatal Condition." *Journal of American Musicological Society* 29 (Summer 1976): 251–53.

Taylor, Deems. 1940. *Walt Disney's Fantasia*. New York: Simon and Schuster.

Taylor, Richard, and Ian Christie, eds. 1988. *The Film Factory: Russian and Soviet Cinema in Documents 1896–1939*. London: Routledge and Kegan Paul.

Temperley, Nicholas. 1985. "Fryderyk Chopin." In Stanley Sadie, ed., 1985. London: Macmillan.

Thomas, Tony. 1973. *Music for the Movies*. South Brunswick, N.J.: A. S. Barnes.

Thomas, Tony, ed. 1979. *Film Score: The View from the Podium*. South Brunswick, N.J.: A. S. Barnes.

Thompson, Kristin. 1980. "Early Sound Counterpoint." *Yale French Studies* 60: 115–40.

Thomson, Virgil. 1966. *An Autobiography*. New York: Dutton.

Tovey, Donald. 1937. *Essays in Musical Analysis*. 6 vols. London: Oxford University Press.

Turner, Michael, and Antony Miall. 1972. *The Parlour Song Book: A Casquet of Vocal Gems*. London: Michael Joseph.

———. 1982. *The Edwardian Song Book: Drawing Room Ballads, 1900–1919*. London: Methuen.

Van Houten, Theodore. 1992. *Silent Cinema Music in the Netherlands*. Buren: Frits Knuf Publishers.

Vertov, Dziga. 1984. *Kino-Eye: The Writings of Dziga Vertov*. Annette Michelson, ed. Berkeley: University of California Press.

Wajda, Andrzej. 1989. *Double Vision: My Life in Film*. Trans. Rose Medina. London: Faber and Faber.

Walker, Alexander. 1974. *Hollywood, England*. London: Michael Joseph.

Ware, John. 1940. *The Lion Has Wings*. London: Collins.

Warrack, John. 1980. "Leitmotif." In Stanley Sadie, ed., 1980, 10: 644–46.

Welles, Orson, and Peter Bodganovich. 1992. *This Is Orson Welles*. New York: HarperCollins.

Wenders, Wim. 1989. *Emotion Pictures: Reflections on the Cinema*. London: Faber and Faber.

———. 1991. *The Logic of Images: Essays and Conversations*. Trans. Michael Hofmann. London: Faber and Faber.

Westermeyer, Paul. 1985. "Grace and the Music of Bach." *The Christian Century* 102: 291–94.

Whitworth, Reginald. 1932. *The Cinema and the Theatre Organ*. London: Musical Opinion.

Willeman, Paul, ed. 1977. *Pier Paolo Pasolini*. London: British Film Institute.

Williams, Ralph Vaughan, and A. C. Lloyd. 1934. *National Music*. London: Oxford University Press.

———. 1959. *Penguin Book of English Folk Songs*. London: Penguin.

Wollen, Peter. 1982. "The Two Avant-Gardes." In *Readings and Writings: Semiotic Counter-Strategies*. London: Verso.

Wright, H. Stephen. 1989. "The Materials of Film Music: Their Nature and Accessibility." In Clifford McCarty, ed., 1989, 3–17.

Zador, Leslie T., and Gregory Rose. 1989. "A Conversation with Bernard Herrmann." In Clifford McCarty, ed., 1989, 209–53.

INDEX